Best Hikes Vancouver

HELP US KEEP THIS GUIDE UP TO DATE

Every effort has been made by the author and editors to make this guide as accurate and useful as possible. However, many things can change after a guide is published—trails are rerouted, regulations change, techniques evolve, facilities come under new management, etc.

We appreciate hearing from you concerning your experiences with this guide and how you feel it could be improved and kept up to date. While we may not be able to respond to all comments and suggestions, we'll take them to heart and we'll also make certain to share them with the author. Please send your comments and suggestions to the following address:

FalconGuides
Reader Response/Editorial Department
246 Goose Lane, Suite 200
Guilford, CT 06437

Thanks for your input, and happy trails!

Best Hikes Vancouver

The Greatest Views, Wildlife, and Forest Strolls

Second Edition

Chloë Ernst

GUILFORD, CONNECTICUT

FALCONGUIDES®

An imprint of The Rowman & Littlefield Publishing Group, Inc.
4501 Forbes Blvd., Ste. 200
Lanham, MD 20706
www.rowman.com
Falcon and FalconGuides are registered trademarks and Make Adventure Your Story is a trademark of The Rowman & Littlefield Publishing Group, Inc.

Distributed by NATIONAL BOOK NETWORK

All photos by Chloe Ernst
Maps by The Rowman & Littlefield Publishing Group, Inc.

British Library Cataloguing in Publication Information available

Library of Congress Cataloging-in-Publication Data
Names: Ernst, Chloë, author.
Title: Best hikes Vancouver : the greatest views, wildlife, and forest strolls / Chloë Ernst.
Other titles: Best hikes near Vancouver
Description: Second edition. | Guilford, Connecticut : FalconGuides, 2021. | Revised edition of: Best hikes near Vancouver. 2014. | Summary: "Featuring over 40 of the best hikes in the Vancouver area, this fully revised guidebook points locals and visitors alike to trailheads within an hour's drive of the city"— Provided by publisher.
Identifiers: LCCN 2020053179 (print) | LCCN 2020053180 (ebook) | ISBN 9781493053667 (paperback) | ISBN 9781493053674 (epub)
Subjects: LCSH: Hiking—British Columbia—Vancouver Metropolitan Area—Guidebooks. | Trails— British Columbia—Vancouver Metropolitan Area—Guidebooks. | Vancouver Metropolitan Area (B.C.)—Guidebooks.
Classification: LCC GV199.44.C22 V3735 2021 (print) | LCC GV199.44.C22 (ebook) | DDC 796.5109711—dc23
LC record available at https://lccn.loc.gov/2020053179
LC ebook record available at https://lccn.loc.gov/2020053180

Contents

Introduction 1
How to Use This Guide 6
Trail Finder 8
Map Legend 12

The Hikes

Vancouver 13
   1. Beaver Lake 14
   2. Stanley Park Seawall 20
   3. Spanish Banks 26
   4. Pacific Spirit Loop 32
   5. Acadia and Tower Beaches 37

North Vancouver 41
   6. Grouse Grind 42
   7. Goat Mountain 47
   8. Lynn Valley to Grouse Mountain 54
   9. Lynn Peak 59
  10. Norvan Falls 64
  11. Deep Cove to Lynn Canyon 69
  12. Mount Seymour 76

West Vancouver 83
  13. Capilano Pacific Trail 84
  14. Lighthouse Park 93
  15. Cypress Falls 99
  16. Hollyburn Ridge 106
  17. Saint Mark's Summit 112
  18. Eagle Bluff 118

Howe Sound 124
  19. Killarney Lake 125
  20. Mount Gardner 131
  21. The Lions Binkert 136
  22. Petgill Lake 142
  23. Sea to Summit 148
  24. Stawamus Chief 154
  25. Alice Lake Provincial Park 160

Burnaby to Indian Arm 166
  26. Burnaby Mountain 167
  27. Buntzen Lake 172
  28. Sendero Diez Vistas 178

Overview

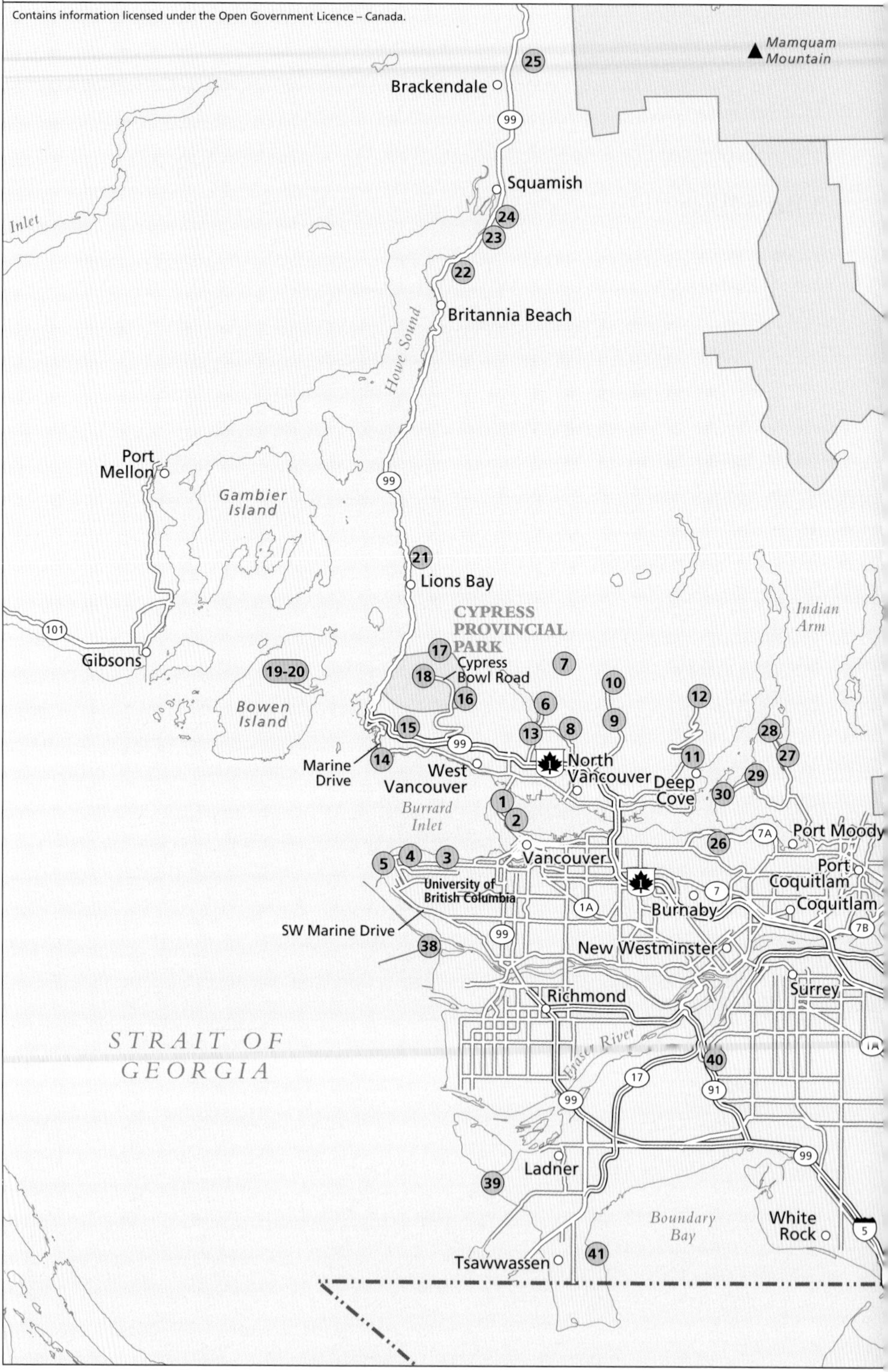

▲ *Mamquam Mountain*

Brackendale ○

25

99

Squamish

24
23

22

Britannia Beach

Howe Sound

Inlet

Port Mellon ○

Gambier Island

99

21

Lions Bay ○

CYPRESS PROVINCIAL PARK

Indian Arm

17   Cypress Bowl Road

7

101

Gibsons

19-20

18

16

10

12

Bowen Island

15

99

6

13   8   9

28

27

14

West Vancouver

North Vancouver

11

29

Marine Drive

Burrard Inlet

1

Deep Cove

30

2

26

7A   Port Moody ○

5   4   3

Vancouver

Port Coquitlam ○

University of British Columbia

1A

7

Coquitlam

SW Marine Drive

38

99

Burnaby

7B

New Westminster ○

Richmond

Surrey

STRAIT OF GEORGIA

Fraser River

40

17

91

1A

99

99

39   Ladner

Boundary Bay

White Rock ○

5

Tsawwassen ○   41

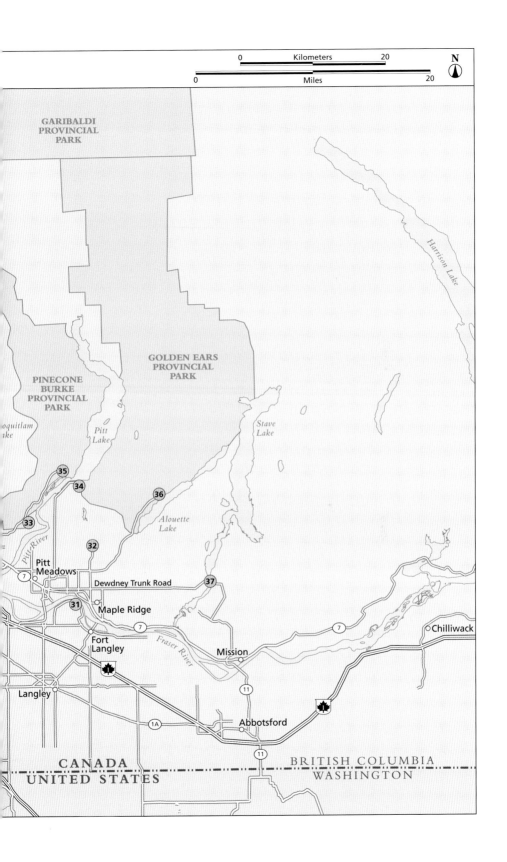

29. Sasamat Lake... 183
30. Jug Island Beach.. 188

Near the Port Mann and Pitt River Bridges.................... 194
31. Derby Reach 195
32. UBC Malcolm Knapp Research Forest 202
33. Minnekhada High Knoll Loop............................. 207
34. Katzie Marsh Loop 214
35. Widgeon Falls... 219
36. Gold Creek Falls.. 226
37. Hayward Lake.. 231

South, Over the Fraser River 239
38. Iona Jetty.. 240
39. Brunswick Point 246
40. Burns Bog 253
41. Boundary Bay... 258

Art of Hiking 263
Clubs and Trail Groups 285
Hike Index 287
About the Author 288

Introduction

Before Vancouver had bridges, provincial parks, or trail markers pointing the way, people were hiking the North Shore Mountains. In the earliest days, reaching Grouse Mountain was a 3-day affair, with women shedding bulky skirts to hike in more practical bloomers.

Today's hikers owe much to those early adventurers, who pushed for protected areas and formed groups like the (literally) trail-blazing British Columbia Mountaineering Club and the Alpine Club of Canada.

It's easy to forget how distant the Coast Mountains would have been to early Vancouverites, especially when you're warming up amid the after-work crowd at the base of the Grouse Grind. Nowadays, the Vancouver-area wilderness is accessible for a quick evening workout or a weekend afternoon walk.

These 41 hikes are all within a 1-hour drive of the City of Vancouver limits, with many close to highly populated neighboring cities like Port Moody, North Vancouver, West Vancouver, and Richmond. Why 1 hour? You can spend 60 minutes or more just waiting for the next BC Ferries sailing, lining up at the Canada-US border, or (if your timing is really unfortunate) merging onto the Lions Gate Bridge. Sometimes, we even battle these time-sucks in the pursuit of getting away.

But heading into the woods is nature's getaway—the running waters, lush forests, and scenic landscapes are a simple spa for the senses. Traveling an hour or less to these hikes maximizes your time on the trail, makes for a more relaxing day, and expends less energy to get you to the trailhead.

Beyond getting there, hiking itself is one of the most readily available pastimes around. Sneakers and a map get you started on most easy trails. It's good to also take along other essentials: sun protection, food, water, extra layers, and a first-aid kit—things you'd normally pack for the beach. If you're traveling on more challenging trails or in the backcountry, add in sturdy boots and a compass, shelter, headlamp, matches, and knife to your packing list. And on any trail, a cell phone with a fully charged battery can be an important communication tool, although it's no substitute for being prepared.

Weather

Start at the Canada-US border and scan north over a map of the Vancouver area: From Tsawwassen past Richmond and up to the Coast Mountains—generally, the farther north you go, the cooler and wetter conditions become. White Rock, to the south, is Vancouver's banana belt—where retirees go for the warm, dry conditions. The City of Vancouver itself experiences a moderate maritime climate, while the North Shore Mountains are the wettest (and snowiest) area covered in this guide.

Vancouver hiking is possible in any season. Year-round trails include those along the coast and at lower elevations, where you just contend with a little rain and occasional icy conditions during winter. But when it's wet and you need to get out-side, remember that the forest is almost like a natural umbrella. At upper elevations the temperature contrast is more considerable and the peaks of the Coast Mountains are usually only snow-free from July through October.

Environment Canada provides weather forecasts online (weather.gc.ca) and by phone (604-664-9010). Conditions are available for Vancouver, Howe Sound, Whis-tler, White Rock, and Fraser Valley, including Chilliwack and Abbotsford. The Van-couver forecast is for the Vancouver International Airport weather station.

Weather Averages for Vancouver

While the averages below are for Vancouver, weather varies greatly by region and elevation. Higher altitudes experience colder temperatures and swiftly changing con-ditions. Mountains tend to have more (sometimes a lot more) precipitation than coastal areas.

Month	Average Maximum	Average Minimum	Rainfall	Snowfall
January	6.9°C/44°F	1.4°C/35°F	157.5 mm/6.2 in	11.1 cm/4.4 in
February	8.2°C/47°F	1.6°C/35°F	98.9 mm/3.9 in	6.3 cm/2.5 in
March	10.3°C/51°F	3.4°C/38°F	111.8 mm/4.4 in	2.3 cm/0.9 in
April	13.2°C/56°F	5.6°C/42°F	88.1 mm/3.5 in	0.3 cm/0.1 in
May	16.7°C/62°F	8.8°C/48°F	65 mm/2.6 in	0 cm/0 in
June	19.6°C/67°F	11.7°C/53°F	53.8 mm/2.1 in	0 cm/0 in
July	22.2°C/72°F	13.7°C/57°F	35.6 mm/1.4 in	0 cm/0 in
August	22.2°C/72°F	13.8°C/57°F	36.7 mm/1.4 in	0 cm/0 in
September	18.9°C/66°F	10.8°C/51°F	50.9 mm/2 in	0 cm/0 in
October	13.5°C/56°F	7°C/45°F	120.7 mm/4.8 in	0.1 cm/0 in
November	9.2°C/49°F	3.5°C/38°F	185.8 mm/7.3 in	3.2 cm/1.3 in
December	6.3°C/43°F	0.8°C/33°F	148.3 mm/5.8 in	14.8 cm/5.8 in

Flora and Fauna

From birds to bears, Vancouver offers up the chance for unforgettable wildlife watch-ing. Keep your eyes open and carry a field guide, and you can discover something unusual in every season. As Vancouver has milder temperatures than much of Canada, spring arrives earlier and autumn lingers longer here.

In spring look for bright skunk cabbage flowers and salmonberry blossoms as early signs of warmer weather. Migratory birds feed on the Fraser River mudflats before continuing their journey north. Bears emerge from winter hideaways.

In summer plants undergo tremendous growth. Though the fall salmon runs are largest, coho spawn from June to November.

Autumn brings some bright fall colors to city parks, but in much of the wilder-ness evergreens prevail. Sockeye and pink salmon return to spawn in the Fraser River as well as smaller creeks and rivers.

In winter many trees and some animals hibernate. Bears are tucked in their dens, but Douglas squirrels are still active in the woods. Snow geese, trumpeter swans, and

Stanley Park is a burst of fall color amid BC's evergeen forests (Stanley Park Seawall hike).

occasionally snowy owls can overwinter in the Vancouver area. Salmon rivers like the Squamish River in Brackendale and areas of the Fraser are known for large convocations of bald eagles—though eagles as well as great blue herons and Canada geese are year-round residents.

Larger mammals generally don't migrate. Cougars inhabit the rugged backcountry terrain (though people have spotted them in many provincial parks). Black bears are common around the North Shore, Howe Sound, Burnaby Mountain, and Indian Arm. Coyotes, raccoons, skunks, and squirrels keep close quarters with humans, living in city areas and nearby parks.

A step along almost any Vancouver-area trail puts you at the base of the coast's mammoth trees. Western hemlock, Douglas fir, and western red cedar are the most common species, with hemlocks tending to dominate second-growth forests—Vancouver is in a Coastal Western Hemlock biogeoclimatic zone after all. But there are other giants along the trails. Around Cypress Provincial Park, yellow cedars (also called cypress) have been dated to more than 1,000 years old.

Within 8 kilometers (5 miles) of the coast, arbutus trees are smaller but spectacular. The broadleaf evergreen is also called madrone and madrona, and its papery bark peels each year to reveal a smooth under-layer.

Wildflowers, shrubs, and other smaller plants are varied. Berries—including huckleberries, salmonberries, thimbleberries, and blueberries—are a particular delight to

find along the trail. While it's delicious to taste a few, provided you can identify the berry with a field guide, leave most for the birds, bears, and other animals intent on survival.

The more you stop to look, the more you can find to look at. Field guides for plants, trees, birds, mushrooms, and mammals all can be helpful in identifying species you spot along the trails.

Tart salmonberries start to ripen in May.

Land in British Columbia

All of Vancouver is unceded Coast Salish Territory, meaning First Nations people lived here for thousands of years before Europeans settled on the coast and laid claim to the lands. First Nations people did not traditionally have the European sense of ownership. Groups often moved with the seasons, and some nations had overlapping territories. In the Vancouver area, many communities were active along the Fraser River during the fall salmon runs.

The hikes in this guide explore the lands of the Coast Salish peoples, including the territories of the Musqueam, Squamish, Tsleil-Waututh, Kwikwetlem, Katzie, Kwantlen, Sto:lo, Tsawwassen, and Semiahmoo First Nations, among others. As we visit these lands we are fortunate for the opportunity to enjoy the region and also continue in a tradition of stewardship and care.

About 94 percent of British Columbia is Crown Land—or lands owned by the federal or provincial governments—but it is city, regional, and provincial parks that make up the main local recreation areas. Metro Vancouver is a conglomeration of twenty-three cities, villages, municipalities, a First Nation, and an island. Regional parks tend to fall under its regional jurisdiction, while individual cities (including Burnaby and Vancouver) manage and maintain their own city parks. BC Parks manages provincial parks, including many campgrounds.

BC Hydro operates hydroelectricity facilities on reservoir lakes such as Buntzen and Hayward, and also provides recreation areas with trails, picnic tables, washrooms, and parking.

Closed watersheds protect city drinking water at Capilano, Seymour, and Coquitlam Reservoirs.

Getting Around

Pack the car, pack bicycle panniers, or pack a pack and hop the bus—there are varied options for transportation in the city. Metro Vancouver's widespread public transportation system includes buses, ferries, and trains. It reaches most areas of the city and many of this book's trailheads. Bicycle routes provide a carbon-neutral way to get to city parks that are closer at hand.

Area Codes

Vancouver has two main area codes: 604 and 778. Additional overlay area codes in the province include 236 and 672. The 250 area code is used on Vancouver Island and in other British Columbia regions.

Roads

There are no highways in Vancouver itself, but the Trans-Canada Highway runs from Horseshoe Bay through the North Shore, Fraser Valley, and to the east beyond. Highway 99 runs north and south, but follows city streets through Vancouver. Keep in mind that rush hour and weekend traffic can add significantly to travel time.

By Public Transit

Buses run throughout the Metro Vancouver area, providing an intricate and convenient transit network. A SeaBus ferry runs between Downtown Vancouver and North Vancouver. SkyTrain lines connect to outlying areas, with the Expo Line running east to Burnaby, Port Moody, and Coquitlam; the Millennium Line running southeast to New Westminster and Surrey; and the Canada Line linking south to Richmond. It's all managed under Translink: find route, fare, and schedule information by phone, (604) 953-3333, or online at translink.ca.

By Air

Vancouver International Airport (YVR) is the main city airport. It's a large, modern facility with daily regional, domestic, and international flights. The Canada Line transit service links the airport and Downtown Vancouver. Floatplanes are often preferred for reaching coastal areas and islands, and these smaller planes (with floats instead of wheels) fly out of the Downtown Coal Harbour and Richmond Fraser River terminals.

By Rail and By Bus

Long-distance bus services and trains operate from the same terminal: Pacific Central Station at 1150 Station St. Greyhound Canada has a wide bus network, and other carriers provide a variety of routes.

Vancouver is the western terminus of a transcontinental railway. Though passenger trains are less common than in years past, there are trains to Kamloops, Jasper, Edmonton, and beyond.

Visitor Information

Tourism Vancouver provides brochures, information, and booking services for visitors. They have free wireless internet too. There are visitor information centers in Downtown Vancouver, at the airport, and near the Canada-US border. Contact them at 200 Burrard St., Vancouver; (604) 683-2000; tourismvancouver.com.

How to Use This Guide

Take a close enough look, and you'll find that this guide contains just about everything you'll ever need to choose, plan for, enjoy, and survive a hike near Vancouver, BC. Stuffed with useful Lower Mainland information, *Best Hikes Vancouver* features forty-one mapped and cued hikes. Here's an outline of the book's major components:

Each section begins with an **introduction to the region**, in which you're given a sweeping look at the lay of the land.

Each hike then starts with a short **summary** of highlights. These quick overviews give you a taste of the hiking adventures to follow. Here's where you can find details about trail terrain and what surprises each route has to offer.

Following the overview you'll find the **hike specs:** quick, nitty-gritty details of the hike. Most are self-explanatory, but here are some details on others:

Distance: The total distance of the recommended route—one way for loop hikes, the round-trip on an out-and-back or lollipop hike, point-to-point for a shuttle. Options are additional.

Hiking time: The average time it takes to cover the route. It is based on the total distance, elevation gain, and condition and difficulty of the trail. Your fitness level will also affect your time.

Difficulty: Each hike has been assigned a level of difficulty. The rating system was developed from several sources and personal experience. These levels are meant to be a guideline only, and hikes may prove easier or harder for different people depending on ability and physical fitness.

- **Easy**—Less than 8 kilometers (5 miles) total trip distance in one day, with minimal elevation gain, and paved or smooth-surfaced dirt trail.
- **Moderate**—Up to 16 kilometers (10 miles) total trip distance in one day, with moderate elevation gain and potentially rough terrain.
- **Difficult**—More than 16 kilometers (10 miles) total trip distance in one day, strenuous elevation gain, and/or rough, rocky terrain.

Trail surface: General information about what to expect underfoot.

Best season: General information on the best time of year to hike

Other trail users: Such as horseback riders, mountain bikers, in-line skaters, etc.

Canine compatibility: Know the trail regulations before you take your dog hiking with you. Dogs are not allowed on several trails in this book, and often must be leashed.

Land status: Provincial park, city park, Crown lands, etc.

Fees and permits: Whether you need to reserve a day-use pass for a particular park, or carry any money with you for park entrance fees and permits.

Maps: This is a list of other maps to supplement the maps in this book. National Topographic System maps are the best source for accurate topographical information, but the local park map may show more recent trails. Use both.

Trail contacts: This is the location, phone number, and website URL for the local organization(s) in charge of all the trails within the selected hike. Before you head out, get trail access information, or contact the park office after your visit if you see problems with trail erosion, damage, or misuse.

Other: Other information that will enhance and help your hike.

Special considerations: This section calls your attention to specific trail hazards, like a lack of water or hunting seasons.

The **Finding the trailhead** section gives you dependable driving directions to where you want to park.

The Hike is the meat of the chapter. Detailed and honest, it's a carefully researched impression of the trail. It also often includes lots of area history, both natural and human.

Distances and Directions identifies all turns and trail name changes, as well as points of interest. **Options** are also given for many hikes to make your journey shorter or longer depending on the amount of time you have.

Lastly, the **Hike Information** section provides information on local events and attractions, restaurants, and hiking organizations.

Don't feel restricted to the routes and trails that are mapped here. Be adventurous and use this guide as a platform to discover new routes for yourself. One of the simplest ways to begin this is to just turn the map upside down and hike any route in reverse. The change in perspective is often fantastic, and the hike should feel quite different.

For your own purposes, you may wish to copy the route directions onto a small sheet of paper to help you while hiking, or photocopy the map and cue sheet to take with you. Snapping a photo on your cell phone is a third option—provided your battery is fully charged! Otherwise, just slip the whole book in your backpack and take it all with you. Enjoy your time in the outdoors and remember to pack out what you pack in.

Enjoy and Respect This Beautiful Landscape

As you take advantage of the spectacular scenery offered by the Vancouver area, remember that our planet is very dear, very special, and very fragile. All of us should do everything we can to keep it clean, beautiful, and healthy, including following the Green Tips throughout this book.

How to Use the Maps

Besides the overview map that gives you a wide look at the region, each hike has its own individual route map.

Overview map: This map shows the location of each hike in the area by hike number.

Route map: This is your primary guide to each hike. It shows all of the main accessible roads and trails, points of interest, water, landmarks, and geographical features. It also distinguishes trails from roads. The selected route is highlighted, and directional arrows point the way.

Trail Finder

Hike No.	Hike Name	Best for Beaches and Coast	Best for Waterfalls	Best on a Rainy Day	Best for Families
1	Beaver Lake				•
2	Stanley Park Seawall	•			•
3	Spanish Banks	•			•
4	Pacific Spirit Loop	•			•
5	Acadia and Tower Beaches	•			
6	Grouse Grind				
7	Goat Mountain				
8	Lynn Valley to Grouse Mountain				
9	Lynn Peak				
10	Norvan Falls		•	•	
11	Deep Cove to Lynn Canyon				
12	Mount Seymour				
13	Capilano Pacific Trail	•		•	•
14	Lighthouse Park	•		•	•
15	Cypress Falls		•	•	•
16	Hollyburn Ridge				•
17	Saint Mark's Summit				
18	Eagle Bluff				•
19	Killarney Lake			•	•
20	Mount Gardner				
21	The Lions Binkert				
22	Petgill Lake				
23	Sea to Summit		•		

Best with Dogs	Best for Peak Baggers	Best for Old Growth Trees	Best for Great Views	Best for Lakes	Best for Canyons	Best for Nature	Best for a Workout
		•				•	
		•	•				•
•			•				•
•						•	
•			•			•	
							•
	•		•			•	
•						•	
	•		•				•
•						•	
			•		•		
	•		•			•	•
•		•	•		•	•	•
•		•	•			•	
•		•			•	•	
•		•		•			
	•	•	•			•	
	•	•	•	•		•	
•		•	•	•		•	
•	•		•			•	
	•		•			•	•
•			•	•		•	
			•			•	•

Hike No.	Hike Name	Best for Beaches and Coast	Best for Waterfalls	Best on a Rainy Day	Best for Families
24	Stawamus Chief				●
25	Alice Lake Provincial Park	●		●	●
26	Burnaby Mountain				●
27	Buntzen Lake	●			●
28	Sendero Diez Vistas	●			
29	Sasamat Lake	●			●
30	Jug Island Beach	●		●	●
31	Derby Reach	●			●
32	UBC Malcolm Knapp Research Forest				●
33	Minnekhada High Knoll Loop			●	●
34	Katzie Marsh Loop				●
35	Widgeon Falls		●		●
36	Gold Creek Falls	●	●	●	●
37	Hayward Lake		●		●
38	Iona Jetty	●			●
39	Brunswick Point	●			
40	Burns Bog				●
41	Boundary Bay	●			●

Best with Dogs	Best for Peak Baggers	Best for Old Growth Trees	Best for Great Views	Best for Lakes	Best for Canyons	Best for Nature	Best for a Workout
	•		•				•
•				•		•	
•							•
•		•	•	•		•	•
	•	•	•	•		•	•
•				•		•	
•			•			•	
•						•	
							•
			•			•	•
			•	•		•	
			•	•		•	
•				•		•	
•				•		•	
•			•			•	•
			•				•
						•	
			•			•	

Map Legend

Municipal

≡🍁≡	Trans-Canada Highway
≡(5)≡	Interstate Highway
≡(11)≡	Provincial/State Highway
══════	Local Road
= = = =	Unpaved Road
┼─┼─┼	Railway
── ── ──	Gondola
▪··▬··▪	International Border
···─···	Provincial Border

Trails

▬▬▬▬▬	Featured Trail
── ── ──	Trail

Water Features

⬭	Body of Water
≈	Swamp/Marsh
∿	River/Creek
≋	Waterfall
∥	Rapids

Symbols

|||||||	Boardwalk
⛴	Boat Launch
⏜⏝	Bridge
▪	Building/Point of Interest
▲	Campground
🅙	Food
🗼	Lighthouse
▲	Mountain/Peak
🅿	Parking
🛆	Picnic Area
🛉	Ranger Station/Park Office
🐾	Scenic View/Lookout
○	Town
①	Trailhead
❓	Visitor Information
🚻	Washrooms or Toilets
🚰	Water

Land Management

▨	Wildlife Refuge
▢	Provincial/Local Park

Vancouver

Talking up Vancouver is a fairly easy job. Various publications and organizations have named the city as one of the most liveable in the world, and no small factor in that is Vancouver's access to wilderness. Just a sip away from grabbing an Americano, there are parks and wild lands supporting bears, raccoons, and migratory birds. Hiking trails twist along shorelines and through expansive, multiuse parks.

Stanley Park is world-renowned for its paved seawall, but step off the tarmac trail and follow needle-packed paths into the interior. Tangled routes lead to lakes, cedar giants, and quiet benches, where the old-growth forest canopy goes a long way to minimizing winter rains. Yes, hiking with an umbrella looks odd, but it's practical here.

Farther west and larger still, Pacific Spirit Regional Park surrounds the University of British Columbia and edges an undeveloped coastline. It's most popular with dog-walkers, but hikers can find narrow woodland routes to gems like Camosun Bog and its carnivorous sundews. The park also envelops a rocky shoreline where World War II searchlight towers and nude sunbathers are an only-in-the-city mix.

On these hikes you don't escape the city; you're hanging out in the backyard with the rest of the Vancouver family. Tourists, cyclists, dogs, parents with strollers, children, in-line skaters, picnickers, and runners may also be sharing the trails. If you can, cycle or take public transit to the trailhead and help reduce pollution and congestion in the city.

1 Beaver Lake

Though best known for its seawall, Stanley Park holds other treasured trails—like this short woodland walk around Beaver Lake. A mix of tourists, Douglas squirrels, and joggers give the park an eclectic life, and the forest path weaves between long-ago-logged stumps, new growth, and some of the park's remaining large cedars and Douglas firs. A pedestrian bridge crosses busy Stanley Park Causeway and connects to more options for easy walks.

Start: RCMP stables parking lot, off Pipeline Road
Distance: 5.0-km (3.1-mile) loop
Hiking time: About 1 hour
Difficulty: Easy due to flat, well-maintained trails and minimal elevation gain
Trail surface: Gravel, dirt, and forested trails
Best season: Year-round
Other trail users: Cyclists, equestrians, tourists
Canine compatibility: Leashed dogs permitted
Land status: City park
Fees and permits: Paid parking

Schedule: Open 24 hours, though daylight hours recommended
Maps: The Vancouver Board of Parks and Recreation (vancouver.ca/parks-recreation-culture .aspx) produces a park map with named trails for the entire park. Government topographic maps include the GeoBC Topographic Map Viewer (gov.bc.ca), as well as map 92G6 in the Atlas of Canada Toporama tool (atlas.gc.ca).
Trail contacts: Vancouver Board of Parks and Recreation, 2099 Beach Ave., Vancouver, BC, V6G 1Z4; 311 locally or (604) 873-7000; vancouver.ca

Finding the trailhead: From Downtown Vancouver, drive northwest on West Georgia Street toward the Lions Gate Bridge. Keep in the Stanley Park lane and take the Stanley Park exit, about a block beyond the Denman Street intersection. At the roundabout, take the second turnoff for Pipeline Road and the miniature train. Pass the Rose Garden and park in the lot on the left-hand side, across from the miniature train parking lot. Trailhead GPS: N49 18.06' / W123 08.26'

The Hike

When you leave the seawall, beaches, and totem poles, you discover Stanley Park's quieter side. Though the park is encircled by a scenic drive and bisected by a high-speed causeway, its interior trails still offer a vibrant forest ecosystem with a calm lake and chattering wildlife. On this hike, you see just how close the urban and natural worlds can coexist.

Beaver Lake sits at Stanley Park's geographic center. The boglike body of water is only about a meter (3 feet) deep and has shrunk by more than a third over the years. It's said that European settlers spotted beavers here and named the lake for them in 1907. Other sources tie the name to the SS *Beaver*, the first steamship that sailed the BC coast and was wrecked on Prospect Point.

Centuries-old cedars are some of the old-growth trees in Stanley Park.

In 2008, a beaver became the first in the lake for nearly 60 years. The years since have seen park staff put protective collars on trees and remove debris that dams Beaver Creek—foiling the rodent's efforts. As of 2020, the beavers (reportedly up to five of them!) are still gnawing away.

The lake is full of diverse life year-round. In spring the pungent waft of skunk cabbage lingers on the lakeshore. Birds are plentiful: Darting passerines land on the outstretched palms of tourists, pecking at crumbs, while mallard and wood ducks swim among the lily pads. It is these water lilies that are clogging the lake and turning it into a bog.

If you're not on a schedule, sit on the lakeside benches and watch for squirrels. The more prevalent eastern gray squirrels are the descendants of those scampering in New York's Central Park. The gray rodents are now considered one of the most invasive species in the world. But it's the Douglas squirrel—smaller, brown, and with a shorter tail—that's native to these woods. Listen for their bossy chatter as you walk along the gravel path.

After rounding the lake, you cross the always-busy causeway using an equestrian-pedestrian bridge, constructed to allow mounted police (the Royal Canadian Mounted Police, that is) to patrol park trails on horseback.

Lilies and other pond plants are clogging up Beaver Lake.

This western half of Stanley Park is home to the park's larger trees. Some edge paved Stanley Park Drive, while others border trails like Tatlow Walk (once a skid road) and Lees Trail. Sadly, these giants are outnumbered by the decay-resistant cedar stumps, many with springboard notches still visible. To reach the straight-grain wood that begins above the tree's flared base, lumbermen stuck scaffolding-like boards directly into the trunk and felled the giant West Coast trees by hand.

Others faded due to their fame, like the Seven Sisters. Once some of the tallest in the world, the trees became one of the park's most popular attractions but for safety reasons were cut down in 1953.

In addition to logging, storms have affected the park's tree-scape: Hurricane Freda felled 3,000 trees in 1962, and in 2006 a windstorm took down another 10,000.

But out of destruction often comes new life, and today you see new and mature trees shooting from these stumps and fallen trunks.

Distances and Directions

0.0 km/0.0 mile   Start from the parking lot next to the RCMP horse stables. Head west, away from Pipeline Road, to find the unmarked trailhead. Continue west on the forest trail.

0.2 km/0.1 mile   At the South Creek Trail junction, turn right (north).

0.3 km/0.2 mile   Keep right (northeast) when the woodland path meets Wren Trail.

0.5 km/0.3 mile   Join with the shoreline Beaver Lake Trail, and turn right (east) to follow the flat gravel path counterclockwise around the lake.

0.6 km/0.4 mile   Pass Tisdall Walk (on the right), which runs a short distance along a creek and back to Pipeline Road.

0.9 km/0.6 mile   When a bike route and Ravine Trail join the trail from the right, continue west around the lake. Ravine Trail descends to Pipeline Road, Stanley Park Drive, and the Seawall.

1.1 km/0.7 mile   The trail forks. The left route continues around the lake; the right (Lake Trail) branches off west. Keep right and head away from the lake.

1.2 km/0.7 mile   Continue straight (west) as you reach the junction with North Creek Trail.

1.4 km/0.9 mile   Cross over the Stanley Park Causeway via the pedestrian bridge. The bridge has a lane for horses too, as it links the two halves of the park.

1.5 km/0.9 mile   Lake Trail continues on the west side of the causeway. Continue straight (west) at the Bridle Path junction.

1.6 km/1.0 mile   Keep right (west) as the trail branches off to Lovers Walk.

1.7 km/1.1 miles   Again, keep straight (west) as Lake Trail meets the short connector, Squirrel Trail. (Note: Park signs and maps vary in labeling Squirrel Trail.)

2.1 km/1.3 miles   Stop to admire the stump of one of Stanley Park's western red cedar giants, then hang a sharp left (south) to walk along Rawlings Trail.

2.2 km/1.4 miles   Continue south along Rawlings at the junction with Tatlow Walk.

2.5 km/1.6 miles   When a trail branches right (north) to Third Beach, turn left (southeast) along an overgrown, singletrack trail that connects with Lovers Walk. (**Side-trip:** Have a full day to enjoy in the park's natural wonders? At Tatlow Walk head west down to Third Beach. A concession stand serves snacks and lunches during summer, and the beach logs allow for an impromptu picnic.)

2.6 km/1.6 miles   Turn left (east) onto Lovers Walk, and immediately pass another giant cedar.

Beaver Lake

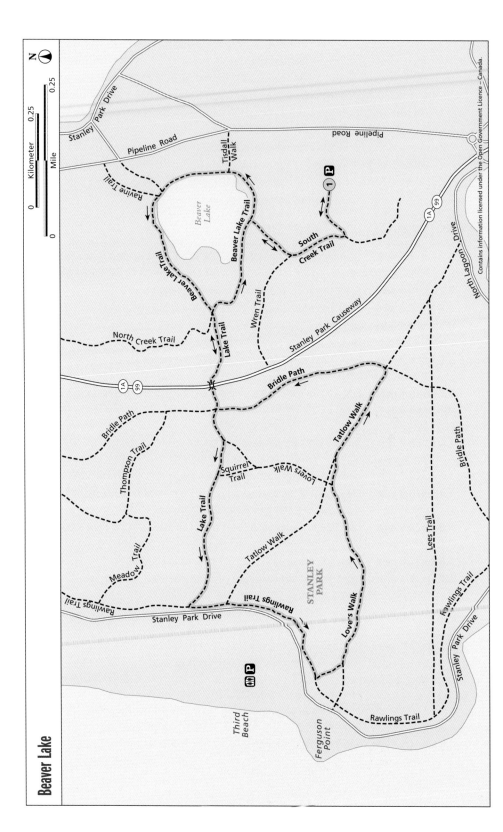

3.1 km/1.9 miles   Turn right (southeast) on Tatlow Walk as it intersects your path, Lovers Walk. (Continuing straight on Lovers Walk is a slightly faster return trip.)

3.5 km/2.2 miles   At Bridle Path, turn left (north) and make the slight ascent back toward Lake Trail. This is where the popular Seven Sisters grew until 1953.

4.0 km/2.5 miles   Turn right (east) onto Lake Trail and cross back over the causeway.

4.3 km/2.7 miles   At North Creek Trail, cut right (southeast) to immediately connect with Beaver Lake Trail. This path completes the counterclockwise loop around the lake.

4.6 km/2.9 miles   Turn right (southwest) onto South Creek Trail and leave the lakeshore.

4.7 km/2.9 miles   Continue south as Wren Trail joins South Creek.

4.9 km/3.0 miles   Turn left (east) onto the connector trail, following the familiar route back to the parking lot.

5.0 km/3.1 miles   Arrive back at the trailhead.

Options: With so many trails in Stanley Park, it's easy to design shorter or longer routes. Most trails in the park are mapped and named so it's easy to chart a route. If you have kids in tow, take Tatlow Walk or Cathedral Trail down to Lost Lagoon. Spot ducks, swans, and herons feeding in the once-tidal lagoon, and then follow the shore around to Stanley Park Nature House on the southeast shore of the lagoon.

Hike Information

Local Information: Stop by the Stanley Park Info Booth for maps and more. 715 Stanley Park Dr., Vancouver, BC, V6G 3E2.

Local Attractions: Call ahead to confirm opening hours, but there are many family-focused attractions in Stanley Park. Kids and adults equally love a visit to see the otters, Steller sea lions, and other marine life at the Vancouver Aquarium (845 Avison Way, Stanley Park, Vancouver; 604-659-3474; vanaqua.org). Park tours include rides on the Stanley Park Railway (690 Pipeline Rd.; 604-257-8531) and Stanley Park Horse-Drawn Tours (735 Stanley Park Dr., Vancouver; 604-681-5115; stanleypark .com).

Restaurants: Savor a fine meal and patio views from Ferguson Point at The Teahouse in Stanley Park (7501 Stanley Park Dr., Vancouver; 604-669-3281; vancouverdine .com). Or in summer season opt for pub grub or takeout at Stanley's Bar and Grill (610 Pipeline Rd., Stanley Park, Vancouver; 604-602-3088; stanleysbargrill.com).

Organizations: Contact the Stanley Park Nature House about any scheduled guided nature walks or the opening hours for exhibits. Southeast shore of Lost Lagoon; (604) 257-8544; stanleyparkecology.ca.

GREEN TIP
Pass it down—the best way to instill good green habits in your children is to set a good example.

2 Stanley Park Seawall

This is Vancouver's iconic walk: an easy, flat path that circumnavigates the 405 hectares (1,000 acres) of Stanley Park. Along the paved, easy-to-follow trail, a scenic blend of mountain views and saltwater shoreline unfold. Plus there are historical sites, wildlife sightings, and picnic spots to relish. Best of all, the route is always busy with Vancouverites and visitors—this is where you come to be part of the city.

Start: Devonian Harbour Park, 1929 W. Georgia St., near the Coal Harbour marina
Distance: 9.3-km (5.8-mile) loop
Hiking time: 2–3 hours
Difficulty: Easy due to sea-level trail with a smooth, paved surface
Trail surface: Pavement, gravel
Best season: Year-round
Other trail users: Dog walkers, cyclists, in-line skaters, camera-happy tourists
Canine compatibility: Leashed dogs permitted
Land status: City park
Fees and permits: Paid parking in some lots

Schedule: Open 24 hours, though daylight hours recommended
Maps: The Vancouver Board of Parks and Recreation (vancouver.ca/parks-recreation-culture.aspx) produces a park map with trail names included. Government topographic maps include the GeoBC Topographic Map Viewer (gov.bc.ca), as well as map 92G6 in the Atlas of Canada Toporama tool (atlas.gc.ca).
Trail contacts: Vancouver Board of Parks and Recreation, 2099 Beach Ave., Vancouver, BC, V6G 1Z4; 311 locally or (604) 873-7000; vancouver.ca

Finding the trailhead: From Downtown Vancouver, drive northwest on West Georgia Street toward the Lions Gate Bridge. Drive in the marked Stanley Park lane and take the Stanley Park exit. At the roundabout, take the first turnoff for Park Drive. Park in any of the lots just off Park Drive. There is also a pay parking lot at 501 Denman St., just off West Georgia. Trailhead GPS: N 49 17.71' / W123 08.16'

The Hike

It took more than 60 years to complete construction of the seawall loop around Stanley Park. What's now a paved path—as popular with cycling tourists as it is with parents pushing strollers—began in 1917 as a way to halt erosion. One man is largely responsible for the city's most popular recreational path; James Cunningham oversaw the project from the late 1920s to 1963. It's said that once, the very dedicated Scottish stonemason even came to check on the seawall construction dressed in his pajamas. In a nod to the seawall's distance (and perhaps also Cunningham's marathon-construction effort), there's a 10-kilometer (6.2 mile) race named for him (lgrr.com/seawall).

But despite this sustained effort through much of the 20th century, it wasn't until 1980 that the city paved the portion between Third Beach and Second Beach, and work was officially declared complete.

Left: The Stanley Park Seawall borders the city.
Right: The Stanley Park Seawall passes sights such as Brockton Point Lighthouse.

Today the Vancouver seawall extends beyond Stanley Park, following the beach-trimmed shore of the West End, passing Yaletown and False Creek, and then curving west again to Granville Island and Kitsilano Beach.

Typically, bicycles and in-line skaters can only travel the Stanley Park Seawall in one direction: counterclockwise. But while COVID-19 restrictions temporarily moved bikes and experienced in-line skaters to the roadway in 2020, walkers still have their pick of which direction to travel.

This very urban hike never leaves the city behind, yet it does put a buffer of nature (forest or ocean) between you and the glass towers.

The counterclockwise loop begins in Coal Harbour. Keep to the right-hand side as you follow the paved trail. The first section travels out along Brockton Point. Here, on the narrow peninsula, are the park's chief attractions: the Brockton Point Totem Poles and the Vancouver Aquarium. Historical plaques help you piece together local history, whether it's the statue of world-record-setting sprinter Harry Jerome or the figurehead of the Pacific-crossing ocean liner the *Empress of Japan*.

As the path leaves the more developed eastern area of the park, look down on the marine life and seaweed that clings to the rocks and seawall masonry. Purple starfish are a particularly fantastical sight, and a favorite with kids.

Passing under the Lions Gate Bridge and then Prospect Point, you reach the more remote end of Stanley Park. Look out onto the Strait of Georgia, perhaps spotting

Walkers and runners get a workout on the Stanley Park Seawall.

year-round residents like gulls and pelagic cormorants. To the landward side, basalt cliffs rise as a steep, impenetrable wall. Near Siwash Rock, there's a plaque that honors James Cunningham.

Another monument near Third Beach marks the resting place of Mohawk poet Pauline Johnson. In her book *Legends of Vancouver*, Johnson weaves magical stories of the park and city, as told to her by Squamish Chief Joseph Capilano. The work was published before Johnson's death in 1913, and the poet was buried in the park.

Of Siwash Rock, a basalt column, Johnson retells the tale of a young warrior who is about to become a father. Tradition dictates that a father must swim to be clean for the birth of his child, but when the young man encounters the canoe of the Great Tyee, he is ordered out of the water. When the warrior refuses to stop swimming, the Great Tyee acknowledges his commitment to his child by saying, "You have placed that child's future before all things.

"You shall stand through all the thousands of years to come, where all eyes can see you. You shall live, live, live as an indestructible monument to Clean Fatherhood."

From Siwash Rock the paved path follows the shore to Third Beach and Ferguson Point. At Second Beach, the route continues to the West End. But to return to Coal Harbour, you must cut inland along Lost Lagoon (the name of which comes from another Pauline Johnson poem). There, watch for ducks, geese, and swans in the fresh water, which was a saltwater lagoon until the Stanley Park Causeway dammed the lagoon's mouth in 1916.

Distances and Directions

0.0 km/0.0 mile Start from the large paved circle alongside the pond in Devonian Harbour Park, just west of Coal Harbour Marina. Follow the seawall north to travel counterclockwise around Stanley Park. This route aligns with the brass kilometer-markers around the seawall.

0.2 km/0.1 mile Pass the historic 1911 Vancouver Rowing Club. Look left across Stanley Park Drive to see the statue of Robbie Burns.

0.5 km/0.3 mile Reach the Stanley Park Info Booth.

1.2 km/0.7 mile A gated road leads right to Deadman's Island, traditionally a First Nations burial site and now the HMCS Discovery naval base. But continue east on the seawall.

1.5 km/0.9 mile One of the busiest tourist sites in the city is the totem pole collection at Brockton Point. Pass the trail to the totems. Or, if you're keen to take a look, be careful in crossing Park Drive. This is also a good point to get drinking water or take a bathroom break.

1.8 km/1.1 miles Plug your ears if it's 9 p.m.—the report of the Nine O'Clock Gun sounds here each night. It once signaled time for ships in the harbor.

2.0 km/1.2 miles Stop at the viewpoint to look out at the North Shore Mountains and back on Downtown Vancouver. The 1914 Brockton Point Lighthouse is just around the corner. It helps guide ships leaving Burrard Inlet through First Narrows.

2.5 km/1.6 miles Pass the north side of the totem poles, where there are washrooms.

2.9 km/1.8 miles Mark the tide's height on the Girl in a Wetsuit statue. At high tide the water laps her flippers; at low tide you can walk out to the rock. A few meters farther, see the colorfully painted bow of the *Empress of Japan,* which sailed across the Pacific more than 300 times between 1891 and 1922. The figurehead is a fiberglass copy, as the original is now in the Vancouver Maritime Museum collection.

Stanley Park Seawall

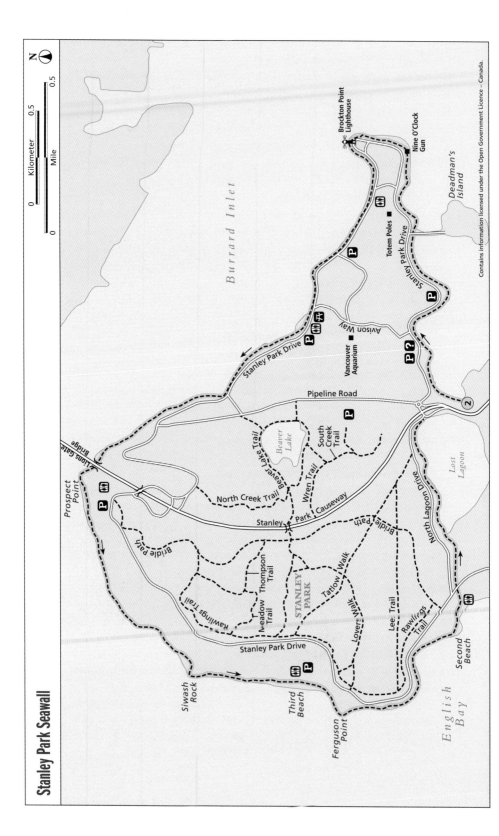

Contains information licensed under the Open Government Licence – Canada.

3.9 km/2.4 miles   Continue northwest on the seawall past Ravine Trail, which leads 300 meters inland to Beaver Lake.

4.3 km/2.7 miles   Need a snack or a bathroom break? Ascend the left trail that climbs up, crosses the Lions Gate Bridge, and reaches Prospect Point.

4.7 km/2.9 miles   Walk under the giant span of Lions Gate Bridge, which connects Downtown Vancouver and the North Shore across First Narrows.

6.2 km/3.9 miles   Pass Siwash Rock and look for a memorial to James Cunningham—the man who oversaw seawall construction.

6.7 km/4.2 miles   Stop at Third Beach, an especially lovely spot at sunset. There are also drinks and snacks available at the concession stand here. (***Option:*** If it's a sunny day and you'd prefer some shade, pick up Tatlow Walk at Third Beach and return to Lost Lagoon under the cool branches of centuries-old cedars.)

7.2 km/4.5 miles   Continue along the seawall at the Ferguson Point stairs. The path ascends to The Teahouse in Stanley Park and a fantastic view atop Ferguson Point (with the Pauline Johnson memorial nearby).

8.2 km/5.1 miles   After passing Second Beach Pool and the concession stand but before reaching the playground and beach, turn left (east) and cross Park Drive. Walk along Lagoon Trail, a gravel route that runs along Lost Lagoon and parallel to North Lagoon Drive.

9.3 km/5.8 miles   End the walk at the Lost Lagoon duck beach. To return to the starting point, follow the underpass beneath Stanley Park Causeway and continue down to the Coal Harbour waterfront.

Options: If you love the experience of walking along the water, try following one of Vancouver's other seawalls. Other popular stretches include along the Coal Harbor waterfront from Canada Place, from English Bay to Yaletown, and from False Creek to Granville Island. Across first narrows, the Ambleside seawall in West Vancouver connects with Capilano Pacific Trail (hike 13).

Hike Information

Local Information: For a full list of all the tours and attractions available in Stanley Park, put an inquiry in at Tourism Vancouver. 200 Burrard St., Vancouver, BC, V6C 3L6; (604) 683-2000; tourismvancouver.com.

Restaurants: Stanley Park has a wide variety of snack stops, takeout, patios, and fine dining restaurants. There are beach concession stands at Third Beach and Second Beach, or stop for coffee, ice cream, or more at Prospect Point Cafe (5601 Stanley Park Dr., Vancouver; (604) 669-2737; prospectpoint.ca).

GREEN TIP
If you see someone else littering, muster up the courage to ask them not to. Or bring a plastic bag and pick up a few pieces of garbage each hike.

3 Spanish Banks

Point Grey's parks are most popular for the more than 3.0 kilometers (1.9 miles) of public beaches from Jericho to Spanish Banks. Beach-going throngs overtake the area in summer (when it's best to retreat under the secluded canopies of adjacent Pacific Spirit Park—see the Pacific Spirit Loop and Acadia and Tower Beaches hikes), yet the well-drained, sand-and-gravel path is a surprisingly good option come heavy rains in November through March. In any season, the spectacular, wide vantage looks out to the North Shore Mountains and Downtown Vancouver.

Start: Jericho Beach parking lot at 3941 Point Grey Rd.
Distance: 7.4-km (4.6-mile) out-and-back
Hiking time: About 2 hours
Difficulty: Easy due to flat, smooth terrain and no elevation gain
Trail surface: Gravel and packed sand trail
Best season: Year-round, but especially during winter
Other trail users: Cyclists, dog-walkers, runners, strollers
Canine compatibility: Leashed dogs permitted along the trail; no dogs permitted on the beaches. (There's a marked off-leash area at the west end of the trail.)

Land status: City park
Fees and permits: Paid parking if free stalls are full
Schedule: Open 24 hours, but daylight hours recommended
Maps: There are no city maps available. Government topographic maps include the GeoBC Topographic Map Viewer (gov.bc.ca), as well as map 92G6 in the Atlas of Canada Toporama tool (atlas.gc.ca).
Trail contacts: Vancouver Board of Parks and Recreation, 2099 Beach Ave., Vancouver, BC, V6G 1Z4; 311 locally or (604) 873-7000; vancouver.ca

Finding the trailhead: From West 4th Avenue or West Broadway Avenue, drive west to Alma Street. Turn right (north) onto Alma. Follow Alma Street to the T intersection with Point Grey Road. Take a left (west) at the stop sign, and drive 3 blocks on Point Grey Road to the Jericho Beach parking lot. Or save on parking and take public transit. Routes 4, 7, 32, 44, and 84 all stop at the intersection of West 4th Avenue and Alma Street. Trailhead GPS: N49 16.28' / W123 11.51'

The Hike

Jericho and Spanish Banks Beaches have witnessed much of Vancouver's history: First Nations lived in a village called Ee'yullmough for untold centuries; Spanish cartographers arrived in 1791; loggers cleared the forests in the late 1800s; the city's first golf course opened in 1889; an air force and military base operated through World War II; and hippies established an enclave called "Cool-Aid" in 1970.

Not too bad for a city that some consider to be light on history.

Today, the shoreline simply serves as one of Vancouver's larger recreational areas. At about 72 hectares (178 acres), the string of three parks (Jericho, Locarno, and

Top: *Spanish Banks East sits apart from, but still in view of, the city.*
Bottom: *Spanish Banks Extension is the end of the trail—but you can continue farther along the shoreline.*

Spanish Banks) has beaches lining the northern edge and woods that provide a buffer from West 4th Avenue, the West Point Grey neighborhood, and the University of British Columbia.

In the hot summer months, crowds of beachgoers prop themselves up against sunbleached logs—the city parks board lines up logs on the beach as makeshift benches.

So it's in fall and winter that this hike is loveliest. The gravel path drains quickly after heavy rain showers, making a 2-hour break in the weather reason enough to embark on this shoreline walk.

The trail starts at Jericho, near the washrooms and concession stand (one of four along the trail). Walk west along the shore, parallel to the beach. Despite there being one freshwater and ten saltwater beaches in Vancouver, Jericho is a rarity for its natural sands. To the south lie large grassy spaces popular with bocce players, Frisbee tossers, and barbecuing groups. After loggers removed old-growth forests in the late 1800s, these lands became Vancouver's first golf course.

As the sand tapers, you reach Vancouver's newest beach area. The city demolished the Jericho Beach Marginal Wharf in 2012. The relic was part of the 1920s air force base and World War II military operation. Other wartime buildings included airplane hangars; tennis courts now stand in the footprint.

At the Jericho Sailing Centre, Discovery Street heads left (south) to the few remaining military buildings, repurposed in various ways. The former junior barracks is now a youth hostel, the recreation hall became the Jericho Arts Centre, and the old officers' mess is a community center.

This hike needs little navigation as you simply follow the main gravel path straight ahead to more beaches: Locarno, Spanish Banks East, and Spanish Banks West string out in a blissfully sandy order. Each has lifeguard stations, washrooms, water fountains, and concession stands that sell burger-and-fries meals as well as drinks.

At low tide, the wide sand flats of Spanish Banks emerge to the north. For an alternative route, head out north over the flat, low tide sands. (You can walk south to rejoin the main trail wherever you choose.) This is an especially nice option come August, when summer vacationers congest the path. Just steer clear of the skim boarders as they surf over the waterlogged sand.

The name Spanish Banks comes from explorers who first entered the harbor. In the late 1700s, activity centered on Vancouver Island's Nootka Sound, with the Spanish, Russians, Americans, and English all vying for the strategic location. But explorers, including Captain George Vancouver, were branching out to map the West Coast's many inlets, rivers, and islands in Puget Sound and along the Strait of Georgia.

ONE LOW TIDE

Vancouver is a saltwater port connected to the Pacific Ocean by the Strait of Georgia. But its tides don't rise and fall to the same rhythm as most coastal areas. While there are two high tides along the Vancouver shoreline, there's only one truly low tide each day. The other drop in ocean level could more fittingly be called a "medium" tide as it falls only about half the distance of other low tides. The reason? The north end of Vancouver Island sits snug to the mainland and other islands, and the narrow straits (often only 2 to 3 km [1.2 to 1.9 miles] wide) restrict water flow and skew tidal heights.

A rower near Jericho Beach

In 1791 José María Narváez anchored at Point Grey and was the first European to visit the harbor. Near Spanish Banks Extension, an anchor sculpture memorializes this arrival. On summer Sundays pre-COVID, drummers often gathered here to pound rhythms into the evening.

About an hour before sunset, the sky and clouds turn from blue to mauve to pink, and orange rays reflect off multimillion-dollar homes on the North Shore Mountains. The trail ends just west of the anchor, with a panoramic view from Bowen Island in the west to downtown Vancouver in the east. A wilder coastline continues, out to Acadia Beach, Tower Beach, Point Grey, and the clothing-optional Wreck Beach. And although downtown Vancouver is only a 20-minute drive away, it looks ever so distant.

Spanish Banks

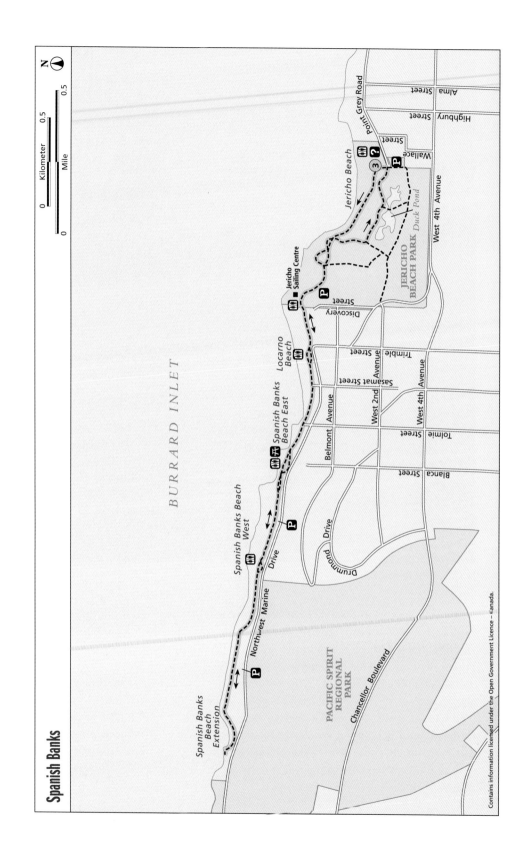

BURRARD INLET

Spanish Banks Beach Extension

Spanish Banks Beach West

Northwest Marine Drive

Spanish Banks Beach East

Locarno Beach

Jericho Sailing Centre

Jericho Beach

JERICHO BEACH PARK   Duck Pond

PACIFIC SPIRIT REGIONAL PARK

Chancellor Boulevard

Drummond Drive

Belmont Avenue

Blanca Street

Tolmie Street

West 2nd Avenue

Sasamat Street

Trimble Street

West 4th Avenue

Discovery Street

Point Grey Road

Wallace Street

Highbury Street

Alma Street

West 4th Avenue

N

0   0.5   1 Kilometer

0   0.5   1 Mile

Contains information licensed under the Open Government Licence – Canada.

Distances and Directions

0.0 km/0.0 mile   Start from the trail at the Jericho Beach concession stand and walk west along the gravel path, passing Jericho Beach.

0.5 km/0.3 mile   There are binoculars at the newest beach area, where the demolished World War II Jericho Beach Marginal Wharf once stood. If you'd like to meet the resident rabbits, head south from the beach to the blackberry bushes. Brazen bunnies will nibble snacks from your hand. In late summer, you can pick a few ripe blackberries for yourself or the rabbits.

0.7 km/0.4 mile   Pass the tennis courts, the old site of air force hangars.

0.9 km/0.6 mile   Bear left at the Jericho Sailing Centre, or stop in for drinks on the mountain-view patio. The nearby pier, to your right (north), is popular with anglers.

1.3 km/0.8 mile   The trail continues west past Locarno Beach.

2.0 km/1.2 miles   Spanish Banks Beach East has a concession stand.

2.5 km/1.6 miles   Spanish Banks West also has washrooms, a concession stand, and a swimming beach.

2.9 km/1.8 miles   The dog off-leash area begins.

3.4 km/2.1 miles   Pass the anchor sculpture commemorating José María Narváez's visit to Spanish Banks. Spanish Banks Extension, also called the "dog beach," is on the north side of the path.

3.7 km/2.3 miles   Reach the turnaround point. After savoring the wide views, return east along the path, back the way you came.

6.9 km/4.3 miles   At the west end of Jericho Beach, head right (south) on a gravel spur. The trail leads away from the beach for a short detour along shaded trails and past a duck pond.

7.4 km/4.6 miles   Arrive back at the trailhead.

Options: At the 2.8-kilometer (1.7-mile) mark, cross south over Northwest Marine Drive to find trails leading into Pacific Spirit Park. The park contains 763 hectares (1,885 acres) of woodlands, where dog-walkers, joggers, and even horseback riders share the trails. The Pacific Spirit Loop and Acadia and Tower Beaches hikes explore the park.

Hike Information

Local Information: For details on beach lifeguards at Jericho, Locarno, or Spanish Banks Beaches, contact the Kitsilano Beach Tower (1305 Arbutus St., Vancouver, BC, V6J 5N2; 604-738-8535 [seasonal]). The Environment Canada Weather office can provide a full local forecast (weather.gc.ca) as well as marine weather.

Restaurants: Grab takeout—perhaps a salmon burger or fish & chips—at The Galley Patio & Grill in the Jericho Sailing Centre. The summer-season patio here is one of the best in the city. 1300 Discovery St., Vancouver; (604) 222-1331; thegalley.ca.

Organizations: Find out about water-related activities and local information at the Jericho Sailing Centre. 1300 Discovery St., Vancouver; (604) 224-4177; jsca.bc.ca.

Other Resources: For more about the military years at Jericho Beach Park, read *Jericho Beach and the West Coast Flying Boat Stations* by Chris Weicht (Creekside Publications, 2008).

4 Pacific Spirit Loop

When the crowds descend on Spanish Banks Beaches, you can escape to the relative tranquility of this woodland ridge trail above the shoreline. Pacific Spirit Regional Park is the largest park in Vancouver, but as it is tucked away near the University of British Columbia, its lands can be fairly untraveled. This short loop connects to a larger network of quiet trails that explore the often flat, forest terrain.

Start: Spanish Banks parking lot, just west of Spanish Banks West
Distance: 5.5-km (3.4-mile) loop
Hiking time: About 1 hour
Difficulty: Easy due to short distance and well-maintained forested trails, though there are some stairs and inclines
Trail surface: Forested trail, dirt path, boardwalk, stairs, and gravel path
Best season: Year-round, especially during winter
Other trail users: Dog-walkers with off-leash dogs
Canine compatibility: Off-leash dogs permitted

Land status: Regional park
Fees and permits: No fees or permits required
Schedule: Daylight hours
Maps: Paper maps are available at the trailhead and online at metrovancouver.org. Government topographic maps include the GeoBC Topographic Map Viewer (gov.bc.ca), as well as map 92G6 in the Atlas of Canada Toporama tool (atlas.gc.ca).
Trail contacts: Metro Vancouver Regional Parks West Area Office, Suite 130, 1200 W. 73rd Ave., Vancouver, V6P 6G5; (604) 224-5739; metrovancouver.org

Finding the trailhead: Drive west along West 4th Avenue, toward Point Grey. After the Jericho Garrison, turn right (north) onto Northwest Marine Drive. Follow the road past Locarno Beach and Spanish Banks East. Park in Spanish Banks Central Parking Lot, just west of the Spanish Banks West Concession. The trailhead is on the south side of the street. Trailhead GPS: N49 16.64' / W123 13.48'

The Hike

About 1,000 dogs (with their walkers) roam these woods every day, but few other folks seem to discover the forested trails of Pacific Spirit Regional Park—even though the park is the city's largest at 763 hectares (1,885 acres). A slightly dizzying trail network cuts through the forest between Spanish Banks in the north and the Fraser River in the south. All are clearly named and signposted; you just need a good park map.

Pacific Spirit doesn't boast the banner attractions of Vancouver's other large parks, like Stanley Park's totem poles or Queen Elizabeth's tropical conservatory. The attractions at Pacific Spirit are the quiet forests, soggy bogs, and wild beaches. This hike connects them all in a rather short but heart-pumping jaunt.

To begin the 5.5-km (3.4-mile) trip, you leave the sand flats of Spanish Banks to disappear into the forest. The route follows a strung-together loop of forest trails, starting with the aptly named Spanish Trail. Though Captain George Vancouver has bragging rights with the city's name, it was the Spanish who were the first Europeans to visit the harbor in 1791. Lieutenant José María Narváez anchored west of Point Grey—a year earlier than Captain Vancouver.

The forested trail winds south, only to pop out alongside busy Chancellor Boulevard. Take great care in crossing here. The speed limit is higher than the usual city 50 kmph/30 mph limit.

On the far side of the road, Spanish Trail starts to bend west, following University Golf Course to the south—barely visible between the trees, and then crosses a bog boardwalk. The wetlands have a refreshingly open feel. But within steps the path returns to the grand, tall trees of the forest and connects with Salish and Sword Fern—the routes back to the beaches.

In the final stretch following Admiralty Trail east, you find yourself with a peekaboo vantage over Spanish Banks. High on the bluff, you can imagine the scene a little over 2 centuries ago, before the City of Vancouver was founded and when the Coast Salish were the region's only inhabitants. (Nearby, the Musqueam have been living at the mouth of the Fraser River for about 4,000 years and other village sites for even longer.)

Looking out between the trees, try to picture Captain George Vancouver sailing into Burrard Inlet in 1792 and mapping the coast. But as his small survey boats returned to the larger HMS *Discovery,* Vancouver ran into two Spaniards—Dionisio Alcalá Galiano and Cayetano Valdés. Though Vancouver thought he was the first to explore this section of coast, two Spanish ships—the *Sutil* and the *Mexicana*—were already in the inlet. And Narváez had been here the year before.

In his own words, Vancouver felt "no small degree of mortification." The explorers shared details from their surveying work, and when Captain Vancouver drew up maps for the area, he named the sand banks in honor of the Spanish.

Left: Ferns unfurl each spring throughout the park.
Right: Mushrooms, mosses, and other small wonders in a slow hike in Pacific Spirit Regional Park

Left: The evergreens of Pacific Spirit Regional Park tower over the trails.
Right: Tall, straight trees give Pacific Spirit Regional Park a grand feeling.

Distances and Directions

0.0 km/0.0 mile Start on the south side of Northwest Marine Drive and walk uphill (south) on Spanish Trail. There's an information board with hardcopy maps; it's good to grab one if you plan on exploring further.

0.1 km/0.1 mile Pass the Admiralty and then Pioneer Trail junctions, which connect in from the right (west).

0.9 km/0.6 mile Continue straight (southeast) on Spanish Trail at the junction with Chancellor Trail.

1.0 km/0.6 mile Keep right (southwest) as an unnamed spur trail forks left.

1.1 km/0.7 mile Safely cross Chancellor Boulevard—a busy, high-speed route to the University of British Columbia. Spanish Trail heads back into the woods on the south side of the road.

1.4 km/0.9 mile As Spanish Trail bends west, follow it past an exit trail to Tasmania Crescent and then a junction with Pioneer Trail. You may glimpse the University Golf Course greens beyond the trees.

2.1 km/1.3 miles When Spanish Trail forks, follow the left branch (west) and then cross Salish Trail.

2.2 km/1.4 miles Turn right (northwest) onto Sword Fern Trail.

2.5 km/1.6 miles Continue straight (north) on Sword Fern as the path intersects Spanish Trail.

2.7 km/1.7 miles A spur trail, on the left, exits west to Acadia Road.

2.8 km/1.7 miles Sword Fern joins Salish Trail just south of Chancellor Boulevard. Head left (northeast) toward the road.

2.9 km/1.8 miles Cross Chancellor Boulevard again. With the elementary school to your right (east), walk north along the Hamber Road sidewalk. Pick up Salish Trail after about 125 meters (410 feet).

Pacific Spirit Loop

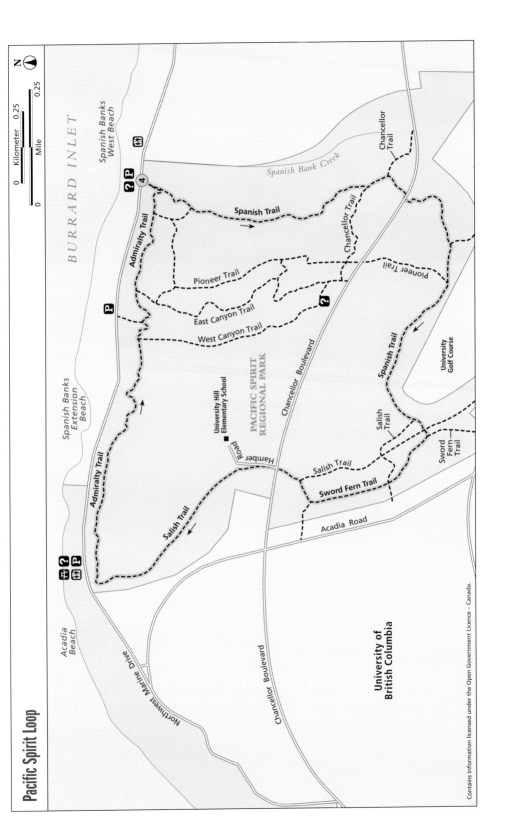

Contains information licensed under the Open Government Licence – Canada.

Quiet, tree-lined trails lace the lands of Pacific Spirit Regional Park.

3.8 km/2.4 miles Just above Northwest Marine Drive, turn right (east) to follow Admiralty Trail along the ridge. Continue past a spur trail to Acadia Beach and through creek canyons.

4.8 km/3.0 miles Continue east past the West Canyon Trail junction. There are stairs down one side of the canyon and up the other. A short spur trail also heads north to the beachside parking lots.

5.0 km/3.1 miles Keep rolling along Admiralty Trail at the East Canyon Trail junction.

5.3 km/3.3 miles Continue straight (east) as Pioneer Trail cuts right toward Chancellor Boulevard.

5.4 km/3.4 miles Turn left (north) and descend Spanish Trail back toward Northwest Marine Drive.

5.5 km/3.4 miles Arrive back at the trailhead.

Option: The park's 73 km (45 miles) of trails are generally well-signposted, so with a full park map it's easy to explore new routes. At Camosun Bog, near West 21st Avenue and Crown Street, you can spot a carnivorous plant: the sundew. The plant lives in the bog's habitats, attracting and feeding on mosquitoes and other insects.

Hike Information

Local Information: Pacific Spirit Park Society holds events, works with the city on restoration projects, and provides information about the park. pacificspiritparksociety .org.

GREEN TIP
When hiking with your dog, stay in the center of the path and keep your pup close by. Dogs that run loose can harm fragile soils and spread pesky plants by carrying their seeds.

5 Acadia and Tower Beaches

On a sunny summer day, you're likely to see hikers—and sunbathers in the buff—along this beach hike. The trail, which is mostly an undefined route along the rocky shore, starts near the University of British Columbia at Acadia Beach. It passes two interesting World War II searchlight towers and ends with a steep climb: the 483 stairs at famous clothing-optional Wreck Beach.

Start: Acadia Beach parking lot on Northwest Marine Drive

Distance: 3.6-km (2.2-mile) point-to-point

Hiking time: About 1 hour

Difficulty: Easy due to the generally flat route, but the rocky terrain and Wreck Beach stairs could pose a moderate challenge

Trail surface: Dirt path, rocky beach, stairs

Best season: Year-round

Other trail users: Nude sunbathers, off-leash dogs Oct–Feb

Canine compatibility: Dogs permitted Oct–Feb

Land status: Regional park

Fees and permits: No fees or permits required

Schedule: Daylight hours

Maps: Paper maps are available in the park and online at metrovancouver.org. Government topographic maps include the GeoBC

Topographic Map Viewer (gov.bc.ca), as well as map 92G6 in the Atlas of Canada Toporama tool (atlas.gc.ca).

Trail contacts: Metro Vancouver Regional Parks West Area Office, Suite 130, 1200 W. 73rd Ave., Vancouver, V6P 6G5; (604) 224-5739; metrovancouver.org

Other: Wreck Beach, where this hike ends, is Vancouver's only nude beach. But on sunny days, the clothing-optional attitude spreads along Tower and Acadia Beaches as well.

Special considerations: Beach rocks can be slippery, and there's not always sand to walk on. There is no fresh water along this hike. At high tide, some sections of the shoreline may be difficult to access (depending on tide height).

Finding the trailhead: Travel west on West 4th Avenue toward the University of British Columbia. Turn right (north) onto Northwest Marine Drive, driving past Locarno and Spanish Banks Beaches. About 1 km (0.6 mile) after Spanish Banks West, watch for the Acadia Beach parking lot on the right (north) side of the road. Trailhead GPS: N49 16.77' / W123 14.50'

The Hike

Though Fort Point Grey never fired a shot against the enemy, the post was heavily armed during World War II. Two hundred fifty men and personnel staffed the guns, bunkers, and observation tower atop the cliff. Some of those original concrete structures remain locked up, others are part of the Museum of Anthropology, and others still lie near the shoreline. This hike takes you past some of these World War II relics and along a wild seashore of tidal scoured rocks, seaweed, barnacles, and the odd mussel.

The walk begins at quiet Acadia Beach, a popular picnic area in summer, but far less busy than neighboring Spanish Banks. A mix of dirt paths and your own

World War II searchlight towers were part of the city's wartime defenses.

improvised beach trail curve around Point Grey toward Wreck Beach. With the cliffs of Point Grey at your back, you can look out on the Strait of Georgia and feel far from civilization.

At the halfway point, an ominous tower looms on the shoreline. This is C.A.S.L. #9. Yes, it looks much like a gun emplacement, but this tower (and its twin, C.A.S.L. #10, just southwest of here) held spotlights. These Coast Artillery searchlights could shine up to 8 km (5 miles) away thanks to the 800-million candlepower bulbs, guiding the gunners to their targets.

The sprawling Museum of Anthropology sits behind and above the searchlights. Architect Arthur Erickson designed the world-class museum to incorporate architectural features of Fort Point Grey. For example, a circular opening that was once the No. 2 Gun lets light stream down on Bill Reid's cedar sculpture, *The Raven and the First Men.*

Steep trails and stairs are the only connection from the shore up to Northwest Marine Drive, which runs along the clifftop. Trail 4 is the last outlet before the official section of Wreck Beach. There are many colorful stories about this stretch of clothing-optional sand, but perhaps the most important is how, in 1974, protesters blocked bulldozers that were targeted on reshaping the cliffs. Though Fort Point Grey never saw enemy action and is now decommissioned, the clash between the university and the naturalist-naturists has been a half-century battle.

Trail 6, also known as the Wreck Beach stairs, is the final leg of this hike. Linger on the friendly beach or head straight from the beach up to Marine Drive, via 483 steps (yes, I counted to check!). To get back to your starting point, follow the road as it curves around the peninsula with a higher vantage, or retrace your steps along the shore.

Acadia and Tower Beaches

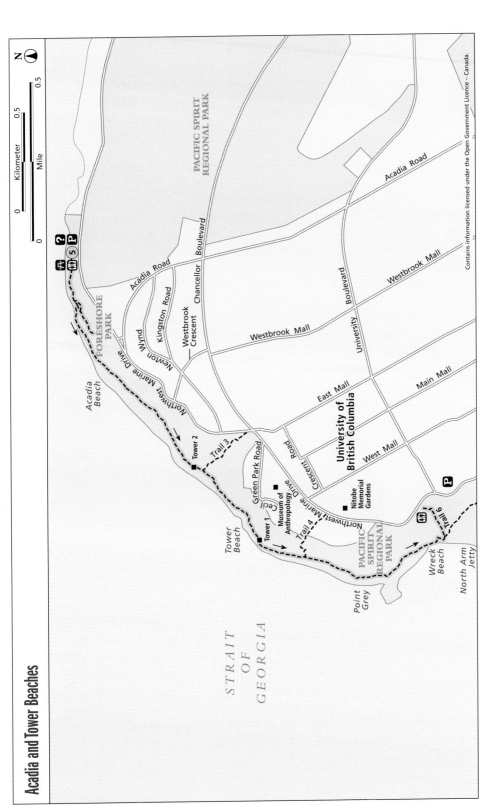

Distances and Directions

0.0 km/0.0 mile   Start from Acadia Beach parking lot and walk west, passing the picnic tables and heading down to the shoreline. A gravel trail runs parallel to the beach.

0.3 km/0.2 mile   Follow a spur trail that leads left (southwest), uphill to the salmonberries in Foreshore Park. The tart berries ripen in May. Or simply continue along the shoreline to skip this side trip.

0.5 km/0.3 mile   Return back down to the shoreline and turn left (southwest) to continue along the beach path.

1.6 km/1.0 mile   Look out to sea from Tower 2–also known as C.A.S.L. #9.

1.7 km/1.1 miles   Continue southwest along the dirt path at the base of the Trail 3 stairs, which connect up to Marine Drive.

2.2 km/1.4 miles   Follow the beach and sections of dirt trail southwest. Stop at Tower 1, or C.A.S.L. #10.

2.5 km/1.6 miles   Walk along Tower Beach and reach the Trail 4 junction. Continue along the shoreline.

2.9 km/1.8 miles   Round Point Grey–the westernmost point in the City of Vancouver.

3.2 km/2.0 miles   Walk along Wreck Beach to the Trail 6 stairs.

3.3 km/2.1 miles   Turn left (northeast) to climb the 483 steps to the top, stopping for a breather at any of the benches.

3.6 km/2.2 miles   Reach the trail's end at Northwest Marine Drive. (*Note:* To make this a full out-and-back hike, either retrace your steps along the beach or turn left [north] and follow Northwest Marine Drive back to Acadia Beach.)

Options: There's one more trail leading up from the beachfront for a slightly longer hike: Trail 7. This set of stairs is tucked along the shoreline and behind the Fraser River log booms. The trail connects to Old Marine Drive near the UBC Botanical Garden.

Hike Information

Local Information: Wreck Beach Preservation Society is a volunteer group that oversees the clothing-optional beach. They can provide more detail on the beach's etiquette and history. wreckbeach.org.

Local Attractions: The University of British Columbia is a hub of educational museums, lush gardens, and world class exhibits. The two not to miss are the Museum of Anthropology (6393 NW Marine Dr., Vancouver; 604-822-5087; moa.ubc.ca), a repository of artifacts and cultural treasures from around the world including BC First Nations communities, and the UBC Botanical Garden (6804 SW Marine Dr., Vancouver; 604-822-4208; botanicalgarden.ubc.ca), with its elevated canopy walkway and rare plantings.

Restaurants: Vendors sell sandwiches, drinks, and baked goods on Wreck Beach. Ask around to see who is selling what on your visit.

North Vancouver

The Capilano River divides Vancouver's North Shore. To the east of the river, the District of North Vancouver and City of North Vancouver sit steps from forest hiking trails and ski runs. (West Vancouver is to the west.)

Watersheds blanket most of the higher-elevation slopes, with restricted access to some areas. This ensures clean drinking water for a metropolitan area of more than 2.5 million people—securing a resource that streams in from the North Shore's creeks, reservoirs, and rivers. Come spring, the freshet funnels down from the mountains, into the creeks, and over waterfalls such as Norvan Falls. But in summer, creekbeds can be dry and almost still.

The North Shore has a long hiking history. In 1894 hikers made the first recorded ascent of Grouse Mountain. That started a flow of visitors that has never stopped. A century ago, hikers would cross Burrard Inlet by ferry and pack in supplies from there. Trips would last 3 days: the first to take the ferry to Moodyville, the second to summit, and the third to ferry back to Vancouver. Though you can still take a boat across Burrard Inlet (the SeaBus), pretty much everything else has changed.

One other thing that's stayed true is that most North Shore hikes have a wicked elevation gain, the best known being the Grouse Grind, which climbs 853 meters (2,799 feet) over 2.9 kilometers (1.8 miles). Many of North Vancouver's higher-elevation hikes are accessible only in summer (and to snowshoers in winter), but others such as the Baden Powell Trail and Lynn Headwaters trails are open to avid hikers year-round—you just have to avoid a little mud and weather a little rain.

But when you think that a century ago people couldn't drive to the trailhead and had to spend days getting here in leather boots with rations of bacon, whole pies, and stale bread, it doesn't seem so taxing.

The BC Mountaineering Club has a photo archive from the olden days of North Shore hiking. It's housed at the North Vancouver Museum and Archives (Archives: 3203 Institute Rd., Lynn Valley; Museum: 115 West Esplanade, North Vancouver; 604-990-3700; nvma.ca).

6 Grouse Grind

Unrelenting. Painful. Steep. Slippery. Crowded. These are all thoughts you may have just in the first quarter of the short but difficult Grouse Grind. Nearing the end of the 2.9-km (1.8-mile) stair-climb, thoughts change to persevere and just finish. The Grouse Grind is perhaps Vancouver's most famous and busiest trail. Mostly because it packs a fantastic training wallop and is ever-so-close to the city, but also because its reputation precedes it: "The Grind" is a hiker's rite of passage.

Start: Southeast of the Grouse Mountain Skyride, near parking lot "D"
Distance: 2.9-km (1.8-mile) point-to-point
Elevation gain: 853 meters (2,799 feet)
Hiking time: 1–2 hours
Difficulty: Difficult due to lots of people traffic and a whopping 853-meter (2,799-foot) elevation gain over a very short length. Much of the steep terrain is technical to navigate with stairs, rocks, dirt slopes, and roots in between.
Trail surface: Forested trail, dirt path, steps, rocks
Best season: Mid-May–Oct
Other trail users: Tourists
Canine compatibility: Dogs not permitted
Land status: Regional park, ski hill
Fees and permits: Parking, and return fare on the Grouse Mountain Skyride (mandatory)

Schedule: Daylight hours
Maps: There's no regional park or Grouse Grind map. Government topographic maps include the GeoBC Topographic Map Viewer (gov.bc.ca), as well as map 92G6 in the Atlas of Canada Toporama tool (atlas.gc.ca).
Trail contacts: Metro Vancouver, (604) 432-6200; metrovancouver.org
Special considerations: One of Vancouver's busiest trails, the Grouse Grind gets a lot of attention. The super-fit finish the hike in as little as 25 minutes, so you'll want to be aware of speedy hikers coming from behind. Keep to the right-hand side of the trail and let them pass. Though The Grind is short in distance, you need adequate water for a 2-hour hike. There is no water available along the trail.

Finding the trailhead: From Downtown Vancouver, head west on West Georgia Street, continuing through Stanley Park and across the Lions Gate Bridge. On the north side of the bridge, keep right for North Vancouver's Capilano Road. From Marine Drive, turn left (north) onto Capilano Road. Follow this uphill route (it becomes Nancy Greene Way) for 5.8 km (3.6 miles) to its end at the Grouse Mountain parking lot. Some people park along the road rather than pay for Grouse Mountain parking. Just be sure you're not blocking a driveway or in a restricted area. Trailhead GPS: N49 22.27' / W123 05.90'

The Hike

Amid the sounds of breathless hikers and trampling runners, listen for the squeaky-pulley sound of the blue grouse. It was this pheasant-like fowl with a stubby tail that gave Grouse Mountain its name, when a hiking party bagged a bird and made the first recorded ascent of the peak in 1894. That was back when vacationing on the North

Top: Rocky, rooty, and uneven steps define the Grouse Grind challenge.
Bottom left: Markers help you measure the pace on the Grouse Grind.
Bottom right: By roots, rocks, and stairs, the Grouse Grind is a continuous climb.

Shore took far more than a drive over a bridge, or hopping on the SeaBus to Lonsdale Quay. It took 3 or 4 days to reach the peak.

Mountaineers built this specific trail, the Grouse Grind, in the early 1980s. They wanted a steep, challenging route for a workout. With its 56 percent (30-degree) slope, the trail certainly suits its name. Although no one is quite sure who christened the trail, the name may have come about with the inaugural mountain run in the 1990s.

Head down the mountain via the Grouse Mountain Skyride.

Today, the mountainous workout is popular with everyone ranging from West Vancouver moms to snap-happy tourists. Locals tote official timing cards (you can see the results at guest services in the Grouse Mountain Chalet), and a close look at the daily time board shows that hikers still use the trail for intense workouts—some people hike The Grind more than once in a day (the record as of August 2019 is 19 times!).

Huge warning signs try to scare off the unprepared at the trailhead—especially as more than 150,000 hike the route each year. If you need to, the beginning, or the first quarter at the most, is the best point to turn back.

After a fairly gentle introduction over a pleasant forest path, the steep climb begins. It is divided into quarters, with a sign marking each progress point as well as markers noting every 1/40th of the hike. The entire length features stairs (some better maintained than others), rock scrambles, and dirt slopes. Ropes and rails offer a hand up on a few sections, but for the most part The Grind is an uphill battle of putting one foot up and in front of the next. A couple of viewpoints give peekaboo glimpses of Vancouver and the North Shore. It's an effort to get the workout reward.

Though it's a short hike and you'll quickly shed layers to keep cool (even on chilly spring mornings), you'll still want essentials like water, warm clothing, and perhaps a snack. Climbing to 1,127 meters (3,698 feet) in elevation can put you in another weather system.

The Snowshoe Grind is a winter route up Dam Mountain, covering 4.3 kilometers (2.7 miles) and 240 meters (787 feet) in elevation gain.

The trail pops out of the dense forest near the ski hill chalet. Early in the season there is still snow on the ground. Warm up with a hot drink and use the clean, well-stocked facilities before taking the Skyride gondola down the hill. Downloading by Skyride is mandatory to keep the trail slightly less busy. The pricing can run a little steep for groups (an annual pass is a better option if you plan to return), but I challenge you to soak up the Vancouver and Strait of Georgia views to get the value.

Grouse Grind

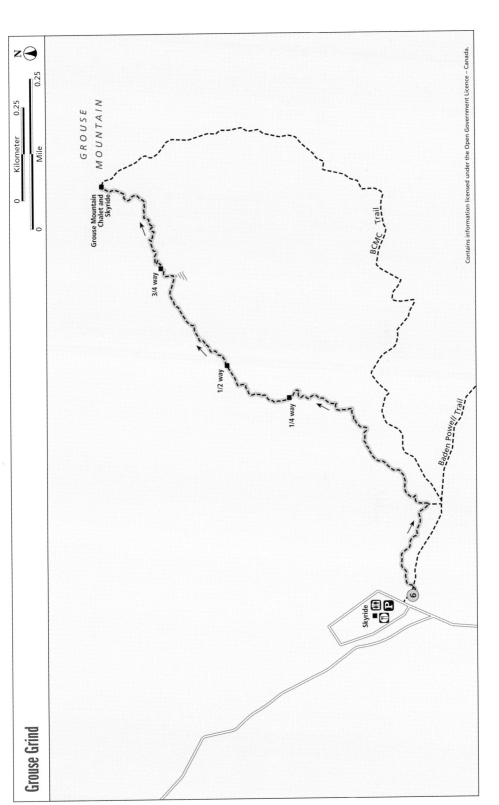

GROUSE MOUNTAIN

Grouse Mountain Chalet and Skyride

3/4 way

1/2 way

1/4 way

BCMC Trail

Baden Powell Trail

Skyride

6

Kilometer
0   0.25

Mile
0   0.25

N

Contains information licensed under the Open Government Licence – Canada.

Distances and Directions

0.0 km/0.0 mile   Start at the gated trailhead, southeast of the Grouse Mountain Skyride and Nancy Greene Way.

0.02 km/0.1 mile   Keep left (northeast) at the junction with the BCMC Trail (which also climbs Grouse Mountain) and the Baden Powell Trail (which continues east to Lynn Headwaters Regional Park).

0.3 km/0.2 mile   There's a second junction with the BCMC Trail. Continue uphill following the Grouse Grind markers.

0.9 km/0.6 mile   Reach the quarter-way marker and assess if this trail is right for you to continue. If you're not keen to go on, simply retrace your steps back downhill—being sure to move aside for those powering uphill. (**Bail-out:** If you need to turn around, do so early on. Bailing at the three-quarter marker will make your fellow Grinders grumpy. Plus, heading downhill with wobbly legs can be risky.)

1.4 km/0.9 mile   Rest at the halfway marker.

2.0 km/1.2 miles   Pass a small waterfall alongside the trail.

2.1 km/1.3 miles   Celebrate passing the three-quarter marker and continue the climb.

2.9 km/1.8 miles   Cross the rocky final stretch and walk up to the trail's official end point—just under the chalet balcony. (**Side-trip:** Now that you've attained this hard-won height, there are hiking options atop Grouse Mountain too. Ask about trails at the Guest Services desk, or see the Goat Mountain hike.)

Option: The British Columbia Mountaineering Club Trail starts out from the same trailhead as The Grind but loops up to the ski resort via a *slightly* less steep route. To follow this alternate route, keep right (east) at the first trail fork and then head left (northeast) uphill as the route leaves the Baden Powell Trail. The elevation gain is the same (853 meters [2,799 feet]) over 3.0 kilometers (1.9 miles). Depending on your fitness level, the one-way route takes an hour or more.

Hike Information

Local Information: With ski hills and suspension bridges, the North Shore is an adventure-seeker's dream destination. Find a long list of things to do from the North Vancouver Chamber (102–124 W. 1st St., North Vancouver, BC, V7M 3N3; 604-987-4488; nvchamber.ca) or online at North Shore Tourism (vancouversnorthshore.com), **Restaurants:** Whether you want a quick bite or full meal, there are plenty of food options available once you reach the top. The Grouse Grind Coffee Bar is a direct stop en route to the gondola line. But fine dining, barbecue, and beaver tails (fried pastry topped with sweet sauces) are also on the mountain menus.

GREEN TIP
Be courteous of others. Many people visit natural areas for quiet, peace, and solitude, so avoid making loud noises and intruding on others' privacy.

7 Goat Mountain

There's so much attention on the Grouse Grind, you often don't hear about Grouse Mountain's other trails. But with its 360-degree views and interesting rocky route, Goat Mountain deserves the limelight. The climb affords a horizon-reaching vantage over southwestern BC. Peaks seem to surround Goat on all sides, including Mount Baker, Mount Judge Howay, Mount Cheam, and Mount Garibaldi. Plus, who can argue with the availability of a celebratory beer at the finish line!

Start: Base of Peak Chairlift on Grouse Mountain
Distance: 7.5-km (4.7-mile) out-and-back
Elevation gain: 307 meters (1,007 feet)
Hiking time: 3–4 hours
Difficulty: Moderate due to length and at times steep and slippery terrain
Trail surface: Forested and rocky trail, dirt path, gravel road, ropes
Best season: July–Sept
Other trail users: None
Canine compatibility: Dogs not permitted
Land status: Ski resort, regional park
Fees and permits: Paid parking and a fee to ride the Grouse Mountain Skyride (or hike in via the Grouse Grind or BCMC Trail)

Schedule: Daylight hours
Maps: Goat Mountain Trail is part of Lynn Headwaters Regional Park, which has maps available online at metrovancouver.org. Government topographic maps include the GeoBC Topographic Map Viewer (gov.bc.ca), as well as map 92G6 in the Atlas of Canada Toporama tool (atlas.gc.ca).
Trail contacts: Metro Vancouver Regional Parks West Area Office, Suite 130, 1200 W. 73rd Ave., Vancouver, V6P 6G5; (604) 224-5739; metrovancouver.org
Special considerations: There is fresh water available near the trailhead, but not during this hike.

Finding the trailhead: From Capilano Road in North Vancouver, drive uphill (north). Continue straight as the route changes name to Nancy Greene Way. The road ends at the Grouse Mountain parking lot. Be careful in choosing a roadside parking spot, or pay to park in the large lots. As the trail starts atop Grouse Mountain, you have a number of ways to get there. The easy route up is on the Skyride gondola; the difficult route is via the Grouse Grind and BCMC Trails. Trailhead GPS: N49 22.92' / W123 04.81'

The Hike

The Skyride drops you off near Grouse Mountain Chalet. The immediate scene is a clash of worlds: Tourists mill about with their cameras and sandals, while Grouse Grinders stretch in what seems like too-little clothing for the chillier mountaintop temperatures. As a hiker, being prepared with hiking boots, poles, and a backpack can make you feel like the odd one out. So, head straight toward the hike's starting point and let the views begin.

Goat Mountain gives 360-degree views of tempting peaks.

Venture north from the Skyride and cross the large patio that serves as a winter skating rink. Follow the paths past the venue for owl talks. Keep the base of the Peak Chair off to your left and pass the grizzly bear habitat, with a quick stop to see if the resident bears are in view.

As the gravel trail leaves the ski resort, look up to the ski resort's peak—soon you'll be looking down it, the Eye of Wind turbine, and the rest of Vancouver.

NOT A BREADCRUMB TRAIL

Some routes come with arrows and neatly labeled signs. But many have improvised or make-shift markings that can help you along the trail though they may also leave you slightly confused. On Goat Mountain you'll spot the usual reflective markers as well as flagging tape. The route has signs and cairns, too, and in rocky sections, spray-painted dots and lines can mark the path.

Some other trails, like The Lions Binkert, have the charm of hand-painted signs that show a local love for the route. For rougher trails, blazed trees and juice-can lids might mark the path. Other trails are simply shown by the bare ground—trampled by feet over time.

If you come across an unmarked trail fork, look for something that may indicate one route or the other is the wrong way. Logs or rocks across the entrance commonly signal a closed trail.

Having now left most of the mountain visitors behind, you soon reach the fringes of Lynn Headwaters Regional Park. The trails within Lynn Headwaters are extensive, and there's a fantastic selection of trickier, back-country ascents. Unfortunately, the markings aren't always clear. On this trail cairns mark major intersections, but—especially in the first 2 kilometers (1.2 miles)—the route can be a bit of an improvisation.

The Grouse Mountain grizzly bears live in an enclosure near the start of the trail.

The trickiest route finding is along Ridge Trail to Dam Mountain. Dirt paths crisscross each other and a green metal water pipe. While it can seem confusing (generally sticking to the left is an easy rule), most trails lead up to the rocky outcrop of Dam Mountain and provide lovely views of Capilano Lake and Burrard Inlet. Yellow reflectors, cairns, and even spray paint also help mark the route in many places.

As the trail continues north from Dam Mountain, the steel-grey outcrops of Crown and Camel Mountains grow ever closer. They have a prehistoric look, especially when free of winter snow. And rightly so. The hornblende diorite is the oldest plutonic rock in the North Shore Mountains.

Goat Mountain looks down on Grouse Mountain and Vancouver.

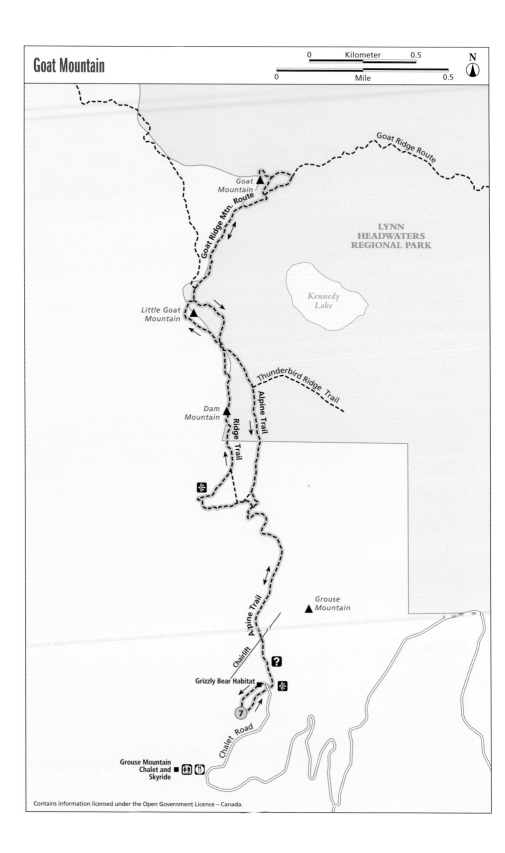

Goat Mountain

Goat Ridge Route

Goat Mountain Route

Goat Ridge Mtn. Route

LYNN HEADWATERS REGIONAL PARK

Kennedy Lake

Little Goat Mountain

Thunderbird Ridge Trail

Alpine Trail

Dam Mountain

Ridge Trail

Alpine Trail

Alpine Trail

Chairlift

Grizzly Bear Habitat

7

Chalet Road

Grouse Mountain

Grouse Mountain Chalet and Skyride

0   Kilometer   0.5

0   Mile   0.5

N

The world gets bigger atop Goat Mountain. Grouse Mountain's white Eye of the Wind turbine looks like a pinwheel; the oil tankers are plastic boats. Casting a view to the horizon, you can easily pick out the Mount Baker massif. Continuing clockwise, your gaze pans over distant mountains on Vancouver Island, Crown and Camel Mountains, Mount Garibaldi and Mamquam Mountain to the north in Squamish, and Mount Judge Howay next to its Golden Ears neighbor, Mount Blanshard.

Starting in 1927, you could drive up Grouse Mountain. The road climbed Mount Fromme and connected over to Grouse Mountain. But due to tremendous construction costs and an accident that closed the Second Narrows Bridge—a critical link to Vancouver—for 4 years, the road quickly pushed its owners to bankruptcy. It's now used by mountain bikers to access the many local trails.

Distances and Directions

0.0 km/0.0 mile   Start from base of the Peak Chair and follow the gravel trail northeast around the grizzly bear habitat.

0.2 km/0.1 mile   Pass the grizzly bear viewing areas.

0.3 km/0.2 mile   Continue straight (north) on a gravel road. A gravel trail continues west around the grizzly enclosure while another gravel road spurs right (northeast) and carves up the peak of Grouse Mountain.

0.4 km/0.2 mile   Reach the information board for Lynn Headwaters Regional Park.

1.0 km/0.6 mile   The trail leaves the road to the left (northwest) and continues as a stone and dirt track. Follow Alpine Trail as it starts to climb.

1.2 km/0.7 mile   Unnamed trails fork and rejoin each other. Generally keep to the left to follow the ridge. The trail also crosses a metal water pipeline multiple times.

1.3 km/0.8 mile   At a cairn, head left (west) to follow Ridge Trail.

1.4 km/0.9 mile   Continue straight at the green water pipeline. Then at a signed intersection, head left (west) on the longer route to Dam Mountain.

2.2 km/1.4 miles   Climb up Dam Mountain and take in the view. (**Bail-out:** Though the views are not as spectacular as Goat, Dam Mountain is also a scenic endpoint and nearly as high at 1,349 meters [4,426 feet] elevation. The round-trip, out-and-back hike covers 4.4 kilometers [2.7 miles].)

2.6 km/1.6 miles   Alpine Trail joins Ridge Trail, but splits again after about 100 meters (328 feet). Continue left (northwest) to Little Goat Mountain.

2.9 km/1.8 miles   Reach the peak of Little Goat Mountain and descend on the north side.

3.0 km/1.9 miles   Turn left (north) at the junction. The trail straight ahead (southeast) will be your return route on Alpine Trail.

3.1 km/1.9 miles   A cairn and signs differentiate the trails to Goat and Crown Mountains. Continue straight (northeast) as a rough trail forks left on the strenuous route to Crown. Follow the ridgeline toward Goat Mountain.

3.7 km/2.3 miles   Some ropes are strung across the steepest section. From here there are two routes to the peak—the hard way or the slightly longer way. Make a steep climb via the left trail (north), or a more gradual ascent via the longer right trail (northeast), which also continues on to Goat Ridge.

Crown and Camel Mountains are rocky, rugged peaks just northwest of Goat Mountain.

3.9 km/2.4 miles Savor the views (and a sandwich) atop Goat Mountain.

4.0 km/2.5 miles Cut down from the peak by either trail and start to retrace your steps.

4.9 km/3.0 miles At the Little Goat trail junction, turn left (southeast) and walk downhill on Alpine Trail. This is an alternate, easterly alternative to Ridge Trail. Follow the yellow trail markings.

5.3 km/3.3 miles Keep left (southeast) as the trail briefly meets Ridge Trail. Continue south on Alpine Trail to the left.

5.5 km/3.4 miles Pass the left spur of Thunderbird Trail. This ridge route heads east to a scenic viewpoint, adding about 1.4 km/0.9 mile return to the total hiking distance.

Asters: one of the alpine flowers growing in the Coast Mountains

5.6 km/3.5 miles Continue straight (south) at a connector (southwest) to Ridge Trail.

6.1 km/3.8 miles Pass the zipline and head right to join Ridge Trail again. Follow the rocky trails as they zigzag the pipeline again, heading generally south back to Grouse Mountain. Alternately, you can loop down past the zipline to reach the main trail.

6.5 km/4.0 miles Rejoin the gravel road.

7.5 km/4.7 miles Arrive back at Peak Chair.

Option: After Little Goat Mountain, a rough and challenging trail forks left toward Crown Mountain. Allow 5 to 6 hours to cover the 10 km/6.2 miles from the Skyride, including a grueling climb to the summit. The reward is an in-your-face experience of Camel Mountain (yes, it looks like a dromedary) and a sweeping vantage from Crown's narrow peak.

Hike Information

Local Information: Grouse Mountain is a mountaintop play land, with dining options, outdoor activities, and shopping. An outfitters shop sells gear and maps. 6400 Nancy Greene Way; (604) 980-9311; grousemountain.com.

Restaurants: There's everything from coffee to upscale cuisine at Grouse Mountain restaurants. But for my money, I like the idea of an outdoor barbecue at The Rusty Rail BBQ as a post-hike meal. It's located near the grizzly bear enclosure. Hours vary, but it's generally open for lunch and until dusk. grousemountain.com/casual-dining.

GREEN TIP
Cotton clothing has a smaller carbon footprint (when washed in cold water) than either polyester or wool. But be warned that cotton stays wet and can accelerate heat loss.

8 Lynn Valley to Grouse Mountain

Share the trails with mountain bikers as you cut across the hillside between Lynn Valley and Grouse Mountain. The trail follows forest paths through thick second growth and across numerous creeks. Short but steep elevation gains provide a moderate, metered-out challenge. A couple of lookouts sneak in a few ever-appreciated views. As with other sections of the Baden Powell, this hike goes from point to point—requiring transport at both ends. Both trailheads are near city bus stops.

Start: Lynn Valley Road, near the trailhead for Lynn Headwaters Regional Park
Distance: 7.6-km (4.7-mile) point-to-point
Elevation gain: 319 meters (1,047 feet)
Hiking time: 3–4 hours
Difficulty: Moderate due to length, short but steep elevation gains, and technical rocky descents
Trail surface: Forested trail, dirt path, boardwalk, stairs, gravel road
Best season: Year-round
Other trail users: Mountain bikers, dog-walkers
Canine compatibility: Dogs permitted, must be leashed in some sections
Land status: Crown land, city parks

Fees and permits: If the free parking spots at Grouse Mountain are full, you'll have to pay for parking.
Schedule: None, but daylight hours recommended
Maps: The trail crosses a mix of land areas and there is no official trail map. Government topographic maps include the GeoBC Topographic Map Viewer (gov.bc.ca), as well as map 92G6 in the Atlas of Canada Toporama tool (atlas.gc.ca).
Trail contacts: With many groups involved in the city-traversing Baden Powell Trail, there is no one source that provides information on the entire length. But check with Metro Vancouver Regional Parks West Area Office, Suite 130, 1200 W. 73rd Ave., Vancouver, V6P 6G5; (604) 224-5739; metrovancouver.org.

Finding the trailhead: From the Upper Levels Highway (Highway 1), take exit 19 for Lynn Valley Road. Drive northeast on Lynn Valley Road, following the busy street through strip malls and traffic lights. After 3 km (1.9 miles), reach a 3-way stop with Dempsey Road. Continue straight (north). Keep left at a fork with Rice Lake Road. Park in the overflow lots for Lynn Headwaters Regional Park. Trailhead GPS: N49 21.50' / W123 01.69'

The Hike

This hike marks the thin border between city and wilderness. It cuts across the steep slopes of the North Shore Mountains, ducking in and out of creek canyons and intersecting with biking paths, mountain roads, and residential streets.

North Vancouverites use this trail as a quick escape into the woods, often connecting with the trail at Skyline Drive and Mosquito Creek. But the full hike starts in the less-traveled section near Lynn Headwaters Regional Park. It's easy to miss the narrow trailhead. Only a small sign (and no map) marks this section of the Baden

Mosquito Creek weaves downhill under a forest canopy.

Powell Trail—a 48-kilometer (30-mile) route that crosses the North Shore Mountains from Horseshoe Bay to Deep Cove. But regular route markers, emblazoned with the Scouts' fleur-de-lis symbol, are simple to follow.

A snaking set of wooden stairs climbs the first hill and envelops you in second-growth forest. There are giant cedar stumps left from long-ago logging operations, now a source of nutrients for interesting plants and fungi. In spring and fall look for clusters of fragile mushrooms, and year-round for red-belted polypores (or conks), which some herbalists claim as a cancer-fighting aid.

The trail soon meets Mountain Highway, where most days you cross paths with armor-clad mountain bikers. There's a water-refill point here too. Over the next 4 kilometers (2.5 miles), Mount Fromme's narrow, marked bike paths intersect the Baden Powell. Each has a name and difficulty rating. Mountain biking trail associations have built the stepping-stone-like paths and small log bridges along the route. Most of Mount Fromme's trails are considered advanced, expert, or extreme in

A wooden staircase marks the start of the Baden Powell's Lynn Valley leg.

difficulty—with almost no trails for beginner riders. The Baden Powell Trail is considered an intermediate mountain-biking route.

At roughly the halfway point, a bench marks a lookout, where you can glimpse views southwest over North Vancouver, Stanley Park, and Vancouver's West Side between the ever-growing trees.

Mosquito Creek marks the end of the mountain-biking trails. Head over the bridge and keep on the Baden Powell as multiple trails head along both sides of the creek. Just west of Mosquito Creek, at Skyline Drive, a steeper and trickier terrain begins. The forest thickens and the trail almost disappears at times in the needle-packed, root-riddled hillside. But keep an eye on the markers and continue across branches of MacKay Creek.

You know the end is near as the trail intersects steep routes to the BC Mountaineering Club cabin, the BCMC Trail (an alternative way up Grouse Mountain), and The Grind itself. It feels odd to arrive at a trailhead where large groups are stretching and warming up to tackle a different hiking route, many perhaps unaware of the route you've just followed.

Distances and Directions

0.0 km/0.0 mile   Start from Lynn Valley Road and climb the wooden stairs to start the Baden Powell Trail.

0.3 km/0.2 mile   Continue straight (west) at a spur trail to Hoskins Road. The tangle of mountain biking trails begins. Generally, the Baden Powell is straight ahead (west) with mountain-biking trails feeding in from the left and right.

0.6 km/0.4 mile   Continue straight (southwest) at branches of the Griffen Trails.

1.0 km/0.6 mile   Reach Mountain Highway, a busy route with mountain bikers. Cross the road and refill your water, and then continue to the west to follow the Baden Powell markers up a woodland trail. Thames Creek runs nearby.

Lynn Valley to Grouse Mountain

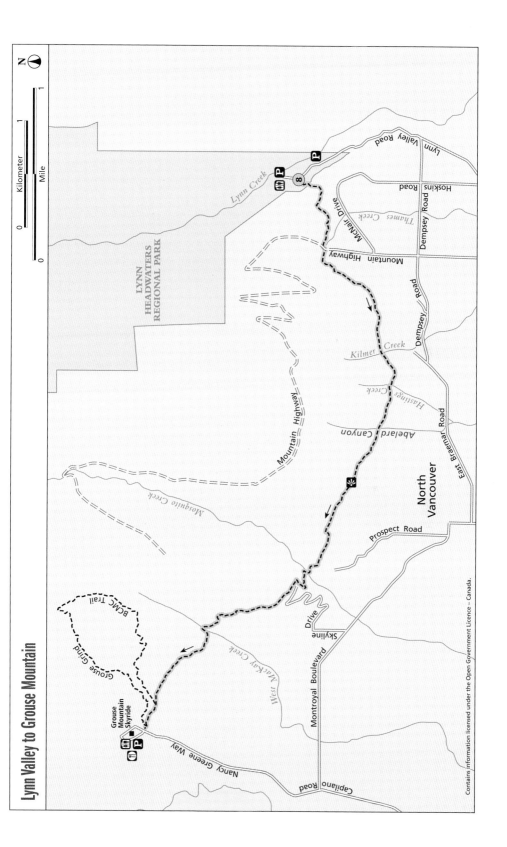

2.3 km/1.4 miles   Cross Kilmer Creek.

2.7 km/1.7 miles   Cross Hastings Creek.

3.2 km/2.0 miles   A volunteer-built bridge gives passage over Abelard Canyon.

3.7 km/2.3 miles   The trail crosses St. George's Trail, a route up Mount Fromme. There's also a North Shore viewpoint here.

4.7 km/2.9 miles   Follow the Baden Powell across Cascades Trail, past two large green water tanks, and then over Mosquito Creek. There are a number of intersecting trail junctions here. (***Bail-out:*** You can cut the route short at Mosquito Creek—though you'll have to factor in transportation.)

4.8 km/3.0 miles   On the west side of the creek, hike uphill on the switchbacks passing Skyline Drive.

5.1 km/3.2 miles   At the top of the ascent, turn right (east) on a gravel road. Round the bend and then keep straight (northwest) as you pass Skyline Trail, which heads farther uphill right (north).

6.0 km/3.7 miles   Pass the Old BCMC Trail.

6.3 km/3.9 miles   Cross West MacKay Creek.

6.5 km/4.0 miles   Larsen Trail branches off right (north), up the hill.

7.3 km/4.5 miles   The trail intersects the BCMC Trail up Grouse Mountain.

7.5 km/4.7 miles   Join the first section of the Grouse Grind, as Grinders heave themselves uphill.

7.6 km/4.7 miles   Arrive at the Grouse Grind trailhead.

Option: The route to Mount Fromme, St. George's Trail, intersects the Baden Powell about 1 kilometer (0.6 mile) east of Mosquito Creek. Mount Fromme is treated a bit like an ugly stepsister among North Shore hikes. The stereotype comes from its gravel road terrain. But at the south summit, you get a view of Crown Mountain, Mount Seymour, and Lynn Peak. The route covers about 10 kilometers (6.2 miles). Allow about 4–5 hours.

Hike Information

Local Information: For using transit to position vehicles and reach the trailheads, contact Translink. (604) 953-3333; translink.ca.

Local Events: Extreme bike and running races use the Baden Powell Trail for endurance events, including the Knee Knackering North Shore Trail Run typically held in July. The route covers the 47.9 kilometers (29.8 miles) of the Baden Powell. kneeknacker.com.

Restaurants: At the trail's end at Grouse Mountain, you can grab a snack at Starbucks. 6400 Nancy Greene Way, Vancouver; (604) 984-0661; starbucks.ca.

Organizations: For more on the area's mountain biking trails—and the sport's explosive local popularity—contact the North Shore Mountain Biking Association. nsmba.ca.

9 Lynn Peak

Pack a picnic and protect your ankles for this hike to a scenic viewpoint almost at the top of Lynn Peak. The route is steep and rocks (ranging from tennis-ball to bowling-ball size) pose a technical challenge. Still, with its three definitive viewpoints and a dense, quiet forest, this is considered a more scenic and less-busy alternative to the Grouse Grind.

Start: Lynn Headwaters Regional Park trailhead
Distance: 8.8-km (5.5-mile) out-and-back
Elevation gain: 742 meters (2,434 feet)
Hiking time: 3.5-4 hours
Difficulty: Strenuous due to uneven terrain and steep, steady elevation gain
Trail surface: Forest trail, dirt path, lots of loose rocks
Best season: May–Oct
Other trail users: Dog-walkers
Canine compatibility: Leashed dogs permitted
Land status: Regional park
Fees and permits: No fees or permits required
Schedule: Daylight hours
Maps: Lynn Peak is in Lynn Headwaters Regional Park, which has maps available online. The trail also appears on maps for the Lower Seymour Conservation Reserve. Government topographic maps include the GeoBC Topographic Map Viewer (gov.bc.ca), as well as map 92G6 in the Atlas of Canada Toporama tool (atlas.gc.ca).
Trail contacts: Metro Vancouver Regional Parks West Area Office, Suite 130, 1200 W. 73rd Ave., Vancouver, V6P 6G5; (604) 224-5739; metrovancouver.org
Special considerations: The peak is snow-bound into mid-spring, and on an early-season hike you'll likely encounter some snow in the final stretch. Fresh water is only available at the trailhead. Some hikers also report bugs—bring repellent.

Finding the trailhead: From the Upper Levels Highway (Highway 1), take exit 19 for Lynn Valley Road. Turn northeast onto Lynn Valley Road. After 3 km (1.9 miles), reach a 3-way stop with Dempsey Road. Continue straight (north). Keep left at a fork with Rice Lake Road. Park in the Lynn Headwaters Regional Park lots. Trailhead GPS: N49 21.64' / W123 01.70'

The Hike

Some local residents come to Lynn Headwaters Regional Park to fill up bottles with fresh mountain water along the roadside. Take their lead and fill up a water bottle here at the trailhead fountain (if it's in service), as this elevation-intense hike will leave you wanting a few long, cool drinks.

You start the 8.8-km (5.5-mile) out-and-back trip across from B.C. Mills House, which is more than a century old. During pioneer days, B.C. Mills Timber and Trading Company produced prefabricated homes for settlers. A catalogue listed this 1908 home for $500. Captain Henry Pybus, who sailed the *Empress of Japan* (a copy of the ocean liner figurehead is along the Stanley Park Seawall), bought the prefab house and built the structure at 147 E. 1st St. in North Vancouver.

Top: Fungi and mushrooms grow on decaying wood.
Bottom: Though not technically the summit, Lynn Peak viewpoint has a superb vantage.

The small structure with a wide balcony stood at that address for more than 80 years. At one time, the leader of the Rhinoceros Party—a bizarre federal political party that has run on platform promises to repeal the law of gravity and move Montreal and Toronto closer—lived in the abode.

Pass the house and its too-bad-walls-can't-speak history to follow the gravel road over rushing Lynn Creek and turn right. When the gravel road continues straight into the Lower Seymour Conservation Reserve, turn left onto Lynn Loop.

It's when Lynn Peak Trail splits off that the rough terrain begins. Make deliberate steps to save your ankles—many of the rocks, large and small, come loose easily. And in my experience, even more care will be needed on the way back down!

IKEA FOR SETTLERS: BC'S PREFABRICATED HOMES

Arriving in British Columbia from around the world and heading off to settle in the province's remote wilderness, many homesteaders needed shelter first, foremost, and extremely fast. The B.C. Mills Timber and Trading Company provided just that: prefabricated homes that could be put together in 4 to 5 days. The company shipped the precut and painted packages of boards throughout the province by rail, complete with instructions. Settlers simply locked the ordered boards together. The small B.C. Mills House, near the trailhead, is one of these homes and cost $500 in 1908.

Historic B.C. Mills House marks the trailhead at Lynn Headwaters.

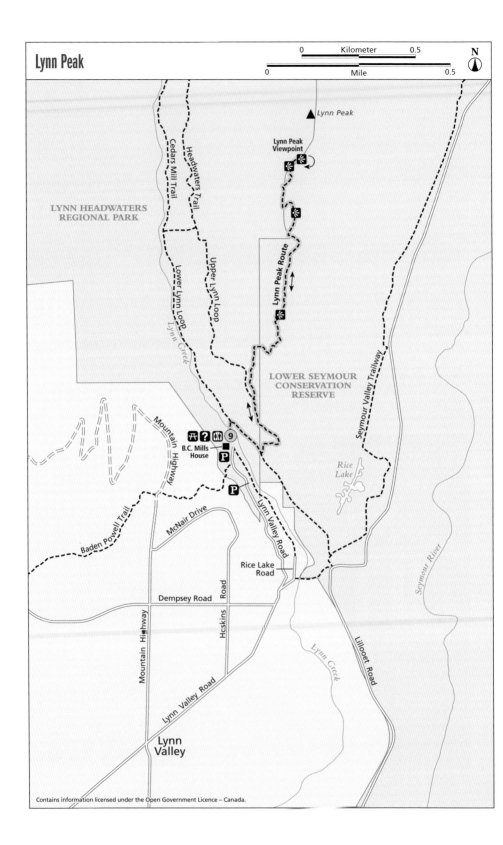

Lynn Peak

Kilometer

0   0.5

Mile

0   0.5

N

▲ Lynn Peak

Lynn Peak
Viewpoint

Cedars Mill Trail

Headwaters Trail

LYNN HEADWATERS
REGIONAL PARK

Lower Lynn Loop

Upper Lynn Loop

Lynn Peak Route

Lynn Creek

LOWER SEYMOUR
CONSERVATION
RESERVE

Seymour Valley Trailway

9

B.C. Mills
House

P

P

Rice
Lake

Mountain Highway

Baden Powell Trail

McNair Drive

Heskins Road

Lynn Valley Road

Rice Lake
Road

Dempsey Road

Mountain Highway

Lynn Creek

Lillooet Road

Seymour River

Lynn Valley Road

Lynn
Valley

The first viewpoint looks east to red-roofed buildings on Mount Seymour. The full-on ascent begins to lessen as you reach a second lookout with better views of Seymour. A third lookout faces west, over Lynn Valley to Grouse Mountain. Large, resident ravens linger on the rocks at this viewpoint, likely having learned that humans come bearing snacks.

At the final viewpoint, slightly lower than the Lynn Peak summit, a rocky bluff is a platform to look down on the city. On a hot summer day, this spot can get pretty crowded, as clear days give you a vantage as far as the US border and Mount Baker.

Overall, the hike elevation gain is about 100 meters (328 feet) less than the Grouse Grind stretched over a 50 percent longer distance. The result is a good workout without the crowds of The Grind. Add in that the season for this hike is slightly longer than some of the other challenging North Shore hikes (it's mostly snow-free in May, versus July for most hikes), and it's a great option for getting your legs summer-season ready.

Distances and Directions

0.0 km/0.0 mile Start from B.C. Mills House and follow the wide, gravel road toward Lynn Creek.

0.1 km/0.1 mile Cross the creek and then turn right (southeast) at the junction.

0.5 km/0.3 mile Turn left (northeast) to follow Lynn Loop Trail. A gravel road continues straight (southeast) into the demonstration forest and to Rice Lake.

1.2 km/0.7 mile After a short uphill stretch, turn right (north) at signs for Lynn Peak. Lynn Loop Trail heads left (northwest).

2.5 km/1.6 miles After a long uphill slog, you reach the first viewpoint, which looks east to Mount Seymour.

3.6 km/2.2 miles Enjoy a second, slightly better viewpoint of Seymour.

4.2 km/2.6 miles Pause at the Grouse Mountain viewpoint, which looks west.

4.4 km/2.7 miles Picnic at the final viewpoint, with a vantage over Burrard Inlet, Vancouver, and Mount Baker across the US border—provided the skies are clear! (**Side-trip:** From the final viewpoint, a rough trail heads north for about 500 meters [0.3 mile] to the actual summit of Lynn Peak, but there are no views.)

8.8 km/5.5 miles Retrace your steps along the same trails to arrive back at the trailhead.

Hike Information

Local Information: Discover Lynn Valley's logging history at the B.C. Mills House. If it's open on your visit, step inside the pretty, prefabricated structure to look at old tools and informational exhibits.

Restaurants: End of the Line General Store sits a couple of minutes south of the Lynn Headwaters trailhead. It marks what was once the final stop of the local streetcar. Streetcars stopped running in North Vancouver in 1947, but the store is still on the route for buses, local residents, and hikers. Stop in for snacks and cold drinks. 4193 Lynn Valley Rd., North Vancouver; (604) 904-2366; eotl.ca.

10 Norvan Falls

Though a longer hike, Norvan Falls is a fairly moderate challenge. Woodland trails and former logging roads cut a level route along Lynn Creek and end at the plummeting 30-meter (98-foot) falls—named for its location in North Vancouver. It's especially lovely during snowbound months when it is harder to venture deep into the forest.

Start: Lynn Headwaters Regional Park trailhead
Distance: 16.0-km (9.9-mile) lollipop
Elevation gain: 229 meters (751 feet)
Hiking time: 4.5–6 hours
Difficulty: Moderate due to some elevation gain and mostly smooth terrain, but longer distance might be strenuous for some hikers
Trail surface: Gravel path, forested trail, stairs
Best season: Year-round
Other trail users: Dog-walkers
Canine compatibility: Leashed dogs permitted (some off-leash areas)
Land status: Regional park
Fees and permits: No fees or permits required

Schedule: Daylight hours
Maps: Lynn Headwaters Regional Park has maps available online (metrovancouver.org). Government topographic maps include the GeoBC Topographic Map Viewer (gov.bc.ca), as well as map 92G6 in the Atlas of Canada Toporama tool (atlas.gc.ca).
Trail contacts: Metro Vancouver Regional Parks West Area Office, Suite 130, 1200 W. 73rd Ave., Vancouver, V6P 6G5; (604) 224-5739; metrovancouver.org
Special considerations: There is fresh water available near the trailhead, but not during this hike.

Finding the trailhead: From the Upper Levels Highway (Highway 1), take exit 19 for Lynn Valley Road. Turn northeast onto Lynn Valley Road. After 3 km (1.9 miles), reach a 3-way stop with Dempsey Road. Continue straight (north). Keep left at a fork with Rice Lake Road. Park in the Lynn Headwaters Regional Park lots. Trailhead GPS: N49 21.62' / W123 01.68'

The Hike

Loggers cut giant trees from this lush valley in the late 1800s and early 1900s. Like along many other Pacific Northwest trails, you can see the giant cedar stumps still decaying, notches marking the spots where loggers slotted in springboards to help reach above the tree's flared base. But seized machinery and rusty wheel spokes also lie among the stumps—logging garbage that has, with time, become a collection of historical artifacts.

This hike begins at a small, early-1900s prefabricated home, B.C. Mills House (read more about this structure in the Lynn Peak hike). After crossing Lynn Creek, the route follows the rushing waterway upstream for most of the hike. On Lower Lynn Loop you are never far from the creek, and the trail continues on a fairly level footing through Cedars Mill Trail. It is this first leg where you see most remnants of logging days.

Logging company Cedars Mill extracted old-growth trees from this valley from 1919 to 1928. At this wide section of Lynn Creek, lumbermen sliced centuries-old trees into shakes, shingles, and lumber. In its early days, Lynn Valley was nicknamed Shaketown, both for its buildings constructed from cedar shakes and logging being the main activity.

Cedars Mill and Headwaters Trail meet at Third Debris Chute, a jumble of rocks that have tumbled down the valley slopes. Continue north on Headwaters Trail as it starts a moderate climb following yellow trail markers. Throughout the lush route mossy forests drip with rain, decaying logs sprout mushrooms, and tangles of lichen dangle from branches.

Bridges and undulating forest trails weave through the woods near Norvan Falls.

Norvan Creek plummets neatly from its rocky ledge.

Just past a right turn to Coliseum Route, another trail leads right to Norvan Falls. But before heading to the falls, cross the cable bridge over the creek. Perhaps for another longer (and much more challenging) adventure, the route continues on to Crown Mountain via Hanes Valley. Another route snakes up to Lynn Lake.

Norvan Creek tumbles 30 meters (98 feet) over a rocky lip. The forest bluff and creekside rocks are both good spots to lunch in view of the falls.

Hikers on the homeward bound journey follow the same route through to Third Debris Chute, where Headwaters Trail forks and offers two options. The higher-elevation Headwaters Trail is more challenging, with multiple sets of stairs and undulating terrain that feels like a fun test for slightly weary legs. Though it's a bit harder, the route does provide access to a group of large boulders—erratics left over from the last ice age.

The easier, and shorter, option is along Cedars Mill Trail, a lower route that returns to the trailhead along rushing Lynn Creek.

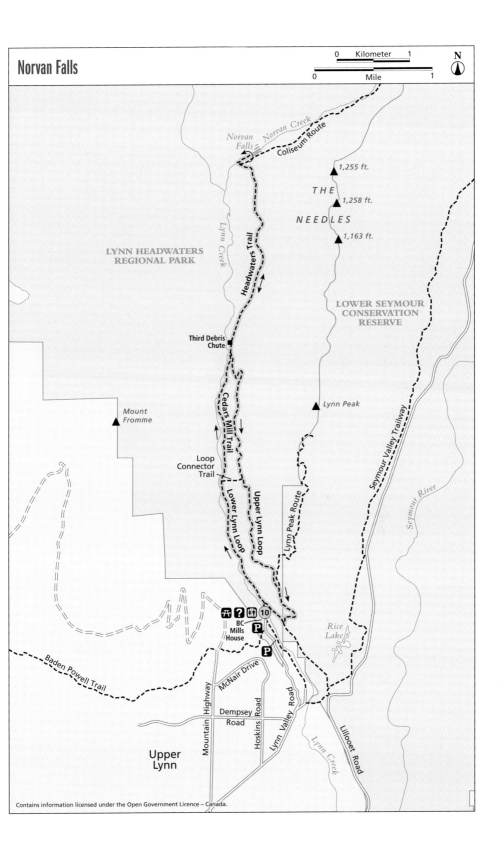

Norvan Falls

Norvan Falls
Norvan Creek

Coliseum Route

1,255 ft.

T H E

1,258 ft.

N E E D L E S

1,163 ft.

Lynn Creek

Headwaters Trail

**LYNN HEADWATERS
REGIONAL PARK**

**LOWER SEYMOUR
CONSERVATION
RESERVE**

Third Debris
Chute

Lynn Peak

Seymour Valley Trailway

Seymour River

Mount
Fromme

Cedars Mill Trail

Loop
Connector
Trail

Lower Lynn Loop

Upper Lynn Loop

Lynn Peak Route

BC
Mills
House

Rice
Lake

Baden Powell Trail

McNair Drive

Mountain Highway

Dempsey
Road

Hoskins Road

Lynn Valley Road

Lynn Creek

Lillooet Road

**Upper
Lynn**

Distances and Directions

0.0 km/0.0 mile   Start from the Lynn Headwaters Regional Park trailhead, by historic B.C. Mills House.

0.2 km/0.1 mile   Cross the creek and then head left (northwest) at the park information sign following Lower Lynn Loop Trail.

2.0 km/1.2 miles   Continue left (north) on Lynn Loop as a trail connects right (east) to Headwaters Trail. A gravel trail and two sets of stairs funnel in to this connector trail.

3.0 km/1.9 miles   Pass the rusty remains of Cedars Mill.

4.3 km/2.7 miles   Head uphill to the right and then bear left (north) on Headwaters Trail at the tumbled rocky stretch of Third Debris Chute. (**Bail-out:** Lynn Loop Trail is a more manageable length for summer after-work hikers and dog-walkers. Simply turn south on Headwaters Trail at Third Debris Chute, or use the midway connector trail for a route that's shorter still. It's a 9-kilometer [5.6-mile] circuit.)

7.0 km/4.3 miles   Pass the right turn to Coliseum Route.

7.1 km/4.4 miles   Turn right (northeast) to Norvan Falls.

7.3 km/4.5 miles   Stop at Norvan Falls for a snack, drink, and rest.

7.6 km/4.7 miles   Return to the Headwaters Trail and retrace your steps south. Or take a quick detour to the suspension bridge.

10.4 km/6.5 miles   At Third Debris Chute, keep left (south) on the upper Headwaters Trail. Cedars Mill Trail branches right and travels along Lynn Creek.

12.7 km/7.9 miles   Continue straight (southeast) on the main trail as the Lower Lynn Loop connector branches right (west).

12.9 km/8.0 miles   Turn left (east) to make the short, 5-minute detour up to a group of glacially deposited boulders.

14.6 km/9.1 miles   Continue straight (south) past the Lynn Peak turnoff, which heads left uphill.

15.4 km/9.6 miles   Loop downhill and turn right (northwest) at the trail junction to Lower Seymour Conservation Reserve.

15.8 km/9.8 miles   Head left (south) at the information sign and cross Lynn Creek.

16.0 km/9.9 miles   Arrive back at the trailhead.

Hike Information

Local Attractions: To the south, Lynn Canyon Suspension Bridge and Lynn Canyon Ecology Centre are both fantastic family destinations (though both experienced COVID-19 closures, so check opening hours before heading out). The suspension bridge was first built in 1912, when making the wobbly crossing cost 10 cents. Lynn Canyon Park, 3663 Park Rd., North Vancouver; (604) 990-3755; lynncanyonecologycentre.ca.

GREEN TIP
Carry a reusable water container that you fill at the tap.
Bottled water is expensive; lots of petroleum is used to make
the plastic bottles, and they're a disposal nightmare.

11 Deep Cove to Lynn Canyon

Waterfront parks, rocky viewpoints, river canyons, a suspension bridge—this point-to-point hike covers the best of the North Shore over a moderate route and a testing elevation gain. This leg is the easternmost section of the Baden Powell Trail, a 48-km (30-mile) route that crosses the North Shore Mountains all the way to Horseshoe Bay, West Vancouver. Note that both the start and end points were affected by COVID-19 closures in 2020—options savor the same sights with an alternate route.

Start: Panorama Drive, near Deep Cove's Panorama Park
Alternate start: Indian River Drive
Distance: 12.0-km (7.5-mile) point-to-point; 9.0 km (5.6 miles) from the alternate start
Elevation gain: 408 meters (1,339 feet)
Hiking time: 3.5–4.5 hours
Difficulty: Moderate due to length and a few steady climbs over well-established forest trails and some stairs
Trail surface: Forested trail, dirt path, paved road, bridges, boardwalks, stairs
Best season: Year-round
Other trail users: Mountain bikers, dog-walkers
Canine compatibility: Leashed dogs permitted, with some off-leash sections
Land status: Provincial park, city park
Fees and permits: No fees or permits required
Schedule: Varies between parks, but generally daylight hours

Maps: There is no one map of the entire route. Portions of the trail are shown on maps for Mount Seymour Provincial Park (available online at bcparks.ca), Lower Seymour Conservation Reserve (available online at metrovancouver.org), and Lynn Canyon Park (available online at lynncanyonecologycentre .ca). Government topographic maps include the GeoBC Topographic Map Viewer (gov.bc.ca), as well as map 92G7 and 92G6 in the Atlas of Canada Toporama tool (atlas.gc.ca).
Trail contacts: Mount Seymour Provincial Park, Mount Seymour Road, North Vancouver; (604) 986-9371; bcparks.ca
Special considerations: With so many intersecting trails, it can be easy to take a wrong turn. Try to keep Baden Powell fleur-de-lis trail markers in sight at all times. Hiking poles may be useful on this hike's steep, rocky descent, positioned about halfway through the route.

Finding the trailhead: Traveling north on Highway 1, take exit 23B—located just north of the Second Narrows Bridge. Drive east on Dollarton Highway. After 12 km (7.5 miles), the route becomes Deep Cove Road when it intersects with Mount Seymour Parkway. Continue straight into Deep Cove. Bear right (east) on Deep Cove Road and turn left (north) onto Panorama Drive. In 400 meters (0.2 mile), the trailhead is on the left (west). Find street parking where you won't be upsetting local residents. To reach the alternate trailhead, turn off Mount Seymour Road onto Indian River Drive and continue for 3 km (1.9 miles). Trailhead GPS: N49 19.80' / W122 56.98'; Alternate Trailhead GPS: N49 20.29' / W122 56.82'

The Hike

Trail closures due to COVID-19 bookended this hike in 2020. But even if there is restricted access to the Baden Powell Trail in Deep Cove and a closed Lynn Canyon

Quarry Rock has a wide vantage over Deep Cove and Indian Arm.

Suspension Bridge, it's still possible to enjoy most of the route's best scenery: just add a little creative route planning.

If we're all lucky enough to enjoy this hike in its fully open form, you can simply begin in Deep Cove. This small community is out-of-sight from Vancouver, giving you a mental distance from the city even if the drive to Downtown only takes about 30 minutes.

Though it's tempting to linger in The Cove (which fittingly enough began as a summer resort for city dwellers), hikers leave the picturesque waterfront town to hike into Mount Seymour Provincial Park and follow this eastern leg of the North Shore—crossing Baden Powell Trail.

The main trailhead is slightly hidden between houses, crowded together for water views. The climb begins almost with the first step off Panorama Drive, as a rooty, rocky forest path threads up through second-growth forest. Plank bridges with railings, steps, and boardwalks help connect the trail over creeks and steep slopes to Quarry Rock, the hike's most spectacular viewpoint.

No exact figures are available, but the Ministry of Energy notes that miners extracted "abundant amounts" of granite from this area. You'll see that much of the rock went into building local jetties and shoreline-protecting riprap.

But mining history aside, it is the views that draw appreciative crowds to Quarry Rock. An expansive marina marks the small village of Deep Cove. Moving your gaze to the left (west), you will see Wickenden Park (with city skyscrapers behind), the more distant Boulder Island, tiny Hamber Island off Turtlehead Peninsula, and the forested stretch of Belcarra Peninsula. Take time for a rest before continuing north on the Baden Powell toward Lynn Canyon.

If trail closures in Deep Cove necessitate an **alternate route**, begin on the quiet road of Indian River Drive instead. Here you miss the Instagram-worthy views at Quarry Rock, but you can head along the Baden Powell through quiet forests and get plenty of picturesque views at Lynn Canyon instead.

From Indian River Drive, the route heads through the woods to Mount Seymour Road, which climbs a series of switchbacks to a wintertime ski hill and summertime hiking trails. Cross carefully and pick up the trail on the west side, readying for another climb.

The Baden Powell first meets Old Buck Trail and then a trail to the park's Historic Mushroom Parking Lot. Starting in the 1930s, people built cabins on

Old and new—markers have long guided hikers along the Baden Powell Trail.

Mount Seymour's slopes. They would leave cars in the "mushroom" parking lot—the end of the road until 1950, and then hike in to the wilderness cabins. But the mushrooms here aren't the edible kind. Hikers and cabin owners posted notes on an information board at this parking lot (this was the text message of the early 1900s), and that information board had a roof shaped like a mushroom cap.

When you leave the provincial park boundaries, you encounter mountain biking trails through to Seymour River. The terrain is rocky, and a 200-meter (656-foot) descent over 1.5 kilometers (0.9 mile)—a trail section dubbed the "Seymour Grind"—will make you thankful for hiking poles, if you have some.

As you cross Hyannis Drive, the trail seems to travel through North Shore backyards. But a hint of raw wilderness reappears as you cross a pipeline bridge over Seymour River. Steep stairs lead you out of the rugged river canyon.

The final trail leg ambles through Lynn Canyon Park, a greenspace that mountaineering twins the Mctavish brothers gifted to the municipality in 1910. In his wide-reaching book *Early Days in Lynn Valley*, pioneer Walter MacKay Draycott describes the park as "an amphitheatre with verdant slopes that nurture the tall stately conifers, deciduous trees, shrubs and ferns."

A century on, Lynn Canyon still has that feeling of natural grandeur. Especially, that is, if you're reaching the park in the early evening when the crowds are gone.

Lynn Canyon Suspension Bridge has been a local fixture since 1912.

Families and tourists flock to the park for the free attractions—a suspension bridge, swimming hole, ecology center, and cafe.

Following Lynn Creek upstream, you first reach Twin Falls Bridge. Cross here, but with luck you'll also be able to cross the creek a few minutes farther along via the suspension bridge. When it's open the bridge charges no fee today—amazingly, that's less than the cost a century ago in 1912, when the bridge proprietors charged 10 cents per person.

Distances and Directions

0.0 km/0.0 mile   Start from Panorama Drive in Deep Cove and climb northeast along the forest trail. Bridges and boardwalks lead over creeks and small canyons.

1.7 km/1.1 miles   At a fork, head right (south) to reach Quarry Rock, stopping at the scenic lookout for views and snacks. (**Bail-out:** The less than 4-kilometer [2.5-mile] out-and-back hike to Quarry Rock is a Deep Cove favorite. If you're short on time or energy, simply savor the view and return along the same route rather than continuing on to Lynn Canyon. It's also easier for coordinating transportation.)

1.8 km/1.1 miles   Head (north) to continue on the Baden Powell, rather than retracing your steps back to Deep Cove.

1.9 km/1.2 miles   Cross a gravel clearing under the power lines and keep straight (northeast) and then turn left (northwest).

2.2 km/1.4 miles Cross a gravel maintenance road, continuing slightly left then straight (northwest) to head toward Indian River Drive.

2.5 km/1.6 miles Short spurs connect to Indian River Drive. Head left (west), parallel to the road, and cross Francis Creek. Continue following the trail markers.

3.0 km/1.9 miles Reach the ***alternate trailhead*** on Indian River Drive. Pick up the forest trail to the left of a metal gate and water tower.

3.8 km/2.4 miles Take care crossing Mount Seymour Road.

4.3 km/2.7 miles Turn left (southwest) at the intersection with Old Buck Trail. Then follow the Baden Powell as it splits off again right (west), just 100 meters (328 feet) on.

5.0 km/3.1 miles Follow trail markers west at intersections with multiple mountain biking trails (the first you meet is Incline Trail).

5.5 km/3.4 miles Turn left (west) when the trail continues straight to the mushroom parking lot.

5.8 km/3.6 miles Carefully make your way down a steep trail section dubbed the "Seymour Grind."

7.1 km/4.4 miles Keep first right and then left (west) to stay on the Baden Powell Trail as the route meets Bridle Path. Then keep right at a connector trail to Marykirk Place.

Left: An owl overlooks a boardwalk near Lynn Canyon.
Right: A pair of rushing cascades are known as Twin Falls.

Deep Cove to Lynn Canyon

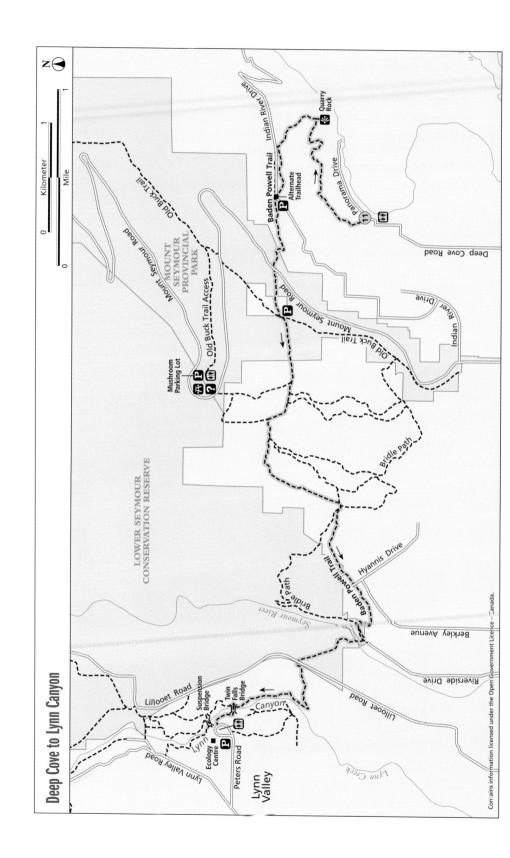

N

0   1   Kilometer   1
0   Mile   1

MOUNT SEYMOUR PROVINCIAL PARK

LOWER SEYMOUR CONSERVATION RESERVE

Old Buck Trail

Mount Seymour Road

Mushroom Parking Lot

Old Buck Trail Access

Old Buck Trail

Mount Seymour Road

Baden Powell Trail

Alternate Trailhead

Quarry Rock

Indian River Drive

Panorama Drive

Deep Cove Road

Indian River Drive

Bridle Path

Baden Powell Trail

Hyannis Drive

Bridle Path

Seymour River

Berkley Avenue

Riverside Drive

Lillooet Road

Suspension Bridge

Lillooet Road

Lynn Valley Road

Twin Falls Bridge

Canyon

Ecology Centre

Peters Road

Lynn

Lynn Valley

Lynn Creek

Contains information licensed under the Open Government Licence – Canada.

8.1 km/5.0 miles   Cross Hyannis Drive.

8.7 km/5.4 miles   Turn left (southwest) on the Baden Powell as Fisherman's/Angler's Trail cuts northeast along the river.

9.0 km/5.6 miles   Straight ahead there's a large bridge leading to Riverside Drive. Turn right (north) to take the pipeline bridge over Seymour River.

9.5 km/5.9 miles   Pass the Powerlines Trail as well as the east and then the west instances of Richard Juryn Trail.

9.8 km/6.1 miles   Carefully cross Lillooet Road and enter Lynn Canyon Park.

10.4 km/6.5 miles   Keep right (north) at the intersections with the Diamond and the Sea to Sky Trails, which head south toward Inter River Park.

11.3 km/7.0 miles   Take in the view and then cross the river on Twin Falls Bridge (west). Then continue right (north) along the creek's west bank.

11.9 km/7.4 miles   Reach the cafe and ecology center.

12.0 km/7.5 miles   If it's open, venture down to the Lynn Canyon Suspension Bridge.

Option: The low-key Two Canyon Loop also follows this Baden Powell section through Lynn Canyon Park. The usual route starts at the suspension bridge, cuts north and then east past the Seymour-Capilano Filtration Plant to Homestead Trail and Seymour River. Then, the loop follows Fisherman's/Angler's Trail south along and then across the river. The Baden Powell heads back northwest to Lynn Canyon for an easy to moderate, 8-kilometer (5-mile) hike that takes 2–3 hours.

Hike Information

Local Attractions: At the end of the trail, visit the Lynn Canyon Ecology Centre exhibits. Or you can continue on park trails, perhaps for a summer swim in 30 Foot Pool. 3663 Park Rd., North Vancouver; (604) 990-3755; lynncanyonecologycentre.ca.

Restaurants: For an excellent weekend lunch before hitting the trail, stop by the lovely Arms Reach Bistro (4390 Gallant Ave., North Vancouver; 604-929-7442; armsreachbistro.com). Or for a grab-and-go option, there's sugar-coated goodness at Honey Doughnuts & Goodies (4373 Gallant Ave., North Vancouver; 604-929-4988; honeydoughnuts.com).

GREEN TIP
Carpool or take public transportation to the trailhead.

12 Mount Seymour

Three progressively higher peaks are a fun workout, but most people hike this route for the views, which start at the parking lot and only get better. Mount Baker, Mount Garibaldi, and Downtown Vancouver all enter the scene. A rocky trail makes for interesting but challenging hiking.

Start: Mount Seymour parking lot
Distance: 8.3-km (5.2-mile) out-and-back
Elevation gain: 417 meters (1,368 feet)
Hiking time: 4-5 hours
Difficulty: Moderate due to length, but difficult elevation gain and steep, rocky terrain
Trail surface: Gravel road, forested trail, dirt path
Best season: July–Sept
Other trail users: Dog-walkers
Canine compatibility: Leashed dogs permitted
Land status: Provincial park
Fees and permits: In 2020, this route required reserving a day-use pass (discovercamping.ca) due to COVID-19 restrictions.
Schedule: None, but daylight hours recommended

Maps: Official maps are available online through Mount Seymour Provincial Park (bcparks.ca). Government topographic maps include the GeoBC Topographic Map Viewer (gov.bc.ca), as well as map 92G7 in the Atlas of Canada Toporama tool (atlas.gc.ca).
Trail contacts: Mount Seymour Provincial Park; (604) 986-9371; bcparks.ca and seatosky parks.com
Special considerations: This rocky route requires sure footing. Hiking poles, boots with ankle support, and fit legs can make a huge difference. There is no water along the route. There can also be bad bugs in June and July—bring repellent.

Finding the trailhead: From Highway 1, take exit 22B—the third turn when heading north on Second Narrows Bridge. Turn right (east) onto Mount Seymour Parkway. After 4.5 kilometers (2.8 miles), turn left (north) onto Mount Seymour Road. The road snakes about 13 kilometers (8.1 miles) uphill to the ski hill parking lot. Trailhead GPS: N49 22.05' / W122 56.95'

The Hike

Until the late 1920s, most Vancouverites didn't know much about Mount Seymour. At that time, Grouse Mountain was already well established as a winter destination, and Hollyburn Ridge had growing numbers of off-grid log cabins. But to the east, the three peaks of Seymour were overlooked.

Today, Seymour is one of three twinkling sets of lights that mark a trio of North Shore ski hills. Visitors in any season get to view the City of Vancouver and Mount Baker from the parking lot. From the peaks, the views on a fine day can extend to Mount Garibaldi in the north and Vancouver Island in the southwest.

Though the Alpine Club of Canada applied for a lease on the mountain's fine skiing slopes, the Depression froze those development plans. The land became a

Top: Mount Seymour offers sweeping and yet tranquil views.
Left: Mount Seymour's slopes are a patchwork of rocky outcrops and heather meadows.
Right: A rocky, rooty trail leads between the peaks of First Pump and Tim Jones, en route to Mount Seymour.

TRAIL SNACKS

When you take something homemade on the trail, you not only save on packaging, but it just tastes better. If you're heading out with friends, take an extra ration or two to share.

PEANUT-BUTTERY GRANOLA BARS

2 cups rolled oats

¼ cup sugar

½ teaspoon salt

¼ teaspoon cinnamon

2½ cups any mix of nuts, seeds, fruits, and chocolate

¼ cup oil

⅓ cup peanut butter

¼ cup honey

3 eggs

1 tablespoon water

1. Mix together dry ingredients.
2. Mix together wet ingredients in a separate bowl.
3. Combine wet and dry ingredients.
4. Grease an 8x8-inch pan or line it with parchment paper. Spread out and pack down the granola bar mixture.
5. Bake for 30 to 40 minutes at 350°F.

CHEWY GRANOLA BARS

2 eggs

⅓ cup maple syrup or honey

1 cup rolled oats

½ cup wheat bran

½ cup skim milk powder

¼ cup whole-wheat flour

½ teaspoon cinnamon

2 cups any mix of nuts, seeds, fruits, and chocolate

1. Beat together wet ingredients.
2. Mix together dry ingredients in a separate bowl.
3. Combine wet and dry ingredients.
4. Grease an 8x8-inch pan or line it with parchment paper. Spread out and pack down the granola bar mixture.
5. Bake for 30 minutes at 350°F.

Navigate snow patches to reach the rocky peak of First Pump on the way to Mount Seymour.

WHOLE-WHEAT BANANA MUFFINS

1½ cups mashed banana (about 3–4 bananas)

¾ cup brown sugar

¾ cup milk with 1 tablespoon vinegar
(a makeshift buttermilk)

1 egg

1 cup whole-wheat flour

¾ cup wheat bran

¾ cup ground flax

2 tablespoons cinnamon

1½ teaspoons baking powder

1 teaspoon baking soda

Handful chocolate chips

1. Mash together wet ingredients.
2. Mix together dry ingredients in a separate bowl.
3. Combine wet and dry ingredients, stirring until combined.
4. Portion the batter into a muffin tray. Makes 12–18 muffins.
5. Bake 20 minutes at 400°F.

TRAIL MIX

There's also the simple option: homemade trail mix. Just throw a selection of nuts (cashews, peanuts, walnuts, pecans, almonds, soy nuts), seeds (sunflower, flax, pumpkin, sesame), and dried fruits (prunes, raisins, cranberries, blueberries, cherries, apricots, apples, bananas) together, perhaps adding some candy-coated chocolate. A few shakes of dried coconut is another tasty extra.

provincial park in 1936, about the same time that Harold Enquist started Seymour Ski Camp, shaping Mount Seymour as you see it today.

It is among these gravel ski runs that this hike begins. The confusion of routes in the early stretch is a bit disorienting, and there are a number of paths to cover the first 1.6 kilometers (1.0 mile). Many hikers tend to favor the non-hiking trail: clomping up Manning ski run to the main trail junction just west of Mystery Peak. This route is simple to follow, though it can get hot on a sunny day. Alternately, a forest route cuts uphill between Dog Mountain Trail and Manning. On this trail, reflective markers show the way. A third option is to follow the rougher Mystery Lake Trail east of Mystery Peak and ascend to Brockton Chairlift.

Mount Seymour is named for Frederick Seymour, governor of the Colony of British Columbia. His term ended rather abruptly in 1869, when he died—reportedly from alcohol poisoning—on a boat heading to Bella Coola on the central coast.

All three routes lead to the same rocky trail that slowly climbs through mountain hemlocks, pink mountain heather, blueberry bushes, and nameless pocket lakes. All trees at this high elevation are evergreens, which keep their needles and therefore can photosynthesize food from spring through fall. This gives coniferous trees a huge head start over deciduous trees—one of the reasons why the West Coast's massive trees are almost exclusively evergreens.

Charles "Chappy" Chapman made the first recorded climb of First Pump and photographed the mountain in 1908, naming the peak for a log that looked like a water pump. That log is long gone, but the name stuck. It also originally lent its name to Second Pump, located down and back up a rocky saddle, until the peak was named for search-and-rescue volunteer Tim Jones in 2017.

It's the third and highest peak that is known as Mount Seymour—and it's worth every step and bug bite to reach.

Distances and Directions

0.0 km/0.0 mile Start from the information sign just north of the ski hill parking lot.

0.1 km/0.1 mile Hike up the central gravel road, passing a turn to Dog Mountain and the forested Mount Seymour Main Trail—both on the left. Follow the main gravel road to the northeast, the wintertime Manning ski run, ignoring lesser trails, runs, and roads as they branch off on either side

0.3 km/0.2 mile A left fork leads north to a small dam. Head up for a quick look, or continue northeast on the main gravel road.

1.3 km/0.8 mile Pass the endpoint for the woodland Mount Seymour Trail—this hike's return route.

1.6 km/1.0 mile Head left (northeast) to follow the rocky trail along a small lake and up toward First Pump. The right fork heads east up the gravel road to Mystery Lake Trail and Mystery Peak.

2.0 km/1.2 miles Admire the view from Brockton Point.

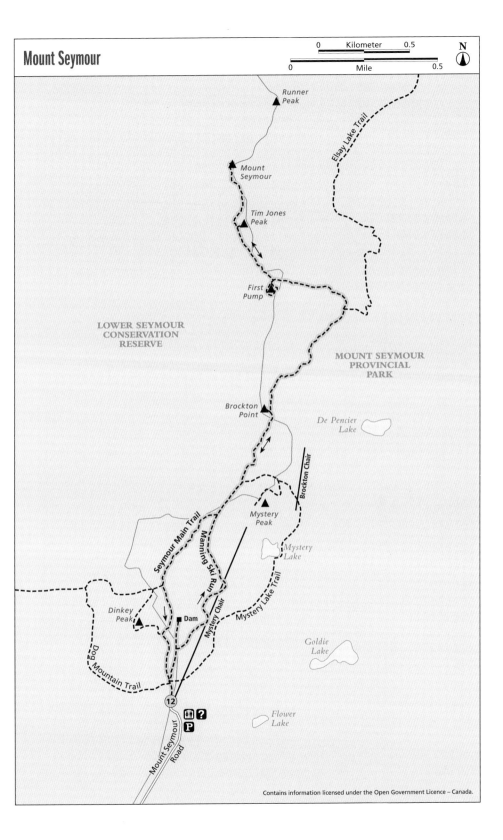

Mount Seymour

0 — Kilometer — 0.5

0 — Mile — 0.5

N

Runner Peak

Elsay Lake Trail

Mount Seymour

Tim Jones Peak

First Pump

LOWER SEYMOUR CONSERVATION RESERVE

MOUNT SEYMOUR PROVINCIAL PARK

Brockton Point

De Pencier Lake

Brockton Chair

Seymour Main Trail

Manning Ski Run

Mystery Peak

Mystery Lake

Mystery Chair

Mystery Lake Trail

Dinkey Peak

■ Dam

Goldie Lake

Dog Mountain Trail

⑫

🚻 ❓

🅿

Mount Seymour Road

Flower Lake

Contains information licensed under the Open Government Licence – Canada.

2.8 km/1.7 miles Continue straight (northwest) and pass Elsay Lake Trail. This backcountry route heads right (east) and a suspended sign warns of avalanche risk.

3.3 km/2.1 miles Turn left (south) to climb the steep rocky face of First Pump. There are various unmarked routes to the top—some require more scrambling ability than others. Head around to the southwest face for the easiest ascent.

3.4 km/2.1 miles Reach First Pump summit. (***Bail-out:*** First Pump has some of the most spectacular views, perhaps on par with the third peak of Mount Seymour. Many opt to turn back at this destination for a 7-kilometer [4.3-mile] hike round-trip.)

3.5 km/2.2 miles Retrace your steps to the main trail, this time turning left (northwest) toward Tim Jones Peak (formerly Second Pump).

3.9 km/2.4 miles Turn right (east) to climb a short trail to the peak.

4.0 km/2.5 miles From Tim Jones Peak, return to the main trail junction and continue north. The route descends along a cliff and into a saddle between the peaks.

4.5 km/2.8 miles After a rocky climb, summit Mount Seymour. Spread out on the peak and enjoy. To return, descend Mount Seymour on the same trail.

6.9 km/4.3 miles Near Mystery Peak, continue downhill right (southwest) along the gravel Manning ski run. There's also a return trail via Mystery Lake if you head left (east) toward Brockton Chair, but overall this route can be tricky to follow if there's any snow on the ground.

7.1 km/4.4 miles Turn right (southwest) to follow the forested footpath down the mountainside.

7.6 km/4.7 miles Trails feed in from the right. Continue straight (south) at the right turn to Dinkey Peak and First Lake.

7.7 km/4.8 miles Continue straight (south) again at the second right turn to Dinkey Peak Lookout. You also pass a memorial to search-and-rescue volunteer Tim Jones.

8.2 km/5.1 miles Continue downhill toward the parking lot—now in sight.

8.3 km/5.2 miles Arrive back at the trailhead.

Option: The hike to Dog Mountain, Dinkey Peak, and First Lake is a favorite with snowshoers and families. The gentle climb covers 5 kilometers (3.1 miles) round-trip. And since it's a loop, it means you can avoid retracing your steps.

Hike Information

Local Information: Mount Seymour operates as a ski hill during winter, roughly December through April. The ski hill has the highest base elevation of the three North Shore ski hills. It offers popular kids' programs, well-reviewed ski lessons, and some of the region's best snowshoeing. 1700 Mount Seymour Rd., North Vancouver; (604) 986-2261; mtseymour.ca.

West Vancouver

The lands to the west of Capilano River form the District of West Vancouver. Above the city's multimillion-dollar homes and shoreline beaches, swaths of evergreen forest stretch up to the rocky peaks of the North Shore Mountains. Only old logging trails, the occasional road, and ski runs cut into the wilderness.

In the early 1900s, people began crossing Burrard Inlet to experience Capilano Suspension Bridge, ski on snowy slopes, and hike forest trails. By the 1930s, more than 200 rough log cabins were slotted into the Hollyburn Ridge forest, many near historic 1926 Hollyburn Lodge, which still stands on the shore of First Lake. Though many off-grid cabins have fallen into disrepair or been removed, others remain as signs of a simpler time.

Over the past century, West Vancouver has found a sometimes-tenuous balance between wilderness, logging, ski hills, hiking trails, and development. Nowhere is this more palpable than in massive Cypress Provincial Park, where shorn summer slopes of a ski resort sit not far from thousand-year-old yellow cedars and amabilis firs.

Though most West Vancouver hillsides have been cut over the last century, there are still stands of old-growth trees in the city. These giant examples of Douglas fir, western red cedar, western hemlock, amabilis fir, grand fir, and yellow cedar stand from an earlier time. Many, but not all, are protected in parklands like Cypress Provincial Park, Lighthouse Park, and Cypress Falls Park.

West Vancouver is also home to the curious arbutus tree, with its papery cinnamon-colored bark flaking away from the smooth trunk. These trees, also called *madrone* or *madrona*, are the only broad-leaf evergreens in the region. With all these leafy gems to find, it's one of the best places in the region to be awed by nature.

13 Capilano Pacific Trail

It's mostly uphill, but the Capilano Pacific Trail has a gentle grade thanks to its beginnings as the Capilano Timber Company rail bed in the early 20th century. From Ambleside Park, which sits within view of Lions Gate Bridge and Stanley Park across First Narrows, you follow Capilano River toward its great concrete wall: Cleveland Dam. Below the dam, a salmon hatchery seethes with fishy activity during the fall spawning, and anglers cast a line at Cable Pool.

Start: Ambleside Park, West Vancouver
Distance: 13.2-km (8.2-mile) lollipop
Elevation gain: 157 meters (515 feet)
Hiking time: About 4 hours
Difficulty: Easy due to smooth terrain and limited, short climbs, though the longer distance could pose a challenge for some
Trail surface: Paved path, gravel road, forested trail, wooden bridges, stairs
Best season: Year-round, but best in Oct and Nov when adult Chinook salmon return to Capilano River
Other trail users: Cyclists, dog-walkers, runners
Canine compatibility: Leashed dogs permitted with some off-leash areas
Land status: Regional park
Fees and permits: No fees or permits required
Schedule: Daylight hours

Maps: Official park maps are available online from Metro Vancouver (metrovancouver.org) and the City of West Vancouver (westvancouver .ca). Government topographic maps include the GeoBC Topographic Map Viewer (gov.bc.ca), as well as map 92G6 in the Atlas of Canada Toporama tool (atlas.gc.ca).
Trail contacts: Metro Vancouver Regional Parks West Area Office, Suite 130, 1200 W. 73rd Ave., Vancouver, V6P 6G5, (604) 224-5739, metrovancouver.org; or City of West Vancouver, 750 17th St., West Vancouver, BC, V7V 3T3, (604) 925-7275, westvancouver.ca
Special considerations: Trails can be muddy and slippery after heavy rains, especially as the North Shore is one of the wettest areas of Metro Vancouver. Off- and on-leash dogs are extremely common on this trail—those who aren't keen on animals may prefer to avoid this hike.

Finding the trailhead: From Downtown Vancouver, take Lions Gate Bridge north across Burrard Inlet. Follow signs for Whistler and merge onto Marine Drive West. Continue 0.75 km (0.5 mile) west past the mall and turn left (south) onto 13th Street. At Argyle Avenue, make a left (southeast) and continue into Ambleside Park, driving to the road's end. Trailhead GPS: N49 19.31' / W123 08.43'

The Hike

For Capilano River to reach the saltwater of First Narrows, it will have flowed down from the Coast Mountains, lingered in Capilano Reservoir, careened down Cleveland Dam spillway, passed under a suspension bridge, and traveled through canyons.

Even with so much diversity, this trail never strays far from water. The trailhead sits near an information sign at the river mouth, adjacent to an off-leash dog area in Ambleside Park. A paved seawall, a cousin to longer paths on the Vancouver side of

Water slides down the Cleveland Dam spillway and into Grand Canyon.

Burrard Inlet like the Stanley Park Seawall, heads in the opposite direction to the hike, skirting the shoreline west through to Dundarave.

There's far less traffic on the Capilano Pacific Trail than the Ambleside seawall, although first the section passes through one of the city's largest developments: Park Royal Mall. This stretch clashes the wild Capilano River on the right side with office towers, condominium residences, and brand-name mall stores to the left.

Yet as you continue in between paved parking lots and other signs of habitation, Brothers Creek still babbles in to join the river—representing West Vancouver's third-largest watershed. The waters have flowed down from the heights of Hollyburn Ridge and beyond (see the Hollyburn Ridge hike), and species of salmon and trout spawn in the creek.

The waterway was originally known as Sisters Creek, but the switch of sex owes itself to confusion: There's another Sisters Creek that flows down from The Lions.

The route draws you away from nature again at Keith Road. Well-marked signs direct you along the side street to a parking area under the Trans-Canada Highway. There are no sidewalks for this 500-meter (0.3-mile) stretch, but keep to the left-hand side of the quiet road. This parking lot can be an alternate trailhead, and puts you closer to the forest trails and salmon hatchery.

As the trail climbs, it skirts the grounds of Capilano Suspension Bridge—one of Vancouver's first tourist attractions built in 1889. There's a substantial admission fee to

Ambleside Beach is a sunny spot in good weather.

cross the 137-meter (449-foot) bridge and admire the rugged canyon from 70 meters (230 feet) up, but you can't access the park from this west side of the river. The main entrance to the attraction is on Capilano Road, on the east side of the river. Lynn Canyon Suspension Bridge, included in the Deep Cove to Lynn Canyon hike, offers a free but less-thrilling alternative.

BUILDING A BRIDGE

In 1932 the beer-making Guinness family purchased 1,619 hectares (4,000 acres) of land on the North Shore Mountains, calling the estate British Properties. The land developers had an agreement to subdivide the land, but the investors realized traveling to the North Shore posed the largest barrier to real-estate success. At that time only ferries linked the two shores.

Despite the challenges of slicing into Stanley Park—the city's major public park since 1889—the Guinness family fronted the $5.6 million to build the Lions Gate Bridge. The 1.8-kilometer (1.1-mile) span, a sister-design to the Golden Gate Bridge, opened in 1938, charging a 25-cent toll.

Continue north along the well-graded 1917 rail beds of the Capilano Timber Company. Loggers felled red cedar in the valley until 1932, and amid the decayed stumps there is now mature second-growth forest (as most North Shore forests are, following fervent logging in the early 20th century). Feeder trails connect to residential streets, and small bridges cross over creeks.

As major hiking trails, including the Baden Powell and the Trans-Canada Trails, join the Capilano Pacific, you know Capilano Lake is nearby, and all trails bottleneck over Cleveland Dam's paved road. In the rainier seasons, the intense sounds of rushing water fill the canyon, but the ultimate experience is standing on the dam above the outlet and feeling the spray from the nearly 91-meter (299-foot) spillway. On the east side of the dam, a rest area has picnic tables, washrooms, and a viewpoint north over Capilano Lake to The Lions. Being at this higher elevation can be much colder than sea level Ambleside Park—bring a warm layer for a rest break here.

From the picnic area, which was once the site of the Grand Canyon suspension bridge (evidently suspension bridges were trendy in early Vancouver!), pick up Palisades Trail to descend the wooden stairs and switchbacks to Capilano Salmon Hatchery.

Capilano Lake sits below many of the North Shore peaks.

Forest trails lead to canyons, a dam, a hatchery, and more attractions.

Salmon use the hatchery's fish ladder to bypass the dam and reach spawning creeks farther upstream. Three types of salmon pass through the hatchery: steelhead adults in March and April, coho adults from June to November, and chinook adults in October and November. If the hatchery is open to the public on your visit, its aquarium-style, underwater windows let you watch the salmon at work.

These salmon are heading to the countless creeks that feed into Capilano River, a waterway that extends more than 17 kilometers (10.6 miles) north of the reservoir. Each salmon has a genetic disposition to a particular creek, to its spawning

Cable Pool Bridge overlooks the river canyon, a popular fishing spot.

ground—it's thought they find their way by smell. The fish ladders and rearing tanks at the concrete hatchery help bolster salmon runs despite the obstacle of the dam.

Fittingly named Coho Loop trail leads south from the hatchery and passes Cable Pool Bridge. This short span crosses back over Capilano River to pick up another section of the loop. Instead, carry on downstream to Cable Pool fishing hole. At a dogleg in the river, watch for the kayakers who regularly run the rapids.

Keep on Coho Loop through to Pipeline Trail Bridge, which crosses the river canyon. On the far side, Coho Loop swings back toward Cable Pool and the Giant

Fir, or Grandpa Capilano, while Shinglebolt Trail heads west to connect again with Capilano Pacific Trail.

From here, it's a familiar, mostly downhill walk back to the river mouth, following a route young salmon take on their way to the ocean.

Distances and Directions

0.0 km/0.0 mile   Start from Ambleside Park and follow the paved trail northeast along Capilano River and under a railway bridge.

0.3 km/0.2 mile   Pass the parking lots and brand-name stores of Park Royal Mall, and then follow the trail under Marine Drive—the river is your constant.

1.2 km/0.7 mile   Pass the site of the old Port Royal Hotel and cross over Brothers Creek.

1.8 km/1.1 miles   Follow the marked trail left (north) away from the river and up to Keith Road. Turn right (east) on the road and follow it to a parking area under Upper Levels Highway.

2.3 km/1.4 miles   Reach a parking lot and alternate trailhead.

2.7 km/1.7 miles   The road ends and a gravel and forest path begins.

3.5 km/2.2 miles   Heading north, reach the grounds of Capilano Suspension Bridge and continue straight past the trail up to Moyne Drive.

3.8 km/2.4 miles   Turn right (northeast) on the trail. The route straight ahead (north) also connects with the Capilano Pacific Trail at the Rabbit Lane junction.

4.2 km/2.6 miles   Continue right (north) on the forest trail at the Rabbit Lane trail junction.

4.3 km/2.7 miles   Admire the views from a canyon lookout.

5.2 km/3.2 miles   Cross over Houlgate Creek.

5.3 km/3.3 miles   Pass a connector trail to Upper Shinglebolt, and then continue straight (northeast) on Capilano Pacific Trail as the Upper Shinglebolt Trail junction heads both left and right.

5.5 km/3.4 miles   The Trans-Canada Trail joins the main route. Turn left uphill on the gravel road.

5.8 km/3.6 miles   Walk straight and pass the Lower Shinglebolt Trail junction.

5.9 km/3.7 miles   The Baden Powell Trail feeds in from the west.

6.1 km/3.8 miles   Walk across Cleveland Dam.

6.4 km/4.0 miles   On the east side of the dam there are washrooms and a

A mushroom bench near Capilano Hatchery

Capilano Pacific Trail

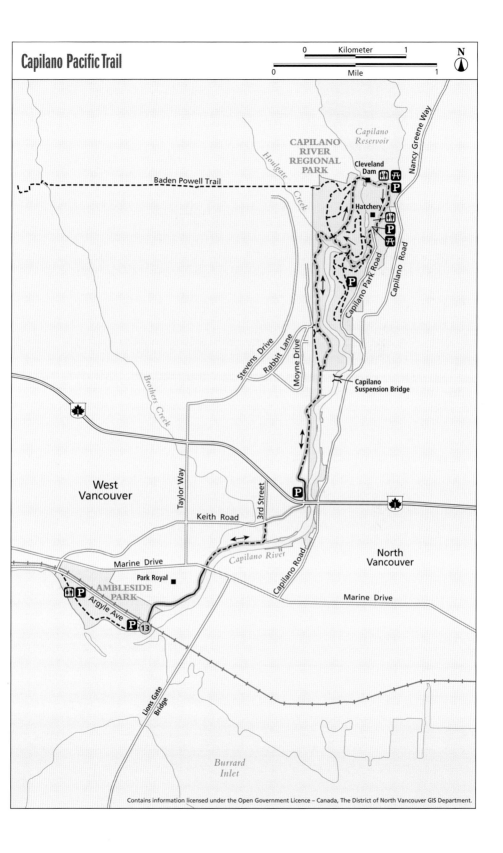

0 Kilometer 1
0 Mile 1
N

Capilano Reservoir

CAPILANO
RIVER
REGIONAL
PARK

Cleveland Dam

Nancy Greene Way

Houlgate Creek

Baden Powell Trail

Hatchery

Capilano Park Road

Capilano Road

Stevens Drive

Rabbit Lane

Moyne Drive

Capilano Suspension Bridge

Brothers Creek

West Vancouver

Taylor Way

3rd Street

Keith Road

Marine Drive

Capilano River

Capilano Road

North Vancouver

Park Royal

Marine Drive

AMBLESIDE PARK

Argyle Ave

13

Lions Gate Bridge

Burrard Inlet

Contains information licensed under the Open Government Licence – Canada, The District of North Vancouver GIS Department.

picnic area. Look for the right (southwest) turn onto Palisades Trail beyond the washrooms and near Capilano Road. Descend the stairs to the hatchery. (***Bail-out:*** You can clip the distance at 6.5 kilometers [4.0 miles] by catching bus 236 down Capilano Road to Marine Drive, and then travel west on the R2 express bus to Park Royal Mall.)

6.6 km/4.1 miles   Cross over Capilano Park Service Road.

7.0 km/4.3 miles   If it's open, watch for salmon at Capilano Salmon Hatchery.

7.1 km/4.4 miles   Pick up Coho Loop Trail, heading south at the hatchery turnaround road loop.

7.2 km/4.5 miles   The trail overlooks the river and Cable Pool Bridge. But stay on the east side of the river and follow the dogleg of the river as it bends west. Continue to follow Coho Loop Trail; it also passes an exit up to Capilano Park Road.

7.6 km/4.7 miles   Turn right (north) on Pipeline Bridge to cross over Capilano River.

7.7 km/4.8 miles   On the far side of the river, immediately turn left (west). Keep left (west) again on Upper Shinglebolt Trail. In 300 meters (0.2 mile) you reconnect with the Capilano Pacific Trail.

8.0 km/5.0 miles   Turn left (west) to retrace your steps along Capilano Pacific Trail.

13.2 km/8.2 miles   Arrive back at the trailhead.

Hike Information

Local Information: Find out what salmon are struggling up the fish ladders from the Capilano Salmon Hatchery. 4500 Capilano Park Rd.; (604) 666-1790; pac.dfo -mpo.gc.ca.

Local Attractions: This hike sits near the North Shore's two largest attractions: Capilano Suspension Bridge (3735 Capilano Rd., North Vancouver; 604-985-7474; capbridge.com) and Grouse Mountain (6400 Nancy Greene Way, North Vancouver; 604-980-9311; grousemountain.com).

Restaurants: Besides good diner-style eats, Tomahawk Barbecue houses a renowned collection of First Nations artworks. 1550 Philip Ave., North Vancouver; (604) 988-2612; tomahawkrestaurant.com.

GREEN TIP
Consider citronella as an effective natural mosquito repellent.

14 Lighthouse Park

With old-growth trees, windswept granite bluffs, and World War II relics, this hike in West Vancouver's Lighthouse Park is simply enchanting. A 4.2-kilometer (2.6-mile) loop connects the park's sights and old groves of arbutus, Douglas fir, and cedar. There are many options to explore side trails and escape down to the shoreline or out to viewpoints. Take picnic supplies and make it a day trip.

Start: Lighthouse Park parking lot
Distance: 4.2-km (2.6-mile) loop
Hiking time: A leisurely 2 hours
Difficulty: Easy due to well-trod forest terrain and little elevation gain, though some may find the rooty trails and occasional hills a moderate challenge
Trail surface: Forested trail, stairs, and dirt path
Best season: Year-round
Other trail users: Dog-walkers with off-leash dogs
Canine compatibility: Off-leash dogs permitted

Land status: City park
Fees and permits: No fees or permits required
Schedule: Daylight hours
Maps: An official trail map is available through the City of West Vancouver (westvancouver.ca). Government topographic maps include the GeoBC Topographic Map Viewer (gov.bc.ca), as well as map 92G6 in the Atlas of Canada Toporama tool (atlas.gc.ca).
Trail contacts: West Vancouver Parks and Community Services, (604) 925-7275; west vancouver.ca

Finding the trailhead: From West Vancouver, follow Marine Drive west toward Horseshoe Bay. About 9 kilometers (5.6 miles) from Park Royal Mall, watch for park signs. Turn left (south) onto Beacon Lane. Continue straight past Water Lane and into the parking area. Trailhead GPS: N49 20.28' / W123 15.81'

The Hike

Point Atkinson marks the place where Burrard Inlet and Howe Sound meet the Strait of Georgia. There's been a lighthouse on the point since 1874, and in 1881 the federal government set aside 75 hectares (185 acres) surrounding the light station. This forest buffer allowed for the light to shine in front of a dark backdrop and also provided a fuel source for the steam-powered foghorn.

But the military reserve had a perhaps unplanned upshot: It preserved virgin stands of coastal forest—today, some of the few old-growth trees left in the Vancouver area.

GREEN TIP
Car shuttles on point-to-point hikes add to the carbon load; loop hikes (like this one in Lighthouse Park) just take foot power.

If the gates are open, you can walk down the road toward Point Atkinson Lighthouse.

From the parking lot, you can walk down a straight gravel road to the lighthouse and large cedars, but I recommend you take a more circuitous path to enjoy the park's other treasures, which include granite bluffs, twisted arbutus trees, and serene cliff vistas.

Lighthouse Park is riddled with trails. Thankfully they are all named and mostly signposted. While it may be easy to get turned around, it's harder to get lost provided you have a map. Inland trails head to salmonberry thickets, quiet bird-watching areas, and groves of towering Douglas firs. Shoreline trails discover beaches, sheer cliffs, and driftwood-clogged coves. All are delightful.

For this route, which covers most of the park terrain, you start at the northern-most branch of Juniper Loop. The route twists through the forest down to Juniper Point and takes in the first Howe Sound views. From this shoreline vantage, you can see a few Howe Sound islands: The Grebe Islets are the small, barren rock islands close to shore to the northwest; Passage Island is the forested, mid-channel island with a few residences; and large Bowen Island sits beyond. Slightly inland, Juniper Loop Trails connect with Shore Pine Trail to head southwest toward more views.

At Shore Pine Point, the namesake trees—shore pines are a stunted lodgepole pine—find gaps in the granite to send down roots. Also along the granite bluffs, arbutus trees find rootholds. The tree's papery bark peels away to expose its young, smooth skin. These trees are the only broadleaf evergreen that grows in the province, and they never grow more than 8 kilometers (5 miles) from the ocean. Each hiker seems to discover his or her area of these smooth granite rocks. It's understandably a favorite picnic spot, and rock climbers also find a challenge on the cliff faces.

Weaving east through the park's many trails, perhaps with a detour over to driftwood-clogged West Beach, you reach the first view of the lighthouse. Even from quite close, the park's trees still provide a dense screen around the light station. Soon, the park's World War II buildings also come into view.

In 1942 eighty personnel were stationed at Point Atkinson. But action was fairly limited. In *Cottages to Community*, author Francis Mansbridge writes of a rare occurrence: firing a warning shot at a tugboat, which was operating without running lights. Across Burrard Inlet, however, 250 men were stationed at Point Grey and the two bases (Point Grey and Point Atkinson) worked to maintain an examination area for all arriving boats.

Picnickers spread out on the rocks at Lighthouse Park.

There's no public access to the current Point Atkinson Lighthouse, a national historic site, which dates to 1912. A century on in 2013, the federal government tried (unsuccessfully) to sell the structure.

The park lies in a Rockfish Protected Area. The Vancouver Aquarium worked to reintroduce the species after anglers depleted the black rockfish population by the 1960s—and there are reports the fish are becoming reestablished.

Trails fan out from Beacon Lane—a World War II gravel road that is the shortest route back to the parking lot. But Valley Trail is the key connection to the park's eastern half. Follow it into the forest, and then turn right (east) onto Arbutus Trail. A walk north on Valley of the Giants Trail lets you discover the park's most treasured secret: its old-growth forest. These 500-year-old Douglas firs and towering cedars were the happy accident of the government declaring this area a military reserve in 1881. It's a quiet, contemplative walk among 2-meter- (6-foot-) wide trunks.

Trails spur off Arbutus Trail, back to the parking lot, including one (Summit Trail) up to a granite outcrop that's the park's highest point.

Distances and Directions

0.0 km/0.0 mile   Two sections of Juniper Loop Trail begin at the northwest corner of the parking lot. Pick up the northernmost trail, located behind a metal barrier. (The southern section of Juniper Loop Trail is near an information board with park maps.)

0.4 km/0.2 mile   At a 3-way intersection, continue right (southwest) onto Juniper Point Trail as the loop trail branches left.

0.6 km/0.4 mile   Walk down the wooden stairs and take the short spur trail to the viewpoint. Look out west to Howe Sound and its islands from Juniper Point.

0.7 km/0.4 mile   Return from the viewpoint and keep right (east) on Juniper Point Trail at the base of the stairs. Then, after 100 meters (328 feet), keep right (east) again when Juniper Loop Trail forks.

0.9 km/0.6 mile   At the large 3-way intersection, keep right (south) on the Shore Pine and Seven Sisters Trails.

1.0 km/0.6 mile   Coming down a slight hill, turn right (southwest) on Shore Pine as Seven Sisters Trail continues straight.

1.5 km/0.9 mile   Reach the granite shoreline of Shore Pine Point (also signed as Jack Pine Point), where there are marked and unmarked viewpoints,

1.8 km/1.1 miles   Turn right (southwest) and opt for the 2-minute walk along a lookout trail.

1.9 km/1.2 miles   A right-hand trail leads south and then west down to West Beach—a small cove clogged with sun-bleached driftwood. After exploring, return back up to the main trail.

2.2 km/1.4 miles   Roughly 30 meters (98 feet) east of the West Beach Trail, take Shore Pine Trail as it forks right (southeast). The Seven Sisters and Songbird Meadow Trails head left (north) at this fork.

2.3 km/1.4 miles   Stop at the lighthouse viewpoint, where informational signs explain the lighthouse history.

Lighthouse Park

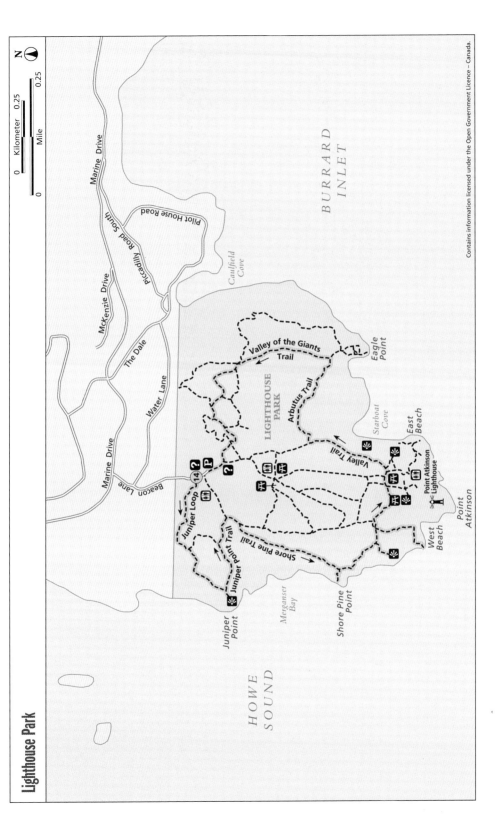

Contains information licensed under the Open Government Licence – Canada.

2.4 km/1.5 miles   Reach the historic World War II buildings, picnic areas, and junction with Beacon Lane. If the gate to the lighthouse is open, visitors are permitted to venture down the roadway for even better views.

2.5 km/1.6 miles   Keep the buildings to your right (south) to pick up Valley Trail and continue into the eastern half of the park. Now heading northeast on Valley Trail, there's a lookout immediately on your right.

2.7 km/1.7 miles   Pass the short trail heading right (southeast) down to Starboat Cove and its driftwood-clogged beach.

2.9 km/1.8 miles   Turn right (east) onto Arbutus Trail and switchback up then down the steepest sections of this hike.

3.3 km/2.1 miles   Make a left (north) onto the Valley of the Giants Trail to walk gently uphill through the park's old-growth forest.

3.6 km/2.2 miles   Meet with Arbutus Trail and turn left (northwest), then head right at the intersection with Summit Trail. It's choose your adventure time: Maple, Summit, Deer Fern, and Salal Loop Trails all branch off this main path—but all lead west toward the parking lot.

4.2 km/2.6 miles   Arrive back at the parking lot and trailhead.

Options: This park is filled with options for shorter or longer trips. For a slightly longer trek, continue on Arbutus Trail to Eagle Point, and then branch off Arbutus Trail to take Summit Trail to the park's 122-meter (400-foot) high point.

Hike Information

Organizations: A volunteer group is actively involved in maintaining park areas and minimizing the impacts of invasive species. You might even catch an occasional lecture, a bird count, or work party. Lighthouse Park Preservation Society, lpps.ca.

GREEN TIP
Use phosphate-free detergent—
it's less harmful to the environment.

15 Cypress Falls

When the snows on Black Mountain at Cypress Mountain ski area melt, they come rushing down Cypress Creek and over the two sets of falls in Cypress Falls Park. These tumultuous cascades are the highlight of this short and interesting route, but the hike's silent costar is the forest, with its old-growth trees, mossy beds, and endearingly haphazard network of trails.

Start: Cypress Falls Park parking lot
Distance: 3.2-km (2.0-mile) out-and-back
Hiking time: 1–1.5 hours
Difficulty: Easy due to short distance and fairly flat forest paths, though steeper sections close to the falls and wayfinding could pose a moderate challenge
Trail surface: Forested trail
Best season: Year-round
Other trail users: Dog-walkers
Canine compatibility: Off-leash dogs permitted
Land status: City park
Fees and permits: No fees or permits required
Schedule: Daylight hours

Maps: There's no map available of the park and its tangle of trails, though some are shown on the municipal map of West Vancouver, available online at westvancouver.ca. Government topographic maps include the GeoBC Topographic Map Viewer (gov.bc.ca), as well as map 92G6 in the Atlas of Canada Toporama tool (atlas.gc.ca).
Trail contacts: West Vancouver Parks and Community Services; (604) 925-7275; west vancouver.ca
Special considerations: There is no fresh water available at the trailhead or during this hike.

Finding the trailhead: From the Upper Levels Highway (Highway 1), take exit 4 for Woodgreen Drive. Make an immediate right at the stop sign onto Woodgreen Drive. After just 350 meters (0.2 mile), turn right onto Woodgreen Place. Bear left on the gravel road and continue into the parking lot. Trailhead GPS: N49 21.12'/ W123 14.45'

The Hike

This is the British Columbia rain forest at its best and most accessible. A rushing creek feeds two impressive waterfalls, and misty airs nourish lichens and mosses that hang from 300-year-old trees—all creating a thick forest canopy that shields you from wetter weather.

But it wasn't always accessible. Some historians, like Elspeth Bradbury in *A View through the Trees,* speculate that these old-growth trees only remain because loggers *couldn't* access them. Whatever the reason for the logging oversight, there is much to appreciate in the park.

A heads-up: Most people feel confused and even lost when walking trails in Cypress Falls Park for the first time. The routes are not mapped and are entirely unnamed, although some orange trail markers

After the last ice age, cedars returned to the landscape only about 6,000 years ago.

have—thankfully—been added in recent years. Use the creek and bridge as your main bearings. To the south of the bridge, there are trails on just the west side of the creek. To the north of the bridge, there are trails on both sides of the creek.

As you start out on the west side of the creek, the woodland trail plunges you quickly into cool forest. Mosses and liverworts (encompassing thousands of species, some of which look like flattened moss) cover rocks and stumps. You soon pass an easy-to-miss trail fork; take either route as both run roughly parallel to the creek and meet again at the first waterfall.

The roaring water echoes in the granite canyon as it plunges down about 15 meters (49 feet) or so. Continue on the main trail and deeper into the park. A bridge offers another view of the falls as you cross the creek and start hiking up the east side. Try to follow the established switchbacks as you continue along the creek bank. Each time I visit the park I tend to uncover a different route—sometimes unintentionally.

When the trail forks near a large Douglas fir, keep left. The right fork leads uphill to the park's boundary and into British Properties lands. Rusted automobiles and a few pieces of scattered garbage edge the needle-packed trails that line the east side of the creek. Slopes can be steep—take time and care. Though the trail continues,

Upper Cypress Falls roars with the spring freshet.

Ghost pipes are a curious species of mushroom flower.

it does venture into private land (British Properties) to cross the creek by Eagle Lake Access Road and thereby link with the west side of the park. Retracing your route back down the east side of the creek avoids the jolt of liability warnings and chain-link fences. As you reach a canyon view, this book's mapped route weaves back along narrow trails closer to the creek.

Back on the west side of the main bridge, I prefer the trail closest to the creek. But this and other trails are marked with orange reflectors. They dot the stand of 300-year-old giants towering above the waterway. These trees, mostly western red cedars and Douglas firs, have survived logging and fires to quietly rule over this park. The thick bark of Douglas firs stands in rough contrast to smooth young hemlocks sidling up alongside.

Farther north, you get another view of the upper waterfall. Again, the trail leaves park boundaries and enters British Properties land, reaching Eagle Lake Access Road. But when the walk is as lovely as Cypress Falls (in few other places can you find old-growth trees and two waterfalls within 1 kilometer [0.6 mile]), a little backtracking is not something to be snubbed.

WHO WAS DOUGLAS?

The Douglas squirrel and Douglas fir are both named for David Douglas, a Scottish botanist and member of the Royal Horticultural Society. Douglas arrived in the Pacific Northwest in 1824, collecting plant samples over a few years to bring back to Britain.

Sitka spruce, grand fir, Douglas fir, and western red cedar are just some of the more than 200 species of plants he introduced to Britain and the world. In doing so, he truly changed the evergreen landscape of the United Kingdom.

But Douglas also has another claim to fame. In 1827 he climbed Mount Brown in the Canadian Rockies. It's the first recorded mountain ascent in Canada, and so Douglas became the nation's first mountaineer. He was just 34 years old when he died in Hawaii, then known as the Sandwich Islands.

Many place names in BC reference a Douglas too. But those generally refer to Sir James Douglas, governor of Vancouver Island, who later became the first governor of British Columbia in 1858.

The Cypress Falls Park forest is a mix of old- and second-growth trees.

Distances and Directions

0.0 km/0.0 mile   Start at the east end of the parking lot.

0.1 km/0.1 mile   Turn left (northeast) to follow the main trail away from the ball field.

0.2 km/0.1 mile   Take either fork of the trail (although the right option is well hidden!).

0.3 km/0.2 mile   Follow a short trail right (east) down to the viewing area above the lower falls.

Cypress Falls

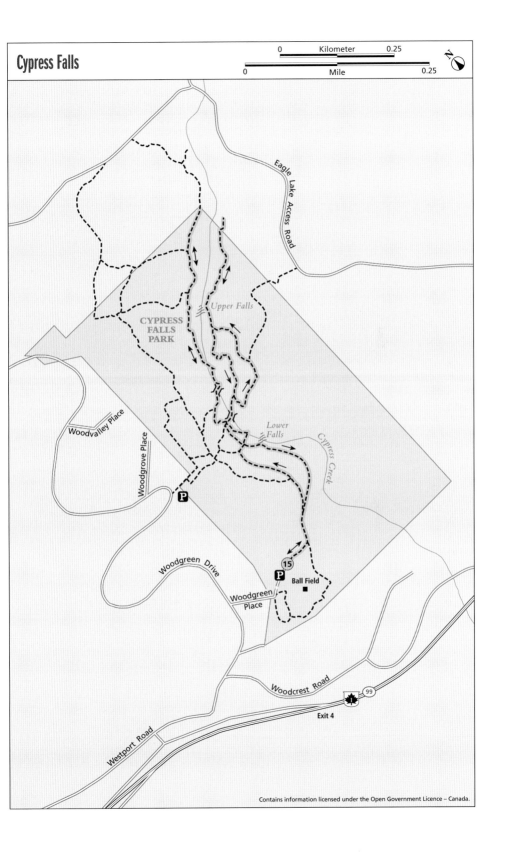

Kilometer

0   0.25

Mile

0   0.25

Eagle Lake Access Road

Upper Falls

**CYPRESS
FALLS
PARK**

Woodvalley Place

Woodgrove Place

*Lower
Falls*

Cypress Creek

P

Woodgreen Drive

15

P   Ball Field

Woodgreen
Place

Woodcrest Road

99

Exit 4

Westport Road

Cypress Falls Park has tucked-away vantages of waterfalls.

0.4 km/0.2 mile Continue upstream and turn right (east), crossing the bridge over Cypress Creek.

0.5 km/0.3 mile Keep right (east) at the first fork, climbing a short but steep hill.

0.6 km/0.4 mile Keep left (north) as the trail forks near a large Douglas fir.

1.0 km/0.6 mile See the upper falls and surrounding canyon, and then return along the same trail toward the bridge.

1.3 km/0.8 mile At a trail fork near the creek, keep right (southwest) along the lower, water-side trails. A couple of paths give you options to explore. Then watch for a route to reclimb the bank and continue southwest toward the bridge.

1.5 km/0.9 mile Return to the bridge and head west across Cypress Creek.

1.6 km/1.0 mile Turn right (north) to pick up the main trail, following the creek's west side. (There are also marked trails heading west away from the creek.)

1.7 km/1.1 miles Cross a small, boardwalk-style bridge and continue northeast.

1.9 km/1.2 miles Pass under the boughs of old-growth Douglas firs.

2.2 km/1.4 miles Reach the park gate on the west side of the creek—the turnaround point. (There are also trails from Eagle Lake Access Road that loop back down into the park.)

2.7 km/1.7 miles Head south and retrace your steps to reach the main bridge.

2.8 km/1.7 miles After passing the main bridge, keep left (southeast). This time follow the lower trail on the creek's west side, which also brings you to a lower falls viewpoint.

3.0 km/1.9 miles The lower trail rejoins the upper trail, heading southwest toward the parking lot.

3.2 km/2.0 miles Arrive back at the trailhead.

Hike Information

Other Resources: Elspeth Bradbury's *A View through the Trees* tells the history of trees in West Vancouver. Logging, recreation, ecology, and other topics all find a place among gorgeous color photographs.

GREEN TIP
Never feed wild animals—including raccoons, squirrels, and birds—under any circumstances. You may damage their health and expose yourself (and them) to danger.

16 Hollyburn Ridge

Pocket lakes, off-grid cabins, and ski lodges, including the historic 1926 Hollyburn Ski Camp, provide interest and lots to look at along this 5.5-kilometer (3.4-mile) forest hike. The route follows a series of trails and snow-free Nordic skiing routes in Cypress Provincial Park for a quiet summer walk during the "off" season.

Start: Hollyburn cross-country skiing parking lot
Distance: 5.5-km (3.4-mile) lollipop
Hiking time: About 1.5 hours
Difficulty: Easy due to the well-established routes, though overgrowth near Blue Gentian and West Lakes can make navigating a challenge
Trail surface: Gravel path, forested trail, boardwalk, gravel road
Best season: June–Oct
Other trail users: Cabin owners, dog-walkers
Canine compatibility: Leashed dogs permitted
Land status: Provincial park, ski resort
Fees and permits: No fees or permits required. This route does not require a day-use pass

under the COVID-19 restrictions that applied to Cypress Provincial Park in 2020.
Schedule: None, but daylight hours recommended
Maps: Some trails are included in the Cypress Provincial Park map, available online at bcparks.ca. Government topographic maps include the GeoBC Topographic Map Viewer (gov.bc.ca), as well as map 92G6 in the Atlas of Canada Toporama tool (atlas.gc.ca).
Trail contacts: Cypress Mountain Guest Relations, end of Cypress Bowl Road, West Vancouver; (604) 926-5612; cypressmountain.com
Special considerations: There is no water available along the trail.

Finding the trailhead: From Upper Levels Highway (Highway 1), take exit 8. Head right (north) on Cypress Bowl Road and follow the route as it switchbacks uphill. After 13 kilometers (8.1 miles), turn right (south) at signs for the cross-country skiing area. Drive past the washrooms and resort rental buildings to the very end of the road. Park in the lot. Trailhead GPS: N49 22.47' / W123 11.56'

The Hike

It was an accident that Rudolph Jules Verne ended up in West Vancouver in May 1922. Verne had been planning to hike Grouse Mountain, but he and a friend boarded the wrong ferry and landed at the 14th Street wharf instead. They followed a trail that took them to the abandoned Nasmyth Shinglebolt Mill and they continued on up to First Lake, where Hollyburn Ski Camp now stands.

Verne recalled the snow as "offering the most perfect skiing imaginable." The entrepreneur set about establishing a ski school, and by 1925 people could rent skis; the next year, Verne opted to move the lodge uphill to better snow conditions. And so—relocated by horsepower—the mill's old cookhouse became Hollyburn Ski Camp on the shores of First Lake.

Hollyburn Lodge from across First Lake

The rust-red building still stands in the same spot, at the western edge of what's now an at-times-dizzying network of trails for Nordic skiing and snowshoeing. In summer, the trails are snow-free but quiet and just as lovely.

Starting along the woodland trail from the parking lot, only a rope strung between trees hints at the height of the wintertime snowpack. Snowshoers use the cord as a hand railing on a brief but steep section. A fire access road leads uphill to Hollyburn Lodge, but be sure to look in the woods on the way.

Between the evergreens, small log cabins are from a simpler time. By 1931 there were more than 200 cabins scattered throughout these woods. Though temporary residents have made many improvements and upgrades since those early days, time and regulation changes have taken their toll on many of the original cabins. As of 2020, about 100 cabins remained and the Hollyburn Ridge Association represents a group of cabin owners, but membership is open to all (including wannabes!).

Hollyburn Mountain was known as Mount Vaughan until 1912.

These structures require continual maintenance. Amid reports of bear break-ins and living without electricity, there are challenges the city-initiated might not expect. Just to keep the roof from caving in, owners may need to shovel off snow a dozen times each winter.

"You're quite welcome here"—to Hollyburn Lodge for winter events and refreshments.

As you reach Hollyburn Lodge on First Lake, you might be the only visitor. Over the years, cabin owners have held summer regattas, swimming and diving competitions, and Loggers Sports Days in this offbeat community. Now blueberry bushes are the liveliest draw.

From First Lake, it's a quiet hike through the woods along the Baden Powell and Nordic skiing trails. Outside the skiing area and into the provincial park, the trails tend to get a bit rougher. In early summer, you may encounter windfall and overgrown bushes across the trail.

Left: The Ranger Station is one of a hundred or so log cabins on Hollyburn Ridge.
Right: Skunk cabbage is a sign of alpine spring on the shores of First Lake.

At Blue Gentian Lake, named for a bright blue flower with five petals, there's a boardwalk and picnic area. Look for the blue blooms in open areas in late September. From the lake, trails continue east to Lost Lake and southeast to Brothers Creek. If you're lucky, you'll have avoided the buggy season.

From Blue Gentian Lake, head northwest to West Lake Trail and cross the small wooden bridge, another example of volunteers bettering the region's trails. Climb uphill over the needle-packed trail, perhaps ducking under a couple of downed trees, depending on the winter beating.

In fall you may spot blue gentians growing on Hollyburn Ridge.

Entrepreneur Ron Brewis dammed Stoney Creek in the early 1930s, creating a lake that is larger than Blue Gentian. Though it looks rather unassuming now, West Lake was the site of Brewis's sixteen-bed lodge and at one time it had the largest ski jump in the Lower Mainland.

From West Lake it's an easy hike along the gravel Jack Pratt and Sitzmark Trails back to Hollyburn Lodge. The lodge and First Lake make for a pretty panorama, especially when the lake waters are calm and reflect the blue skies, evergreen trees, and the lodge's red shingles. And perhaps you will even find some blueberries, which ripen in July—though keep in mind berries are also a favorite with bears.

Distances and Directions

0.0 km/0.0 mile   Start from the southeast end of the parking lot and follow the trail southeast into the woods.

0.4 km/0.2 mile   Turn left (northeast) at Hollyburn Fire Access Road.

0.8 km/0.5 mile   Turn right (south) at the rust-red Hollyburn Lodge.

0.9 km/0.6 mile   Pass the small log cabin Ranger Station, Forks Trail, and First Lake.

1.0 km/0.6 mile   Cross a bridge over Marr Creek.

1.1 km/0.7 mile   Bear right (southeast) on Baden Powell Trail. Here the trail also intersects Sitzmark and Lower Wells Gray Trails.

1.3 km/0.8 mile   Continue right (east) on the Baden Powell Trail (also marked as the ski run Grand National) at the first junction with Jack Pratt Trail.

1.7 km/1.1 miles   Again, continue right (southeast) on Baden Powell Trail at a second junction with Jack Pratt Trail.

1.9 km/1.2 miles   If the weather is clear, you'll have a view of Vancouver. Keep left, following the tree line east as you head downhill.

2.1 km/1.3 miles   The gravel road reappears. Near a clearing, continue straight (southeast) and pass the left turn to West Lake (an alternate but more overgrown route to Blue Gentian Lake).

Hollyburn Ridge

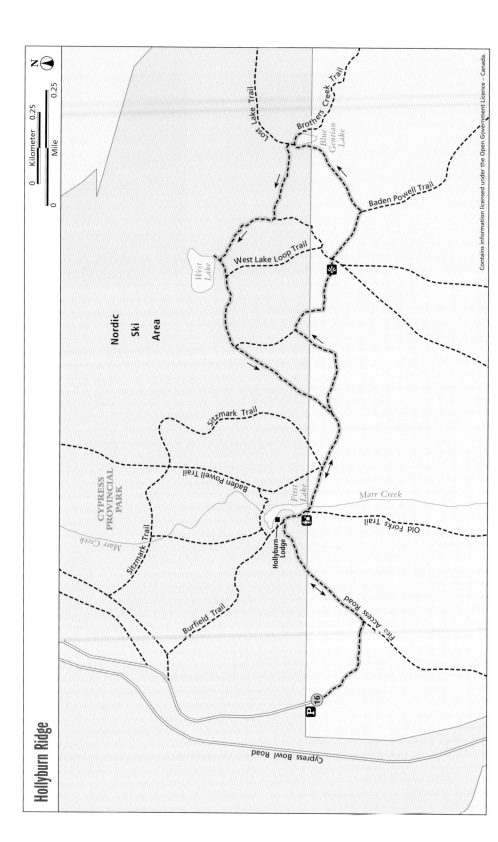

Nordic Ski Area

CYPRESS PROVINCIAL PARK

N

Kilometer   0.25   0.25

Mile

0

Lost Lake Trail

Brothers Creek Trail

Blue Gentian Lake

Baden Powell Trail

West Lake Loop Trail

West Lake

Sitzmark Trail

Baden Powell Trail

Marr Creek

Sitzmark Trail

Marr Creek

First Lake

Old Forks Trail

Hollyburn Lodge

Burfield Trail

Firs Access Road

Cypress Bowl Road

P 16

2.3 km/1.4 miles Turn left (northeast) and leave the Baden Powell (which continues southeast to Craigmohr Drive).

2.6 km/1.6 miles Explore the small shore of Blue Gentian Lake along the boardwalk.

2.7 km/1.7 miles Follow the boardwalk to the lake's north end. At a three-way signposted junction, follow signs north to West Lake. A few strides on, head left (west) at the second junction. The north route continues to Lost Lake.

3.0 km/1.9 miles Hiking uphill (west) on a rooty trail to West Lake Trail, turn right (northwest) to climb the hill to the lake.

3.3 km/2.1 miles Explore the short stretch of West Lake shoreline, and then follow signs west to the parking lot.

3.5 km/2.2 miles A trail, West Lake Weir, feeds in from the right. Continue straight (west).

3.6 km/2.2 miles Continue straight (southwest) uphill on Jack Pratt as another branch of Jack Pratt heads left (southeast). Lower Mobraten heads uphill to the right (northwest).

4.1 km/2.5 miles Continue straight (west) as the Baden Powell Trail rejoins the route from the left. Follow the wide trail toward Hollyburn Lodge.

4.3 km/2.7 miles Head left (west) on Sitzmark as the Baden Powell cuts north.

4.7 km/2.9 miles Pass Hollyburn Lodge and keep left (southwest) to follow the fire access road downhill.

5.1 km/3.2 miles Don't miss the right turn (west) to the parking lot.

5.5 km/3.4 miles Arrive back at the trailhead.

Options: Lost Lake Trail and Brothers Creek Trail are nice options for longer hikes, with the added bonus of a potential swim at Lost Lake. Trails also lead uphill for a more challenging hike to Hollyburn Peak. Either follow the Baden Powell east from the downhill ski area (about 7 km/4.3 miles return) or north from the cross-country area (about 8 km/5.0 miles return) to connect with Hollyburn Mountain Trail. Reaching the peak takes about 3 to 4 hours. In 2020, a day-pass was required for this trail due to COVID-19 restrictions.

Hike Information

Local Attractions: Hollyburn's giant alpine neighbor is Cypress Mountain ski area. The runs cover three mountains with a 610-meter (2,010-foot) vertical rise. Cypress Bowl Road, West Vancouver; (604) 926-5612; cypressmountain.com.

Organizations: Hollyburn Lodge has had near-brushes with being torn down over its long history, and many other local ski lodges have burned down. Hollyburn Heritage Society has been instrumental in saving the lodge, and the structure received funding as a 2010 Winter Games legacy project. It officially reopened after renovations in 2017—90 years after Rudolph Jules Verne held the first opening. The heritage group also collects local histories about Hollyburn and its off-grid cabin community. hollyburnheritage.ca.

GREEN TIP
Reuse ziplock bags.

17 Saint Mark's Summit

Views of Bowen Island and The Lions are in the scope of this rugged but well-traveled hike, which follows a portion of the 29-kilometer (18-mile) Howe Sound Crest Trail. Centuries-old yellow cedar and amabilis fir giants line much of the route to the summit, where narrow trails explore the peak and its rocky cliffs.

Start: Cypress Creek Day Lodge
Distance: 11.4-km (7.1-mile) lollipop
Elevation gain: 430 meters (1,411 feet)
Hiking time: 4–5 hours
Difficulty: Moderate due to mid-range length but steep switchbacks and continual elevation gain could be a challenge for some
Trail surface: Gravel, forested trail, dirt path
Best season: July–Sept
Other trail users: Dog-walkers
Canine compatibility: Dogs not permitted at Yew Lake, but leashed dogs permitted in the park
Land status: Provincial park, ski hill
Fees and permits: In 2020, this route required reserving a day-use pass (discovercamping.ca) due to COVID-19 restrictions.

Schedule: None, but daylight hours recommended
Maps: Official Cypress Provincial Park map and Howe Sound Crest Trail map are available online at bcparks.ca. Government topographic maps include the GeoBC Topographic Map Viewer (gov.bc.ca), as well as map 92G6 in the Atlas of Canada Toporama tool (atlas.gc.ca).
Trail contacts: Cypress Mountain Guest Relations, end of Cypress Bowl Road, West Vancouver; (604) 926-5612; cypressmountain.com
Special considerations: There is fresh water available near the trailhead, but not during this hike.

Finding the trailhead: From Upper Levels Highway (Highway 1), take exit 8. Head right (northwest) on Cypress Bowl Road and follow the route as it switchbacks uphill. After about 15 kilometers (9.3 miles), the road reaches Cypress Mountain's buildings and cleared ski hills. At the end of the road, turn right (northwest) to Cypress Creek Day Lodge and park in the lot. The trailhead is just north of the lodge. Trailhead GPS: N49 23.81' / W123 12.26'

The Hike

Catholic Saint Mark's symbol is a winged lion, so it's fitting that Saint Mark's Summit ends with a vantage over The Lions—the twin peaks that are a Vancouver emblem. But the views don't stop there; exploring the various trails on the treed summit brings you to rocky viewpoints over Howe Sound too.

Saint Mark's is just one stop on the 29-kilometer (18-mile) Howe Sound Crest Trail. This route starts at the south terminus of the trail, but it continues north from Saint Mark's on to Mount Unnecessary, the base of West Lion, Mount Brunswick, Deeks Lake, and finally ending near Porteau Cove.

Amid the glory of these heights, peaks, and views, the quieter discovery is the old-growth forest along an astounding portion. Though the route begins with a flat

A rocky vantage at Saint Mark's Summit overlooks Howe Sound.

amble near Yew Lake and around an old-growth loop, the impressive trees stretch far beyond, nearly all the way to Saint Mark's. On the steep slopes, it's easy to forget looking for the trail markers as you admire tree after tree. I lost count of the yellow cedar (also called yellow cypress—hence the park's name), amabilis fir, and mountain hemlock that measured more than a meter (3 feet) across.

While big trees are the most impressive, even smaller park trees can be centuries old. A tree that measures only 2.0 meters (6.6 feet) tall could be a very grandfatherly

CYPRESS GIANTS

At these higher altitudes, trees that are centuries old can appear to be much younger. A 2-meter (6.6-foot) tree could be up to 200 years old. In Francis Mansbridge's *Hollyburn*, the writer tells of a tree that measured no more than 19 centimeters (7.5 inches) in diameter when cut, but was 280 years old. Note that coastal trees more than 250 years old are considered old growth by the Ministry of Forestry standards, giving a whole new perspective to Cypress's evergreen landscape.

Though you will be left guessing at the ages of most alpine trees, a couple stand out for their astounding age.

Alongside Cypress Bowl Road, just west of the Hollyburn Ridge turnoff, a yellow cedar measures 2.28 meters (7.5 feet) across and stands 39.6 meters (130 feet tall). But those aren't the most impressive statistics: The tree is more than 1,200 years old.

The Hollyburn Giant, another yellow cedar, is located along Old Strachan Trail. Its girth measures more than 3 meters (9.8 feet) across. It too is thought to be in the quadruple digits. While this sounds almost unbelievable, yellow cedars (also called cypress) can live up to 2,000 years.

Other trees reach the millennial mark too. Mountain hemlock and western hemlock can reach more than 1,000 and 1,200 years old respectively, while amabilis firs can be up to 750 years old.

Randy Stoltmann discovered many of the huge trees around Cypress and wrote about these living antiques in his book *Hiking Guide to the Big Trees of Southwestern British Columbia*

200 years old due to the slow rate of alpine growth. When the trail crosses windfall, and park rangers have cleared the path with a chainsaw, look at the tightly packed rings on the dissected tree. Start counting, but you won't finish unless you forego the hike altogether.

It's a good moment to be thankful that some conscientious citizens put up a fight for these forests and helped protect the land as a provincial park. In the 1960s, a logging company started cutting swaths of forest on Cypress Bowl's Black and Strachan Mountains under the guise of developing a ski hill. The logging extended beyond the proposed area, so concerned locals rallied to stop the destruction of old-growth trees. They banded together, later becoming the Friends of Cypress Provincial Park, an organization that's still actively involved in the park.

The outcry also helped establish Cypress Provincial Park in 1975. The logging company exited the picture and BC Parks took over ski hill development, building Cypress Bowl Road. Later on a private resort company took over operations.

Some similar themes of conservation reemerged in the lead-up to the 2010 Winter Games. Cypress was host mountain for freestyle skiing and snowboarding events

Bowen Island from Bowen Lookout in Cypress Provincial Park

(a set of Olympic rings and a stone inukshuk are still at the ski hill base), and bringing the mountain up to international competition levels required extensive work. But in the face of this much more recent challenge, the park had a nonprofit advocacy group and provincial park status in its corner. This means the park's treasured old-growth trees are still slowly growing today—some upwards of 1,000 years old.

Despite the many trees in Cypress Provincial Park, there are no yew trees at Yew Lake.

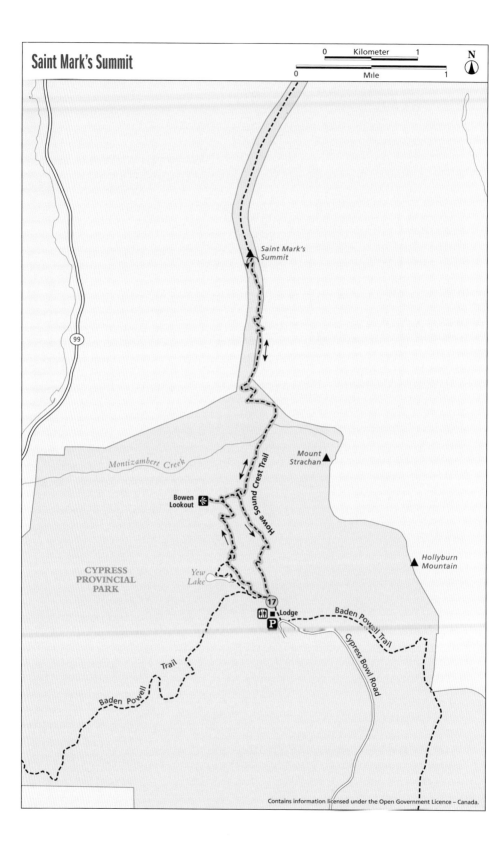

0   Kilometer   1

0   Mile   1

N

Saint Mark's
Summit

99

Montizambert Creek

Mount
Strachan

Bowen
Lookout

Howe Sound Crest Trail

Hollyburn
Mountain

CYPRESS
PROVINCIAL
PARK

Yew
Lake

17

Lodge

P

Baden Powell Trail

Cypress Bowl Road

Trail

Baden Powell

Distances and Directions

0.0 km/0.0 mile   Start from Cypress Creek Day Lodge and follow Yew Lake Interpretive Trail north along the east side of Cypress Creek.

0.05 km/0.0 mile   Head straight (northwest) along the flat, gravel path (signed as Bowen Lookout) as the Howe Sound Crest Trail East Access Trail forks right up to Pumphouse Road.

0.2 km/0.1 mile   Continue straight (northwest) at the left turn to the Baden Powell Trail and Black Mountain.

0.7 km/0.4 mile   Turn right (northeast) toward the old-growth loop. Yew Lake Trail continues its loop to the left (west).

0.8 km/0.5 mile   Follow the old-growth loop around in either direction. As it's only 200 meters (0.1 mile) long, consider completing the whole circle and then doubling back.

1.1 km/0.7 mile   Turn left (northwest) at the intersection with gravel Pumphouse Road, heading toward Bowen Lookout.

1.3 km/0.8 mile   Keep on the trail as it makes a sharp right (north) and crosses over a bridge.

2.0 km/1.2 miles   Take the short trail left (west) down to the lookout.

2.2 km/1.4 miles   From the viewpoint, see Bowen, Keats, and Gambier Islands with tiny Bowyer Island close to shore. Then return uphill to the main trail and continue northeast. (*Bail-out:* Bowen Lookout makes for a short and scenic route that's about 4.4 kilometers [2.7 miles] round-trip.)

2.7 km/1.7 miles   Turn left (north) onto Howe Sound Crest Trail. The right-hand route (southeast) returns to the lodge and parking lot.

3.5 km/2.2 miles   Cross Montizambert Creek.

6.3 km/3.9 miles   By way of many switchbacks, reach Saint Mark's Summit.

6.4 km/4.0 miles   View The Lions from a northeast-facing viewpoint. Linger over the scene before returning back along Howe Sound Crest Trail toward Cypress.

9.9 km/6.2 miles   Continue straight (southeast) along a trail to Pumphouse Road. The right turn (west) goes to Bowen Lookout, the old-growth loop, and Yew Lake.

10.6 km/6.6 miles   After a creek, turn right (southwest) to follow a wooded trail back toward the ski hill. Or simply continue along the road (although the road route is slightly longer).

10.9 km/6.8 miles   Pass a water tower. Then the trail joins the gravel Pumphouse Road.

11.4 km/7.1 miles   Arrive back at the trailhead.

Hike Information

Organizations: Friends of Cypress Park formed to help keep development and logging in the mountain area's old-growth forests in check. Their environmental focus sees members leading hikes and helping to maintain trails. cypresspark.ca.

GREEN TIP
If at all possible, camp in established sites. If there are none, then camp in an unobtrusive area at least 61 meters (200 feet) from the nearest water source.

18 Eagle Bluff

After an initial steep climb alongside the ski slopes of Cypress Mountain resort, this hike turns into a lovely relaxing amble past subalpine lakes and out to Eagle Bluff. There, you sit at the corner of Vancouver, looking down on Lighthouse Park, Horseshoe Bay, and Point Grey, before losing the crowds to visit the peak of Black Mountain. Bring a bathing suit and towel for a summer lake swim too.

Start: Cypress Creek Day Lodge
Distance: 8.9-km (5.5-mile) out-and-back with a short loop
Hiking time: 3–4 hours
Elevation gain: 302 meters (991 feet)
Difficulty: Moderate due to mid-range length and steep climbs on a smooth, well-marked trail
Trail surface: Gravel, forested trail, dirt path, boardwalk
Best season: July–Sept
Other trail users: Dog-walkers, tourists
Canine compatibility: Dogs not permitted at Yew Lake, but leashed dogs permitted in the park
Land status: Provincial park

Fees and permits: In 2020, this route required reserving a day-use pass (discovercamping.ca) due to COVID-19 restrictions.
Schedule: None, but daylight hours recommended
Maps: An official Cypress Provincial Park map is available online at bcparks.ca. Government topographic maps include the GeoBC Topographic Map Viewer (gov.bc.ca), as well as map 92G6 in the Atlas of Canada Toporama tool (atlas.gc.ca).
Trail contacts: Cypress Mountain Guest Relations, end of Cypress Bowl Road, West Vancouver; (604) 926-5612; cypressmountain.com
Special considerations: There is fresh water available near the trailhead, but not during this hike.

Finding the trailhead: From Upper Levels Highway (Highway 1), take exit 8 for Cypress Bowl Road. Turn right and follow Cypress Bowl Road as it switchbacks uphill. After about 15 kilometers (9.3 miles), the road reaches the Cypress Mountain Resort buildings and cleared ski hills. Turn right and drive toward Cypress Creek Day Lodge. Park in the expansive lot. The trailhead is just north of the lodge. Trailhead GPS: N49 23.82' / W123 12.26'

The Hike

Eagle Bluff, the turnaround point for this hike, overlooks a busy scene. The waters of Burrard Inlet and Howe Sound meet at Lighthouse Park; ferries steam out of Horseshoe Bay to Nanaimo, the Sunshine Coast, and Bowen Island; motorboats churn up water; tankers hang on their anchors; sailboats cut slow, smooth paths.

It's the type of scenery that's usually hard-won through a long climb. But in the case of this hike, after the first steep and dusty climb, the elevation profile is fairly friendly to tired legs.

Top: Eagle Bluff looks down on West Vancouver.
Bottom: Yew Lake Lookout has a superb view of The Lions.

Begin just north of Cypress Creek Day Lodge, where trails point to Yew Lake, Howe Sound Crest, and the Baden Powell route. Most of this hike follows the Baden Powell Trail, but as that multisection hike stretches across the North Shore from Horseshoe Bay to Deep Cove, it's important to head in the westerly direction. Heading east will bring you to Cleveland Dam near Grouse Mountain. And while it's also a lovely route, it's a long way from Cypress Mountain Resort.

The first and major climb covers about 250 meters (820 feet) elevation gain over 1.5 kilometers (0.9 mile). Keep going, resting in the shaded areas as you need. Beyond a small buffer of trees to the left, bare hillsides mark the routes of winter ski runs.

At an unnamed lake there's a right (northwest) turn to Cabin Lake. This hike visits Cabin Lake on the return, so head left (southeast) on the Baden Powell Trail. Soon, the shore of Sam Lake beckons off to the left (southeast). Sam and Theagill Lakes both drain into Cypress Creek, which spills over the rushing Cypress Falls about 5 kilometers (3.1 miles) downstream (see the Cypress Falls hike).

Road cyclists love the challenge of biking up the steep switchbacks of Cypress Bowl Road—called the Cypress Challenge. Though the cyclists are slow on the way up, expect them to go just as fast as cars on the way down.

Wide red cedar boards provide a mud-free terrain between freshwater lakes and mountain hemlock forest and also help protect fragile plant life. Though paw prints in the muddy sections on either side of the boardwalk are usually dog-size, keep an eye out for anything larger. This is black bear country.

Owen and Cougar Lakes fall quickly along the trail before you head into the forest through to Eagle Bluff.

The southwest-facing bluff absorbs the hot summer sun. Likely a couple of giant ravens will be lingering there too. From Eagle Bluff the Baden Powell Trail goes

Eagle Bluff views are a panorama.

Ravens on Eagle Bluff

down, down, down to Horseshoe Bay. It's an incredibly steep and rocky route that is safest to attempt on the ascent rather than the descent.

When the Sea to Sky Highway was upgraded for the 2010 Winter Olympics, the new vehicle route sliced through a rare arbutus grove on Eagleridge Bluffs and the original Baden Powell trailhead. Despite community and First Nations protests, the paving went ahead. There's now an alternate Baden Powell trailhead at Nelson Creek.

On the return journey to Cypress Mountain, make the detour to Cabin Lake—a popular spot for swimming after a sweaty hike. The loop first passes a Black Mountain viewpoint before continuing on to the lakeshore. Though it's a lovely spot to linger, save for when the bugs are in season, cut the visit a few minutes short to follow the viewpoint trail up to a valley lookout.

It's called Yew Lake Lookout, but personally, I can't say I noticed Yew Lake. Instead, the ever-impressive scene takes in the stark and impressive profiles of The Lions rising far above evergreen slopes.

Distances and Directions

0.0 km/0.0 mile   Start from Cypress Creek Day Lodge. There are many short stretches of trail near Yew Lake, but generally you'll be heading west on the Baden Powell Trail toward Horseshoe Bay.

0.1 km/0.1 mile   From the trail on the east side of Cypress Creek, turn left (northwest) at two trail intersections for Howe Sound Crest and Yew Lake Trails.

Eagle Bluff

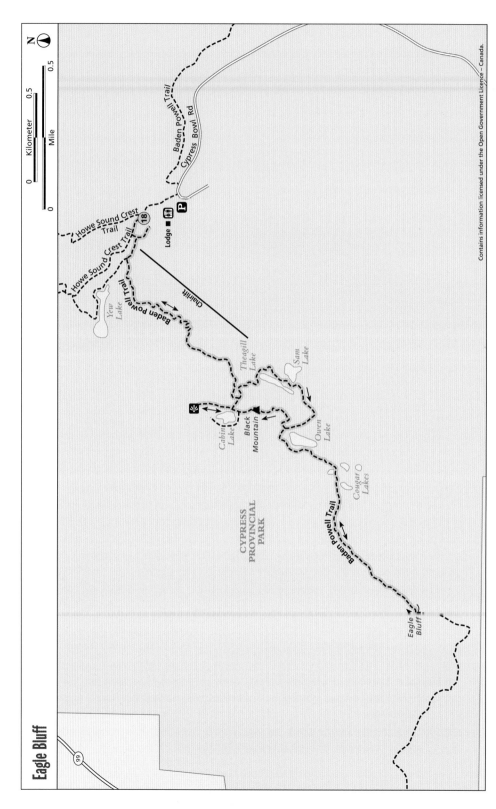

0.2 km/0.1 mile   Cross the creek and then turn right (west), walking away from Eagle Express Chair.

0.3 km/0.2 mile   Keep left (west) as a trail branches right (northwest) to Old Growth Loop. You begin to gain elevation and the climb intensifies over the next 1.5 km (0.9 mile).

1.8 km/1.1 miles   Follow the Baden Powell Trail left (southeast) rather than starting the Cabin Lake loop.

2.1 km/1.3 miles   Head right (southwest), following the Baden Powell Trail. The left route returns to the Eagle Express Chair.

2.3 km/1.4 miles   Reach Theagill and Sam Lakes.

2.9 km/1.8 miles   Continue left (west) on the Baden Powell Trail. This is the other end of the Cabin Lake loop, and your route for the return journey. (***Bail-out:*** For a shorter, 5.7-kilometer [3.5-mile] lollipop route, head right at this second turnoff for Cabin Lake. The route loops around Black Mountain and along the lakeshore before rejoining with the Baden Powell.)

3.1 km/1.9 miles   Pass Owen Lake.

3.4 km/2.1 miles   Thread over the bog boards between the small group of Cougar Lakes.

4.5 km/2.8 miles   Take a break on Eagle Bluff before turning around and returning by the same trail.

6.0 km/3.7 miles   Turn left (northeast) to follow the Cabin Lake trail uphill.

6.3 km/3.9 miles   Stop at a rocky knoll on Black Mountain, being sure to admire the views on both sides of the trail. Continue along the trail north toward Cabin Lake.

6.5 km/4.0 miles   Reach the shoreline of Cabin Lake. After spending some time here, follow the main trail and turn left (north) onto the viewpoint trail.

6.8 km/4.1 miles   Climb up to the lookout, which faces Howe Sound Crest to the north.

7.0 km/4.3 miles   At the base of the lookout trail, turn left (southeast) and follow the Cabin Lake trail down to the Baden Powell junction.

7.1 km/4.4 miles   Keep left (northeast) to return to Cypress Mountain ski area.

8.9 km/5.5 miles   Arrive back at the trailhead.

Options: Yew Lake Interpretive Trail focuses on marsh habitat and wildlife. The gravel path is 2 kilometers (1.2 miles) long and is wheelchair accessible.

Hike Information

Local Attractions: As Cypress hosted snowboarding and freestyle skiing events during the 2010 Winter Olympics (you may remember hearing about a Vancouver ski hill that had no snow—this was it), there are a few reminders of the international event. A set of green Olympic rings and a stone inukshuk (Vancouver's games mascot) are just to the north of the main parking lot. Cypress Mountain, end of Cypress Bowl Road, West Vancouver; (604) 926-5612; cypressmountain.com.

Restaurants: From mid-June to early September, you can grab a to-go bite at Cypress Mountain's Crazy Raven Bar & Grill. Cypress Creek Day Lodge, end of Cypress Bowl Road, West Vancouver; (604) 926-5612; cypressmountain.com.

Howe Sound

Mountains trim either side of Howe Sound, providing just barely enough room for the narrow Highway 99, the main route between Vancouver, Squamish, and Whistler. While the twisting Sea to Sky Highway is a fantastic way to see the scenery, making the tough climb to a mountaintop vantage and enjoying the views from there is truly unforgettable.

That's why so many tourists find themselves climbing up to First Peak of the Stawamus Chief, wondering how they are going to negotiate the route's ladders, chains, and steep rock trails. They've seen the photos of teal-blue waters, ash-gray granite, and evergreen-treed slopes, and they want to be there themselves.

But Howe Sound offers some of the toughest hikes near Vancouver. Volcanoes and glaciers have carved a harsh and challenging landscape. Geologically dramatic, the clash of fire and ice forged many of the area's unusual features. Ice smoothed the granite of the Stawamus Chief monolith; lava erupted to form Mount Garibaldi, its western flank forming on top of an ice sheet only to collapse as the ice melted; 2-kilometer-thick glacial ice reached the top of BC's third-highest waterfall, Shannon Falls, 13,000 years ago; and glacial sediment refracts and reflects light, giving Howe Sound its dense teal-blue color.

Still, amid the drama there's also relaxation along Howe Sound. Outdoor enthusiasts congregate in Squamish to go rock climbing, fishing, hiking, scuba diving, and mountain biking. Lakes—including family-friendly Alice Lake and Killarney Lake on Bowen Island—are a chilled-out alternative to the epic ascents of The Lions and the Sea to Summit trail near Upper Shannon Falls. Campgrounds are plentiful, and many book up far in advance.

When you start exploring the area, and find out what lies just minutes away from the Sea to Sky Highway, you suddenly understand the crowds. Because this is scenery worth seeing for yourself.

19 Killarney Lake

Bowen Island feels like a simpler place than the rest of Metro Vancouver, and that starts with walking off the ferry ahead of the cars. Tranquil Killarney Lake is at the island's quiet heart. Here, a mostly flat, easy amble circuits the lake on a well-established forest trail. You can walk to the trailhead from the ferry terminal and also get in a few interesting sights like a salmon hatchery, a fish ladder, and a giant Douglas fir nicknamed Opa.

Start: Across from the Bowen Island Gas Station and recycling depot, Mount Gardner Road
Distance: 6.2-km (3.9-mile) loop
Hiking time: About 2 hours
Difficulty: Easy due to mostly flat, well-established trails
Trail surface: Forested trail, dirt path, boardwalk, gravel road
Best season: Year-round
Other trail users: Dog-walkers, equestrians, mountain bikers
Canine compatibility: Leashed dogs permitted
Land status: Regional park

Fees and permits: No fees or permits required, though there is ferry fare to get to the island
Schedule: Daylight hours
Maps: Maps are available online at metro vancouver.org. Government topographic maps include the GeoBC Topographic Map Viewer (gov.bc.ca), as well as map 92G6 in the Atlas of Canada Toporama tool (atlas.gc.ca).
Trail contacts: Metro Vancouver Regional Parks West Area Office, Suite 130, 1200 W. 73rd Ave., Vancouver, V6P 6G5; (604) 224-5739; metrovancouver.org

Finding the trailhead: From the Snug Cove ferry terminal on Bowen Island, follow Bowen Trunk Road/Government Road west into the business district. Turn right (northwest) onto Mount Gardner Road and park at the trailhead—about 1.5 kilometers (0.9 mile) from the ferry dock. Trailhead GPS: N49 22.94' / W123 21.06'

The Hike

Killarney Lake sits in the low-lying land between Bowen's highest peak, Mount Gardner, and its second highest, Mount Collins. The lake is dappled with lilies and surrounded by forest, making for a picturesque scene. In the early 1900s, Bowen Island welcomed many visitors and tourists to its idyllic setting. Terminal Steamships and then Union Steamship Company brought thousands of picnickers and vacationers to the island. Just the *Lady Alexandra* alone was designed to transport 1,400 people. Cottages, picnic grounds, and a dance pavilion for up to 800 couples were part of the getaway draw.

Starting out at the trailhead off Mount Gardner Road, a wide gravel path leads past Terminal Creek Hatchery. The volunteer-run hatchery works to improve salmon runs, and each fall collects and incubates eggs so they can release chum and coho into local creeks come spring.

Deer are a common sighting on Bowen Island.

The trail passes the hatchery and heads northeast to Terminal Creek Meadows. This wide, grassy area is a shade of the once large and award-winning Terminal Farm, which supplied food to steamships and holiday-makers during the early 20th century. Now, you may see birds of prey circling, looking for lunch in the grasses.

After a bog area and views of Mount Gardner to the northwest, the trail parallels Killarney Creek through to the lake. The level gravel trail cuts under a second-growth forest canopy. Terminal Steamships also owned the land around the lake, now part of Crippen Regional Park.

At the first boardwalk, a steep gravel road leads to a side trip to Opa—a mammoth Douglas fir that's greatly loved by locals. It's about 30 minutes out-and-back (see side-trip for details). Boardwalks at the north end of the lake connect over low-lying areas before the trail gets into the hillier east side of the lake. But the slight climbs (about 40 meters [131 feet] elevation gain) on this stretch are worth the effort.

Continuing along the forest trails on the lake's east side, you quickly rejoin with Magee Road, where Cedar Trail provides an alternate forest route back to Killarney Creek Trail. At the junction with Meadow Trail, opt to return to the same trailhead if you're driving. If you're returning to the ferry on foot, continue straight along Killarney Creek toward Miller Road. Though the hike ends here, you can return to the ferry dock via the fish ladder and Bridal Veil Falls—to see where the salmon return come autumn.

A picnic area on the shore of Killarney Lake

DAVIES ORCHARD COTTAGES

You can still rent cottages on Bowen Island for a weekend away from the city, and a couple of local cottages are original to the Union Steamship days.

The company built more than 180 cottages on Bowen Island. Today, Union Steamship Marine Resort rents a much smaller number of refurbished 1920s cottages that are walking distance from the ferry terminal. The small buildings are set in the Davies Orchard, where day-trippers would come to picnic and play games in the 1920s. Clawfoot tubs and wide verandas give each a quaint charm.

Contact Union Steamship Marine Resort for more details: (604) 947-0707 or ussc.ca.

A tempting selection of restaurants and cafes lines Government Road to the ferry, ready with quick service for those waiting in line.

While picnickers once flocked to Bowen Island, so did the partiers. In the 1940s, Bowen Island booze cruises were rather infamous. "Nice girls weren't allowed to go on them, though they went just the same," writes Irene Howard in *Bowen Island 1872–1972*. She tells of local boys hunting about for bottles hidden under the trees on Saturday night—because alcohol wasn't allowed in the dance hall. And if you think Granville Street is bad on a weekend, consider that police rounded up thirty people on Bowen Island during the May long weekend in 1948!

> The Squamish people hunted and fished on Bowen Island before settlers arrived. It was also a neutral territory and a place to rest on longer canoe journeys.

Distances and Directions

0.0 km/0.0 mile   Start from the trailhead near the recycling depot and gas station, heading east along the gravel trail.

0.1 km/0.1 mile   Pass Terminal Creek Hatchery.

0.2 km/0.1 mile   Continue straight (northeast) as Hatchery Trail goes right. You soon pass an equestrian ring.

0.7 km/0.4 mile   Turn left (west) toward the lake at Killarney Creek Trail.

0.8 km/0.5 mile   Keep left (west) on Killarney Creek Trail at the forked intersection with Cedar Trail.

1.4 km/0.9 mile   Turn left (southwest) and briefly walk along Magee Road.

1.5 km/0.9 mile   Turn right (northwest) and follow Killarney Lake Loop Trail clockwise, passing a lakeshore picnic area.

2.1 km/1.3 miles   Admire views of the lake from a small rocky beach that lies near a creek mouth.

2.2 km/1.4 miles   On your left, two short spur trails connect up to Mount Gardner Road.

Killarney Lake

2.7 km/1.7 miles   Cross a boardwalk—here a trail and gravel road branch left (northeast) uphill. (*Side-trip:* To visit Opa, a giant Douglas fir in the region of 1,000 years old, follow the gravel road uphill from this boardwalk. Keep right on Fernie Road and walk for 450 meters [0.3 mile]. At Smith Road, turn right and proceed downhill, past the Xenia Labyrinth. Opa is on your left after 100 meters [0.1 mile]. The total distance is 2 kilometers [1.2 mile] there and back to the lake.)

3.3 km/2.1 miles   Reach the second boardwalk.

3.9 km/2.4 miles   Continue clockwise around the lake and reach a spur trail to the hilltop viewpoint.

4.5 km/2.8 miles   Keep right (southwest) on the main trail as a spur heads left to Magee Road.

5.1 km/3.2 miles   Turn left (northeast) on Magee Road and pick up Cedar Trail just 50 meters (164 feet) on. Cedar Trail cuts right (southeast) off Magee Road.

Spring and fall bring scads of mushrooms and fungi to decaying logs.

5.6 km/3.5 miles Connect again with Killarney Creek Trail and continue southeast.

5.7 km/3.5 miles Turn right (southwest) onto Meadow Trail to return to the same trailhead, or continue straight (southeast) to return to the ferry via Miller Road.

6.2 km/3.9 miles Reach the Miller Road parking lot.

Hike Information

Local Information: For local information and accommodations, contact Bowen Island Visitor Info Centre. 432 Cardena Rd., Bowen Island, BC, V0N IG0; (604) 200-2399; tourismbowenisland.com.

Local Attractions: Watch for young salmon in spring or spawning salmon in fall at Terminal Creek Hatchery, which is run entirely by volunteers from Bowen Island Fish and Wildlife Club. bowenhatchery.org.

Restaurants: For an after-hike meal, there's no finer taste than the excellent thin crust pizzas at Tuscany. 451 Bowen Trunk Rd., Snug Harbour; (604) 947-0550, tuscanypizza.com.

GREEN TIP
When you just have to go, dig a hole 15–20 centimeters (6–8 inches) deep and at least 61 meters (200 feet) from water, camps, and trails. Carry a ziplock bag to carry out toilet paper, or use a natural substitute such as leaves instead (but not poison ivy!). Fill in the hole with soil and other natural materials when you're done.

20 Mount Gardner

Though Mount Gardner, at 719 meters (2,359 feet) high, doesn't stack up against The Lions or Mount Seymour, it does award with similarly epic views. The mountain proves a formidable climb, especially as you start near sea level. But the challenge is as much in the navigation as the elevation gain—you need a keen eye to negotiate a series of old gravel logging roads and skid roads to the summit.

Start: Metal gate on Hikers Trail Road, off Mount Gardner Road
Distance: 9.3-km (5.8-mile) loop
Elevation gain: 590 meters (1,936 feet)
Hiking time: 4-6 hours
Difficulty: Moderate due to length, though challenges include navigation and steady climbing through steep terrain
Trail surface: Forested trail, gravel road
Best season: Year-round
Other trail users: Dog-walkers
Canine compatibility: Dogs permitted
Land status: Crown land
Fees and permits: No fees or permits required, though there is ferry fare to get to the island

Schedule: None, but daylight hours recommended
Maps: Island maps show Mount Gardner's many trails. Hard copies are available at the Bowen Island Visitor Info Centre on Cardena Road. Government topographic maps include the GeoBC Topographic Map Viewer (gov.bc.ca), as well as map 92G6 in the Atlas of Canada Toporama tool (atlas.gc.ca).
Trail contacts: None, but island info is available at Bowen Island Visitor Info Centre, 432 Cardena Rd., Bowen Island, BC, V0N 1G0.
Special considerations: There is no fresh water available at the trailhead or during this hike. The route is poorly marked in places. Don't head out without directions in hand.

Finding the trailhead: From the Snug Cove ferry terminal on Bowen Island, follow Bowen Trunk Road/Government Road into the business district. Turn right (northwest) onto Mount Gardner Road, and drive 2 kilometers (1.2 miles) to Hikers Trail Road. Drive up the gravel road and park just before the metal gates. Overall it's about 3 kilometers (1.9 miles) from the ferry dock. Alternately, you can hike along the western shore of Killarney Lake and cut up to Mount Gardner Road at the signposted junction. Trailhead GPS: N49 23.43'/ W123 21.89'

The Hike

Looking at a 1950s aerial photo of Mount Gardner, it's easy to see the effects of logging on the island and its tallest peak. Bald areas fan out from the riddled gravel roads, which twist up the mountain slopes.

Large-scale logging, the kind that plucked most of the large trees from the coastal rain forest, didn't begin on Bowen until the 1920s. But it still had a sweeping effect. Nearly all of Bowen Island has been logged—and I've heard there are just two old-growth trees left on the island (one of which is Opa, the side-trip in the Killarney Lake hike).

Mount Gardner has a view west to the Sunshine Coast.

Today, hikers use these logging roads as well as skid road trails to access Mount Gardner's two summits. Alongside the trails regenerating forest is mostly second-growth cedar and hemlock.

The route to Mount Gardner can be a bit complicated on a first trip. (In fact, I've long wondered if getting turned around on Mount Gardner's logging roads may be a rite of passage.) But obelisk-like wooden posts now mark many of the trail junctions to give hikers a helping hand.

The hike begins, fittingly enough, on Hikers Trail Road, a gravel road that cuts an unforgiving route uphill. But within meters, a skid road trail cuts into the woods to the left (southwest). This trail winds up along a creek, the forest canopy providing refreshing shade on summer days. At the first fork, head right (you'll return via the left fork from South Summit Trail) on the gravel road. A series of slightly confusing turns at those ever-helpful wooden posts take you through the logging gravel roads, skid trails, and logging routes that loop around the mountain. Orange markers also punctuate the routes into the woods.

After the first viewpoint, which takes in Keats Island in the foreground and the growing community of Gibsons on the Sunshine Coast behind, the trail turns into the woods toward the peak. Each year felled trees may crisscross the trail and fresh sawdust could show where some folks are actively working to clear a route—a never-ending job among BC's trails. Keep a sharp eye on the trail markers to thread your way through.

Continue left to the North Summit when the trail forks, and in a short while you'll be using ropes to help yourself up the short but challenging final haul.

Two helicopter pads provide patio-like lunch spots on the peak. The humming and clicking of cell phone towers in between is a bit distracting from the views: northwest to the Sunshine Coast and southeast to Vancouver. Head south to find the trail for the ride home and make a grand loop around the South Summit (which doesn't have any views).

> In the early 1900s, Bowen Island was a draw for mining speculators. Though silver and copper were both found on the island, quantities never made investors rich.

Distances and Directions

0.0 km/0.0 mile Start from the metal gate on Hikers Trail Road and walk southwest up the gravel road.

0.1 km/0.1 mile Turn left (southwest) at Skid Trail and climb through the woods. (The road you're leaving also covers part of the distance to the summit.)

0.9 km/0.6 miles When the trail forks at a wooden post, go right (north) on the forested North Mount Gardner Trail. This hike returns via the left trail.

1.0 km/0.6 mile As the trail meets an old road, keep right (north) at another wooden post.

1.1 km/0.7 mile At a creek, turn right (northeast) walking downhill briefly on a gravel road.

1.15 km/0.7 mile About 50 meters on, watch for a left turn (west) to take the bridge over the creek.

1.4 km/0.9 mile At a junction, continue following the orange markers along a wooded trail, heading back toward the creek. You'll pass the location of the old creek crossing.

2.4 km/1.5 miles Turn left (south), following orange markers uphill. Handloggers Trail continues straight (northwest) and is also marked with orange reflectors.

2.6 km/1.6 miles The wooded trail meets a gravel road. Turn right (south) and head downhill. (Left heads up to a small peak to the east.)

2.9 km/1.8 miles At a trail fork under power lines, turn right (south) and hike uphill.

3.0 km/1.9 miles Continue uphill (northwest) on the gravel road. A wooden post marks where a wooded trail forks left (south).

3.3 km/2.1 miles Watch carefully for the trail and turn sharply uphill to the left (southwest). A metal pipe continues straight.

3.6 km/2.2 miles Keep straight (southwest) on North Mount Gardner Trail as signposted Handloggers Trail feeds in from the right (west).

3.8 km/2.4 miles Reach the Sunshine Coast and Keats Island viewpoint.

4.4 km/2.7 miles Head left (south) to the North Summit when the trail forks. The right-hand loop trail skips the north summit.

Mount Gardner

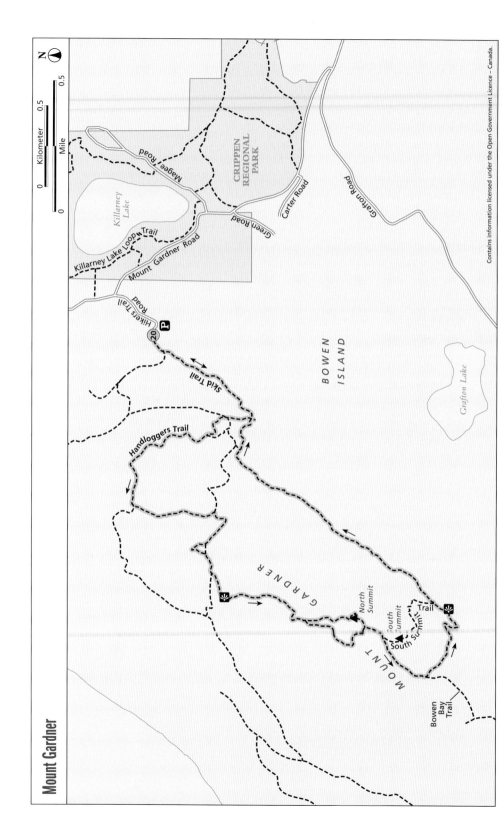

4.6 km/2.9 miles   Carefully climb the steep final hill, putting limited trust in the available ropes.

4.7 km/2.9 miles   Reach the first of two helicopter pads.

4.8 km/3.0 miles   Relax on the second helicopter pad, overlooking Vancouver.

4.9 km/3.0 miles   Venture south to pick up the trail near the cell towers. At the trail fork, keep left (southwest) toward South Summit and Bowen Bay.

5.0 km/3.1 miles   Continue straight (southwest) rather than turning left to the South Summit (south) and follow the trail as it loops around the peak.

5.4 km/3.4 miles   Pass the Bowen Bay Trail. Your route then switchbacks downhill.

6.2 km/3.9 miles   Pass South Summit Trail junction, which heads steeply uphill to the left (north/northwest).

7.1 km/4.4 miles   Follow the orange markers downhill, keeping right (northeast) at a trail spur that's just after a short section of corduroy (log) road.

8.2 km/5.1 miles   At the bottom of the steep descent, both right and left trails connect to Skid Trail. Turn right (northeast). This is then a familiar forest route back to Hikers Trail Road.

9.3 km/5.8 miles   Arrive back at the trailhead.

Options: Rather than hiking the longer route around South Summit, retrace your steps along the trail to North Summit. Others like to hike the route in reverse, coming around South Summit first.

For a short pump of a hike that's not a full day like Mount Gardner, head east of Snug Cove to Dorman Point. It's about 2.5 kilometers (1.6 miles) round-trip from the ferry dock and takes about an hour. The final viewpoint looks out east across Queen Charlotte Channel.

Hike Information

Organizations: There are many rich memories of Bowen Island's steamship days and logging to be explored. Bowen Heritage is the best resource. bowenheritage.org.

GREEN TIP
For rest stops, go off-trail so others won't have to get around you. Head for resilient surfaces without vegetation.

21 The Lions Binkert

Seeing The Lions from Vancouver will become a reminder of the up-close views that this strenuous, full-day hike gives. You can say to yourself: I was there. A long, uphill slog brings you to an unrivaled vantage over Howe Sound. Continue on up to a rocky ridge to see West Lion, East Lion, and the city far below.

Start: Sunset Drive, Lions Bay
Distance: 14.2-km (8.8-mile) out-and-back
Elevation gain: 1,341 meters (4,400 feet)
Hiking time: 7–8 hours
Difficulty: Difficult due to long distance, intense elevation gain, and steep terrain
Trail surface: Dirt road, forested trail, dirt path, rocky ledges
Best season: July–Oct
Other trail users: None
Canine compatibility: Not recommended for dogs
Land status: Crown land
Fees and permits: No fees or permits required
Schedule: None, but daylight hours recommended.
Maps: The first section of the trail is included on The Village of Lions Bay trail map, which is available online at lionsbay.ca. Government topographic maps include the GeoBC Topographic Map Viewer (gov.bc.ca), as well as map 92G6 in the Atlas of Canada Toporama tool (atlas.gc.ca).
Trail contacts: N/A
Other: There are limited (about a dozen) parking spots at the trailhead. If you don't arrive early, you will have to park at Lions Bay Community School on Bayview Road.
Special considerations: Snow near the ridge can stick around well into July. The fast-melting slopes can create slippery and dangerous conditions. It's best to go prepared with hiking poles and even crampons. There is no fresh water available at the trailhead, but there are rushing creeks during this hike.

Finding the trailhead: From the Sea to Sky Highway (Highway 99), drive north from Horseshoe Bay. At the highway passes through Lions Bay, take the Lions Bay Avenue exit. Drive uphill around the first left (north) turn onto Crosscreek Road, and then the next right (southeast) onto Centre Road. At Bayview Road, turn left (northeast) and continue uphill past Lions Bay Community School. This is the alternate parking point if all spots at the trailhead are taken. Bear left (northeast) at Mountain Drive, and then make a final left (north) onto Sunset Drive. Trailhead GPS: N49 28.25' / W123 14.07'

The Hike

If limited parking spots forced you to park at Lions Bay Community School, your legs will already be warmed up by the time you reach the metal gate and old logging road. The first third of the trail is unremarkable, zigzagging uphill along a gravel road. Even as you hit the forest and a couple of rushing creeks, the reward is only fleeting as your mind returns to the climb. It's not truly until you leave the tree line at the 5.9-kilometer (3.7-mile) mark that all that effort fades into the background. There,

Climbing on the Binkert Trail may take you into and then above the clouds.

a ridge lets you look back and down on Howe Sound, and the rocky cliffs of West Lion sit immediately ahead.

The Lions are perhaps Vancouver's most storied peaks.

"They catch the earliest hint of sunrise, they hold the last colour of sunset," wrote Pauline Johnson in her poetic local history *Legends of Vancouver.*

The earliest tales of the twin peaks go back to First Nations history, when a warring chief had two daughters who had just reached womanhood. Despite an ongoing conflict with people from the North, the chief was preparing a great feast to honor his daughters' coming of age—as they could now be married and bear warrior children.

When the daughters asked their father to invite the Northern enemy to the feast, the chief rejoiced and hosted a potlatch for friends and former enemies—the Northern people arrived with gifts and food instead of weapons. The feast led to peace between the nations, and for their unselfish intentions, the Great Chief immortalized the two young women as these mountains. Thus, the two peaks above the Capilano River are also known as The Chief's Daughters or The Two Sisters.

Most Vancouverites, and maps, however, do use the name The Lions—a tie to the city's English roots. It seems early settlers thought the peaks resembled the lions in Trafalgar Square.

But The Lions are not the only peaks with a tale. Before Paul Binkert established the Binkert Trail (which you're hiking), the primary route to The Lions was along the Howe Sound Crest Trail. En route to The Lions, the trail climbs up and over Mount Unnecessary—the name speaking to the hiker's fatigue of climbing an extra mountain before reaching your destination.

From the first major viewpoint above the tree line, there is a wide panorama from Mount Harvey and West Lion around to Howe Sound and its islands. The trail continues with a climb up through the rocky slopes to the southeast, following rocks dotted with spray paint. The route leads to a ridge that runs between Mount Unnecessary and West Lion. You can head right (southwest) to Mount Unnecessary, but left (northeast) toward The Lions is more spectacular.

Close to West Lion you can perhaps see people scrambling up the side to summit—a dangerous pursuit that's not recommended without safety gear and climbing skill. This fantastic vantage also looks down on East Lion, Capilano Reservoir, and the North Shore beyond—all reasons that make it the perfect spot for a good, long break.

Views are a fantastic reason for a break on the way up the Lions Binkert Trail.

This ridge is a fine thread between The Lions and Mount Unnecessary.

Distances and Directions

0.0 km/0.0 mile Start from the Lions Bay trailhead on Sunset Drive and begin the climb uphill.

0.3 km/0.2 mile Pass a water service building.

1.0 km/0.6 mile Continue straight (southeast) on the road as you pass a gated road on the left.

1.9 km/1.2 miles Keep right (south) on Binkert Trail as a trail spurs off north to Brunswick Mountain.

2.5 km/1.6 miles Continue straight (southeast) on Binkert Trail as an overgrown road heads left to Mount Harvey via Magnesia Creek.

2.8 km/1.7 miles There is a second, narrow trail heading left to Mount Harvey.

3.0 km/1.9 miles Cross Alberta Creek. The bridge here was out in 2020 but the creek was easily passable—still, be cautious.

4.5 km/2.8 miles Turn right (southeast) at the Lions sign and head downhill. (The trail straight ahead continues northeast to Harvey Basin, Magnesia Meadows, and Howe Sound Crest.)

4.6 km/2.9 miles A bridge crosses Harvey Creek. Then the trail climbs again.

5.1 km/3.2 miles Stop for a breath and take in the Howe Sound views.

The Lions Binkert

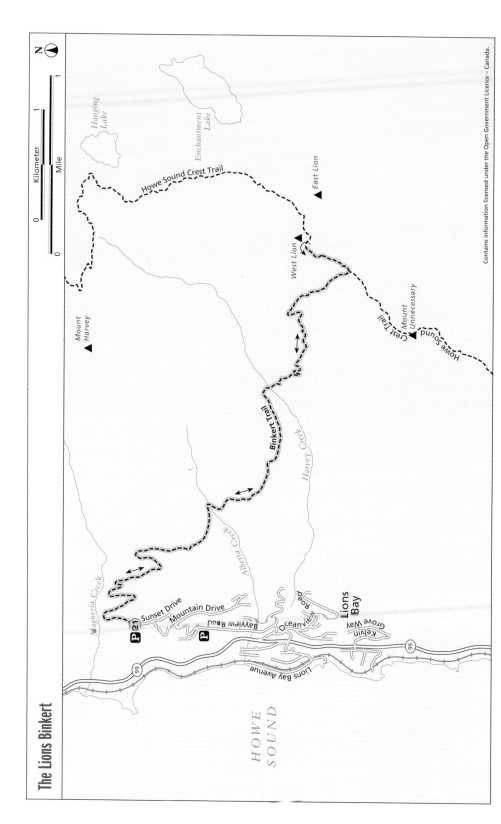

N

Kilometer
0   1

Mile
0   1

Mount Harvey ▲

Hanging Lake

Enchantment Lake

Howe Sound Crest Trail

West Lion ▲

East Lion ▲

Binkert Trail

Harvey Creek

Mount Unnecessary ▲

Howe Sound Crest Trail

Alberta Creek

Magnesia Creek

Sunset Drive

Mountain Drive

P 21

P

Bayview Road

Oceanview Road

Lions Bay

Kelvin Grove Way

Lions Bay Avenue

99

99

HOWE SOUND

5.9 km/3.7 miles   Emerge from the tree line to views of Mount Harvey and West Lion. Turn right (southeast) toward the ridge. (**Bail-out:** When you reach the tree line, the views of West Lion are immediate and astounding. Though the hike continues on, you can also just catnap here and give your legs a break.)

6.0 km/3.7 miles   Again, stop to admire the Howe Sound panorama. Follow spray-painted markings up the steep ascent.

6.7 km/4.2 miles   Turn left (northeast) along a ridge to West Lion. The trail also branches right (southwest) to Mount Unnecessary.

7.1 km/4.4 miles   Reach The Lions Viewpoint.

7.6 km/4.7 miles   Head back to the Mount Unnecessary junction. Turn right (northeast) and retrace your steps along the same route.

14.2 km/8.8 miles   Arrive back at the trailhead.

Options: Once you've attained the height of Howe Sound Crest, a couple of other peaks are in fairly close reach. To the north lies Mount Harvey, and to the southwest Mount Unnecessary.

Hike Information

Restaurants: Lions Bay General Store and Café is a Sea to Sky classic. It's located near the Sea to Sky Highway and has a lovely patio. 350 Centre Rd., Lions Bay; (604) 921-6344.

With luck, an overcast morning at sea level could be spectacular above the clouds.

22 Petgill Lake

Lake swimmers have options with this hike. There's a refreshing dip at Browning Lake in Murrin Provincial Park near the trailhead, as well as Petgill Lake at the turnaround point. In between, forest trails, perfectly positioned viewpoints, and rocky bluffs make for a delightful and slightly challenging route.

Start: Murrin Provincial Park parking lot
Distance: 9.5-km (5.9-mile) out-and-back
Elevation gain: 633 meters (2,077 feet)
Hiking time: 4–5 hours
Difficulty: Moderate due to length, though steady elevation gain could be challenging for some
Trail surface: Forested trail, dirt path, gravel, logging road
Best season: Mar–Oct
Other trail users: Dog-walkers, logging crews
Canine compatibility: Dogs permitted
Land status: Crown land
Fees and permits: No fees or permits required

Schedule: None, but daylight hours recommended
Maps: No official maps available. Government topographic maps include the GeoBC Topographic Map Viewer (gov.bc.ca), as well as map 92G11 in the Atlas of Canada Toporama tool (atlas.gc.ca).
Trail contacts: None, but consult Murrin Provincial Park info for parking (bcparks.ca and seatoskyparks.com)
Special considerations: The hike follows a section of logging road. There is no fresh water available at the trailhead or during this hike.

Finding the trailhead: On the Sea to Sky Highway (Highway 99), drive north of Horseshoe Bay. About 3 kilometers (1.9 miles) north of Britannia Beach, watch for the Murrin Provincial Park turn-off on the left (west). Pull in and find a parking spot. Trailhead GPS: N49 38.88' / W123 12.11'

The Hike

Some hikers head out on the trail with the primary purpose of swimming. In Squamish, the options for a freshwater dip are many. While Alice Lake can be overrun with campers and day-trippers in summer, other destinations can be overlooked. Perhaps they are not in a provincial park with hot-water facilities, or the access is only via a bumpy gravel road.

On this hike you see the contrast between an accessible lake and one that's at the end of a somewhat challenging hike. At the start, Browning Lake sits in view of the highway in Murrin Provincial Park. But Petgill Lake, at the hike's destination, is hike-in only. One buzzes with energy, the other (at times) with bugs.

Start from Murrin Provincial Park and cross the highway. With so many cars exceeding the speed limit, don't rush this. Wait for a safe opportunity. The trailhead is on the east side of the highway, 200 meters (0.1 mile) north of the provincial park turnoff.

A carved wooden sign marks the trailhead, though as of 2020 the sign had seen better days, and a thin trail disappears up the rock face. The route is interesting to follow and quickly pulls you away from the traffic noise. This first climb is one of many, as the route descends into creekbeds only to climb up the far side. It's like being in a boat going over huge rollers.

Three viewpoints are on the north side of the trail within the first 1.0 kilometer (0.6 mile) and provide ample chance for a breather. The second view to Mount Garibaldi is particularly picturesque, with the gray volcanic rock of the dormant volcano and the granite Stawamus Chief fusing with evergreen slopes. Squamish is wedged in between the forest and Howe Sound, the water's glacial sediment refracting sunlight from the (ideally) blue sky.

The forest is second growth, and there is lingering evidence of clear cutting. A section of the trail follows logging roads. For years this was an old, disused section, but there are also fresh marks of logging on the landscape. While cut areas are jarring, they can at times offer new views and it's also a good reminder that we all could consume less to stem the harvesting of natural resources.

The waters of Howe Sound often can look teal due to suspended glacial flour, or sediment.

A perfect vantage over Squamish takes in Mount Garibaldi and the Stawamus Chief.

SQUAMISH SWIMMING LAKES

Freshwater swimming is a gold standard in Squamish—especially after a hot day of hiking, mountain biking, or climbing. Murrin Provincial Park's Browning Lake is a very easy option to reach, as is Alice Lake in Alice Lake Provincial Park (located north of Squamish on Highway 99).

Brohm Lake is another lake near the highway, and there are also trails through the recreation site's interpretive forest. The access road for Cat Lake is just across the highway from Brohm. This small lake offers a warm summer swim with basic, walk-in campsites around the shoreline.

Some would debate that hike-in lakes are the most rewarding, as you've put in hours of boots-on-the-ground time to get there. Petgill Lake is a moderate hike and for a greater sweat-to-reward ratio, head up the challenging 18-kilometer (11.2-mile) route to Deeks, Hanover, and Brunswick Lakes.

Be aware that swimming in the area's glacial lakes can be very dangerous. The ice-cold water can shock the body and cause hypothermia.

At the destination lake, a slightly overgrown trail circles the water, while a worthwhile spur trail climbs up for Howe Sound views from an outcropping—perhaps the best view of all.

Take a walk around. The more hikers use trails, the more chance they have of being protected and retained.

Distances and Directions

0.0 km/0.0 mile   Start from the trailhead, alongside the Sea to Sky Highway (it's near the utility pole marked 7/12), and follow orange trail markers northeast up the rocky incline.

0.6 km/0.4 mile   Reach the first viewpoint, which looks west out to Howe Sound.

0.7 km/0.4 mile   The second viewpoint takes in the dormant, glacier-topped peak of Mount Garibaldi and the Stawamus Chief to the north.

0.8 km/0.5 mile   Stop at the third viewpoint to overlook Squamish, protruding between the Squamish River and Mamquam Blind Channel.

1.1 km/0.7 mile   Emerge from the forest to join a logging road and head northeast.

1.8 km/1.1 miles   Cross a creek.

2.1 km/1.3 miles   Cross a third creek and bear right (southeast) as a logging road joins the route.

2.4 km/1.5 miles   Another logging road emerges. Head uphill to the right (south).

2.7 km/1.7 miles   Turn left (east) along a wooded trail. (Unfortunately there's no good landmark for this turn, but it's just before a hill with a clearing beyond.) Follow the trail markers and signs.

3.6 km/2.2 miles   Hike up and over an exposed rocky area.

4.1 km/2.5 miles   Continue straight at the junction with Goat Ridge Trail, which branches off right—this is also the return path of the loop around the lake.

4.3 km/2.7 miles   Pass Petgill Lake and turn left (northwest) to climb up to the viewpoint, then keep left at the second junction.

4.5 km/2.8 miles   Linger over very worthwhile Howe Sound views.

4.7 km/2.9 miles   Return to Petgill Lake, perhaps going for a swim or just resting on the logs. Then, follow the lake trail clockwise along the shoreline to circumnavigate the water. The trail can be swampy and/or difficult to find at times—it branches off before the climb to the lookout.

4.9 km/3.0 miles   Continue around the lake as an overgrown trail branches left to Shannon Falls, though I've not hiked this route and can't vouch for its condition. This second half of the lake trail is more overgrown—you may prefer to retrace your steps rather than complete the loop.

5.3 km/3.3 miles   Turn left (southwest) to follow the main trail back to the highway.

6.8 km/4.2 miles   Turn right (north) to walk back along the logging road.

7.1 km/4.4 miles   Keep left (north) at a fork in the logging road. Then 300 meters (1/4 mile) on, keep left at another fork.

8.4 km/5.2 miles   The forest trail leaves the logging road to the left (west).

9.5 km/5.9 miles   Arrive back at the trailhead.

Petgill Lake

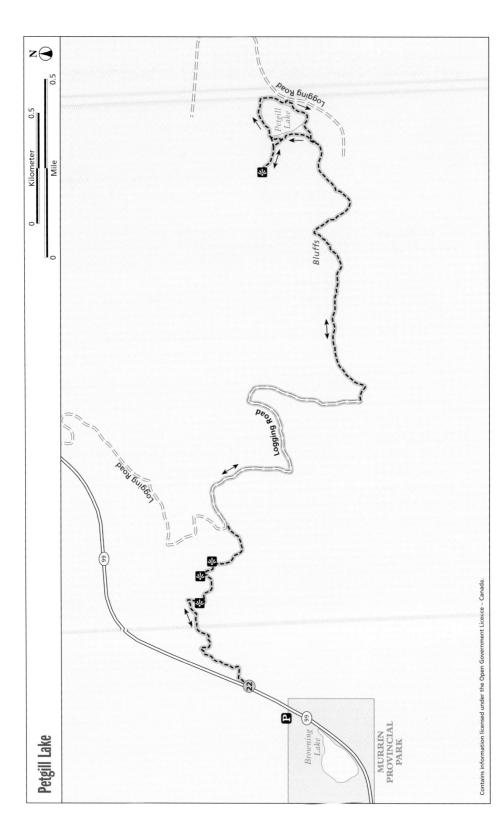

The Petgill Lake trailhead is right alongside busy Highway 99.

Hike Information

Local Attractions: Britannia Mine Museum, less than a 5-minute drive south, is a surprisingly fascinating visit. An underground tour lets visitors see old mining equipment in action. The multistory building, a highway landmark, is a treat to step inside. 1 Forbes Way, Britannia Beach; (604) 896-2233; britanniaminemuseum.ca.

GREEN TIP
Especially for day hikes, use a camp stove for cooking so there's no need to make a fire.

23 Sea to Summit

This route climbs from the base of Shannon Falls, the third-tallest waterfall in British Columbia, to the summit lodge of the Sea to Sky Gondola. But this hike gives you vastly different vantages throughout the 6.7-kilometer (4.2-mile) climb as it ascends to the upper falls, rocky bluff viewpoints, and finally the mountaintop attraction.

Start: Shannon Falls Provincial Park picnic area
Distance: 6.7 km (4.2 miles) one way
Elevation gain: 918 meters (3,012 feet)
Hiking time: 3–4 hours
Difficulty: Moderate due to elevation gain and a varying terrain that includes steep, rocky sections with difficult footing and ropes
Trail surface: Gravel, forested trail, dirt path, wooden stairs, granite outcrops with ropes
Best season: Apr–Nov
Other trail users: Dog-walkers, tourists
Canine compatibility: Leashed dogs permitted
Land status: Provincial parks, Sea to Sky Gondola
Fees and permits: In 2020, this route required reserving a day-use pass (discovercamping.ca) due to COVID-19 restrictions. A ride-down pass is available but not mandatory for the Sea to Sky Gondola ($15 in 2020).

Schedule: Daylight hours
Maps: A park map is posted at the trailhead and available through the provincial park website, bcparks.ca. The Sea to Sky Gondola has trail maps of routes near the summit, seatosky gondola.com. Government topographic maps include the GeoBC Topographic Map Viewer (gov.bc.ca), as well as map 92G11 in the Atlas of Canada Toporama tool (atlas.gc.ca).
Trail contacts: Sea to Sky Gondola, (604) 892-2550 or toll free (855) 732-8675, seatoskygondola.com; or Shannon Falls and Stawamus Chief Provincial Parks, bcparks.ca and seatoskyparks.com
Special considerations: As a popular tourist stop, Shannon Falls parking lot can be full to capacity on weekends. But turnover is usually quick, as most people only make the 5-minute walk to the lower falls. There is fresh water available near the trailhead, but not during this hike.

Finding the trailhead: On the Sea to Sky Highway (Highway 99), drive north of Horseshoe Bay. About 7 kilometers (4.3 miles) north of Britannia Beach, watch for the Shannon Falls Provincial Park turnoff on the right (east). Pull in and find a parking spot. Trailhead GPS: N49 40.25' / W123 09.60'

The Hike

Though Shannon Falls is the third highest waterfall in the province, it is tops when it comes to accessibility. Pull off Highway 99, walk 5 minutes on a paved path, and you have a full view of the impressive waterfall. Follow a forested trail a few minutes farther and you can feel the cold spray. But that's about as far as the huge majority of the more than 600,000 annual visitors go.

This hike follows a horseshoe route to a lookout above the falls and then climbs to the summit of the Sea to Sky Gondola. Hikers get to look down on the 335-meter

(1,099-foot) waterfall and then ascend to Howe Sound views. Plus, downloading by gondola is a blessing for tired knees.

Although rarer views await, start by following the paved path to the falls and admire the tumult from the belvedere-like viewing area. During the spring freshet, the waterfall spray feels cool and refreshing. An upper trail gets you a little closer to the base.

Retrace your steps to the Lower Falls Trail heading to the Stawamus Chief, and follow the gravel path as it becomes a narrower forest trail, passes the tourist base of the gondola (parking here is limited to three hours), and starts to climb. At Olesen Creek, pause on the bridge to feel the rush of cold air—the trail gets very close with company on the next stretch.

If day-use passes are in effect, there may be a park ranger checking your reservation where the trail joins Chief Peaks Trail. In summer 2020, reservations for this park were one of the most popular.

Here you begin a serious climb that's often busy with other hikers. Most are heading to the First, Second, and Third Peaks of the Stawamus Chief—a granite rock face that climbers see in their dreams.

Upper Shannon Falls almost looks like a waterslide. (Of course, it's not.)

The Sea to Summit Trail intersects the gondola at various points.

CUTTING THE CORD

In August 2019, in the predawn hours, a person or persons severed the 4-kilometer (2.5-mile) cable supporting the forty cars of the Sea to Sky Gondola. Months of effort in repairs and millions of dollars later, the gondola reopened to once again take visitors from basecamp up to the summit lodge at 885 meters (2,904 feet)—a 10-minute trip and worth every second.

Then, in September 2020, the same vandalism happened again and halted both visitors to the attraction as well as those hiking routes such as the Sea to Summit Trail. At the time of writing, repair work was avidly underway.

It's unfortunate for tourism in the region, as the gondola is a way for folks to see the views without overreaching their limits on hikes like The Chief. Here's to hoping for a brighter future for this attraction!

Exposed bluffs rise along the Sea to Summit Trail.

After countless wooden steps, you branch off right (east) on the Sea to Summit/ Upper Shannon Falls Trail. On this route, the crowd thins, the path narrows, and the grade eases. The trail passes under the route of the Sea to Sky Gondola. Eight-person cabins transport visitors the easy way to Summit Lodge at around the 885-meter (2,900-foot) level on Mount Habrich.

The next stretch poses the trickiest terrain of the trail—a steep, rocky slope that tests the knees and balance. But wider views and the upper falls are worth the climb.

As you reach the top of the waterfall, keep back from the edge. The Upper Falls race by at an intimidating speed, roaring around corners only to tumble over the rocky lip and down the cliff. After a quick break, push on past the creek and continue the climb to a rocky bluff, through evergreen forest, and then up a final granite outcrop with fixed ropes to assist the ascent.

Finally—hours of steep and sweaty climbing in—you reach the bustling summit with the gondola, suspension bridge, eateries, and nature trails. Catch your breath and admire the views of the Sea to Sky Highway, Howe Sound, and Squamish knowing you took the hard-but-worthwhile route to the top.

Distances and Directions

0.0 km/0.0 mile   Start from the Shannon Falls picnic area, just south of the parking lot. There's the rare luxury of bathrooms with running water here!

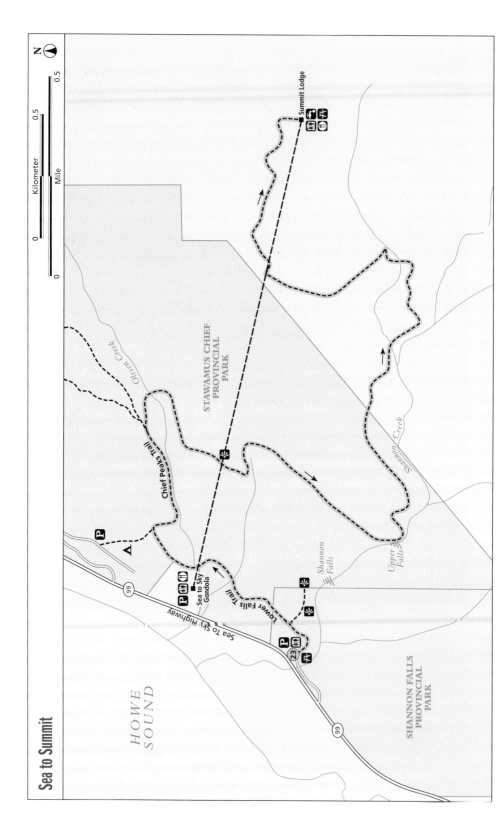

Sea to Summit

HOWE
SOUND

Olesen Creek

Chief Peaks Trail

STAWAMUS CHIEF
PROVINCIAL
PARK

Summit Lodge

Shannon Creek

Sea to Sky Highway

Sea to Sky Gondola

Lower Falls Trail

Shannon
Falls

Upper
Falls

SHANNON FALLS
PROVINCIAL
PARK

0   Kilometer   0.5   0.5

0   Mile   0.5

N

0.1 km/0.1 mile   Follow the paved path northeast toward the viewing area.

0.2 km/0.1 mile   If you want to see the lower falls, pass the Chief/Lower Falls Trail turnoff, which leads to the Stawamus Chief. Or turn left (northeast) here to start the hike now.

0.3 km/0.2 mile   Reach the Shannon Falls viewing platform, and then climb the left spur trail to get a little closer.

0.6 km/0.4 mile   Return to the Chief/Lower Falls Trail junction and follow the wide gravel path northeast toward the Stawamus Chief.

1.1 km/0.7 mile   Pass the base of the Sea to Sky Gondola. Continue on the trail (northeast). Here you also pick up the Sea to Summit Trail markings, which are diligently spaced every 50 meters (164 feet).

1.4 km/0.9 mile   Turn right (northeast) and join the busy Chief Peaks trail. This is where BC Parks may be checking day-use pass reservations. Start the intense climb.

1.9 km/1.2 miles   Turn right (east) to the gondola and Upper Falls. Chief Peaks Trail continues left (northeast).

2.6 km/1.6 miles   Stop at a Howe Sound viewpoint that sits under the Sea to Sky Gondola.

3.5 km/2.2 miles   A spur leads down to an Upper Falls viewpoint. Pause at the powerful section of Shannon Creek before continuing the climb.

4.0 km/2.5 miles   Stop for a snack with a view on the rocky bluff. The trail continues behind the bluff to travel northeast.

4.8 km/3.0 miles   Turn left (northeast) as the forest trail joins a logging road signposted as Shannon Basin Loop. The right turn heads down to the gondola base.

5.2 km/3.2 miles   Turn left (northwest) on the more challenging route to the peak. The road continues to the right (south and east), snaking up to the summit with an easier grade but longer route.

5.9 km/3.7 miles   Use the fixed ropes to help navigate up a steep rocky section.

6.7 km/4.2 miles   Reach the summit of the Sea to Sky Gondola. Download via the gondola or retrace the same trail on the descent.

Hike Information

Local Information: Squamish is a town in transition. Having once thrived on logging, the wealth of the woods is now in mountain biking and hiking trails. For more local excursions, contact the Squamish Adventure Centre. 101-38551 Loggers Lane, Squamish; (604) 815-4994 or (877) 815-5084; exploresquamish.com.

Camping: There's camping available at neighboring Stawamus Chief Provincial Park, but for a waterfront location, head to Porteau Cove Provincial Park—about 16 kilometers (9.9 miles) south. Highway 99; (604) 986-9371; bcparks.ca.

GREEN TIP
Stay on the trail. Cutting through from one part of a switchback to another can destroy fragile plant life or erode the slope.

24 Stawamus Chief

This granite monolith stands sentinel on the Sea to Sky Highway, a rain-gray face that rises up suddenly near the mouths of the Stawamus and Squamish Rivers. At this point, where Howe Sound begins, hikers make a tough climb over technical terrain for fantastic views from all three peaks of the Chief. And it's those views that lure in a full house of visitors on any (and every) summer day.

Start: Stawamus Chief Provincial Park campground
Distance: 6.1-km (3.8-mile) lollipop
Elevation gain: 627 meters (2,057 feet)
Hiking time: About 4 hours
Difficulty: Difficult due to trail congestion, intense elevation gain, and technical skill needed to navigate the ladders and steep slopes
Trail surface: Forested trail, stairs, granite rock face, ladders
Best season: Mar–Nov
Other trail users: Dog-walkers, tourists
Canine compatibility: Off-leash dogs permitted on the Chief Peaks trail
Land status: Provincial park
Fees and permits: In 2020, this route required reserving a day-use pass (discovercamping.ca) due to COVID-19 restrictions.

Schedule: Daylight hours
Maps: A park map is posted at the trailhead and available through the provincial park website, bcparks.ca. Government topographic maps include the GeoBC Topographic Map Viewer (gov.bc.ca), as well as map 92G11 in the Atlas of Canada Toporama tool (atlas.gc.ca).
Trail contacts: Stawamus Chief Provincial Park, bcparks.ca and seatoskyparks.com
Special considerations: Even with the restricted flow of the day-use pass system, the trail can be busy with tourists and hikers. Bottlenecks occur at the ladders below First and Second Peaks, and impatience has led to some hikers being injured when they try to skip the queue and find alternate routes. There is no water available beyond the campground.

Finding the trailhead: On the Sea to Sky Highway (Highway 99), drive north of Horseshoe Bay. About 8 kilometers (5.0 miles) north of Britannia Beach, watch for signs directing you to Stawamus Chief Provincial Park. (You'll know you're close when you pass Shannon Falls Provincial Park.) Take the Stawamus Chief turnoff on the right (east). Pull in and find a parking spot. Trailhead GPS: N49 40.55' / W123 09.20'

The Hike

In many ways, the Stawamus Chief is like the Grouse Grind. Both are steep, have countless steps, and are popular with visitors. Both are also a strenuous workout and reward with I-can't-believe-I'm-here views. But be fairly warned that the challenge is not exaggerated for either.

"Is it much farther?" seems to be a familiar refrain on the Chief Peaks Trail. First Peak sits 540 meters (1,772 feet) higher than the trailhead. It's a hefty elevation gain

First Peak is the least challenging, but also busiest, of the three Stawamus Chief peaks.

over 1.5 kilometers (0.9 mile), especially for novice hikers who can sometimes make up much of the traffic. Second and Third Peaks mean more climbing, to 590-meter (1,936-foot) and 630-meter (2,067-foot) summits, respectively. But despite the trail's popularity, hiking the Chief Peaks is unquestionably worth the trip.

This hike starts with a steady climb to Third Peak and steps down to Second and then First. Should you have your fill of the views or simply find the route too busy, it's easy to skip the final ascents. On the flip side, the ladder waits tend to be longest at First Peak, making it good to have a little fatigue in your legs to help you appreciate the rest.

Left: Catch a glimpse of Mount Garibaldi en route from Third to Second Peak.
Right: A Douglas fir has wedged its roots between a rock and hard place.

Wooden stairs and natural stone steps mark the first intense stretch. As the trail continues on to Third Peak, however, the grade eases and the forest grows quieter. Even on a busy summer day you can hear the trees creak. Climbing to the peaks themselves requires hiking over steep granite slopes—often worn smooth with foot traffic.

Besides hikers, rock climbers are the other major visitor to the provincial park. Yet you rarely see them other than when passing through the campground. When not at camp, the climbers are dangling somewhere on the Grand Wall, bouldering near the base, or threading up through the trees on the severely sloping Apron. It's only on the descent (along the hiking trail) that you may spot a climber, with waterproof pack loaded with ropes and gear.

While humans seem to crawl all over the surface of this granite monolith, claimed as the second-largest in the world after the Rock of Gibraltar, there are other creatures that inhabit the coastal forest and granite landscape. The park closes some climbing routes in spring for peregrine falcon nesting season. Chipmunks regularly scamper across the peak, angling for a piece of your sandwich. And perhaps a northern alligator lizard will cross the forest path near Olesen Creek. Keep your eyes focused and you'll soon see: Tourists aren't the only ones here.

Distances and Directions

0.0 km/0.0 mile   After following the gravel path through the campground, start from the trailhead near the information sign and begin climbing the stairs.

0.1 km/0.1 mile   Continue climbing on Chief Peaks Trail at the junction with Lower Falls Trail. This route leads right (southwest) to Shannon Falls. Shortly after this junction, BC Parks may be checking reservations for day-use passes.

0.5 km/0.3 mile   Head straight (northeast) uphill as a trail branches off right (east) to the Sea to Sky gondola summit and Upper Shannon Falls (see the Sea to Summit hike).

0.55 km/0.3 mile   Keep right (northeast) for Third Peak when the trail splits and follow yellow markers on this leg of the hike. The left trail is a shorter route to First and Second Peaks, and the return route for this hike.

1.2 km/0.7 mile   When Slhaney Trail branches off right (east), continue straight (northeast) on Third Peak Trail.

1.8 km/1.1 miles   Pass the left turn to Second Peak. Continue on the trail toward Third Peak. Keep right (northeast) again at a second turn to Second Peak.

2.2 km/1.4 miles   Ascend to Third Peak. When the trail leaves the trees, it almost doubles back on itself and climbs up the steep granite rock face.

Second Peak has one of the largest areas to explore. But be mindful of the edges: It's a long way down.

Stawamus Chief

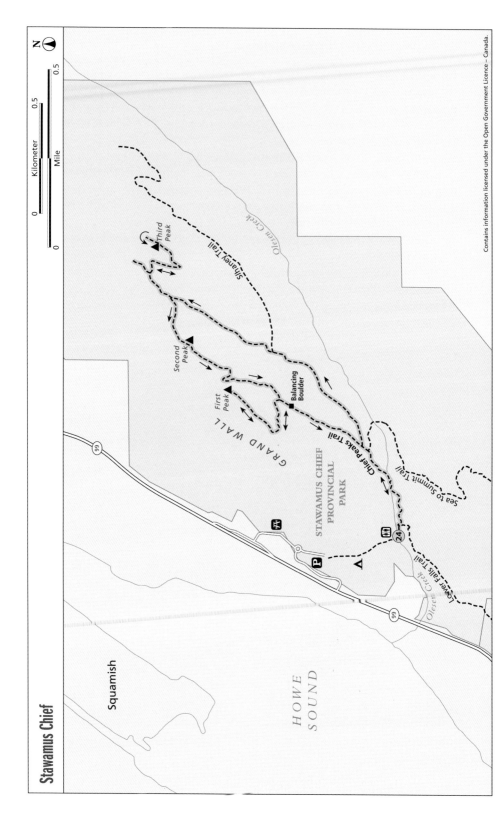

Squamish

HOWE
SOUND

Olsesn Creek

99

99

Lower Falls Trail

24

STAWAMUS CHIEF
PROVINCIAL
PARK

P

Chief Peaks Trail

Sea to Summit Trail

GRAND WALL

First
Peak

Balancing
Boulder

Second
Peak

Third
Peak

Shaney Trail

Olsen Creek

N

0   0.5   Kilometer
0   0.5
           Mile

2.4 km/1.5 miles Reach the quiet, treed setting of Third Peak, also called North Summit. To continue hiking, retrace your steps on the same trail, toward the junction with Second Peak Trail.

2.9 km/1.8 miles Pause for a view of Mount Garibaldi to the north.

3.0 km/1.9 miles Return to the Second Peak junction; this time follow the trail right (west) and then straight, looking for the red and white trail markers to Second Peak.

Steller's jays are a boisterous resident on The Chief.

3.3 km/2.1 miles Reach Second Peak, or Centre Summit.

3.5 km/2.2 miles Follow the main trail southwest down a steep slope, using the chains and ladders for safety. Reflective markers guide you on the route.

4.0 km/2.5 miles At the First Peak trail junction, turn right (west) and follow orange trail markers to make the climb to the final peak.

4.5 km/2.8 miles Ascend to First Peak, or South Summit.

5.0 km/3.1 miles After returning along First Peak Trail, turn right (southwest) on the main trail.

5.1 km/3.2 miles Take a photo of a balancing boulder, just east of the trail. It is conveniently perched by a viewpoint.

5.5 km/3.4 miles Keep right (southwest) on Chief Peaks Trail. Trails from Third Peak and Upper Shannon Falls trails join this main route.

6.0 km/3.7 miles Continue down the stairs at the junction with the Lower Falls and Sea to Summit Trails.

6.1 km/3.8 miles Arrive back at the trailhead.

Option: I've described the route for bagging all three peaks, but completing only Third and Second Peaks is a popular alternative. Hiking just to First Peak only is also an extremely popular choice.

Hike Information

Restaurants: It's common for outdoor adventurers to gather at a number of Squamish eateries after a day on the trails (whether hiking, biking, or skiing). The house-brewed beer and patio at Howe Sound Brewpub are a favorite. 37801 Cleveland Ave., Squamish; (604) 892-2603; howesound.com.

25 Alice Lake Provincial Park

There's a family of four lakes in Alice Lake Provincial Park. This hike links them all and also stops at the debris-clogged banks of the Cheekye River. After you've made the quick, easy 6.4-kilometer (4.0-mile) circuit, you can swim on sandy beaches, kayak Alice Lake, fish for rainbow trout, or settle into the provincial park campground. It's a summer playground that's a favorite for families.

Start: Stump Lake trailhead on Alice Lake Road
Distance: 6.4-km (4.0-mile) loop
Hiking time: About 1.5 hours
Difficulty: Easy due to short length and flat, forest trails that are all well marked
Trail surface: Forested trail, gravel path
Best season: Year-round
Other trail users: Mountain bikers, families, campers, dog-walkers
Canine compatibility: Leashed dogs permitted
Land status: Provincial park
Fees and permits: No fees or permits required
Schedule: Daylight hours
Maps: A park map is available through Alice Lake Provincial Park website, bcparks.ca.

Government topographic maps include the GeoBC Topographic Map Viewer (gov.bc.ca), as well as map 92G14 in the Atlas of Canada Toporama tool (atlas.gc.ca).
Trail contacts: Alice Lake Provincial Park, Alice Lake Road, Squamish; (604) 986-9371; bcparks.ca and seatoskyparks.com
Special considerations: Squamish is cougar country, and the large wild cats have been spotted in the area. Children and dogs are especially vulnerable. Never turn and run from a cougar. If one follows you, maintain eye contact and make noise. If a cougar attacks, fight back with sticks, stones, or anything else on hand. For more information, see wildsafebc .com.

Finding the trailhead: From Squamish, drive north on the Sea to Sky Highway (Highway 99) toward Whistler. About 10 kilometers (6.2 miles) past downtown Squamish, turn right (northeast) onto Alice Lake Road. Continue straight, passing a right (south) turn into the park. The trailhead is about 1.6 kilometers (1.0 mile) from the highway, across from the campground entrance. Trailhead GPS: N49 47.02' / W123 07.29'

The Hike

Alice Lake became a provincial park in 1956, but locals loved it long before. Amid the intense outdoor activities that tend to define Squamish (like rock climbing on the face of the Stawamus Chief or mountain biking through forest trails), Alice Lake is a comparatively tranquil spot. Families huddle around campfires roasting marshmallows, kids swim out to lake rafts, Canada geese herd their goslings in the picnic area, and anglers in hip waders fish for trout.

Four Lakes Trail—taking in Stump, Fawn, Edith, and Alice Lakes—samples the best of this recreation scene. But it also discovers quieter areas of the park like the sometimes-turbulent Cheekye River and lily-dotted Stump Lake.

There's a swimming area, dock, and raft at Alice Lake Beach.

Start at the trailhead on Alice Lake Road and follow the flat forest trail north toward Stump Lake. The trail forks around the lake, with one-way restrictions in place due to COVID-19 in 2020. Just north of the lake, Cheekye River runs east to west. It originates from glacier-cloaked Mount Garibaldi—a towering stratovolcano that formed partly on top of a glacier during an ice age. As the ice retreated, the volcano partially collapsed. As turbulent as that sounds, don't let it ruffle your vacation feathers. Mount Garibaldi last erupted more than 9,000 years ago.

You may like to add to the rock sculptures along the Cheekye's riverbanks, stacking smooth stones into a finely balanced tower. It has a meditative quality—a natural zen garden feel.

Return to the trail from the river and follow the path southeast as it climbs a short series of switchbacks. Lovely Fawn Lake deserves a quick visit before continuing on. The trail widens and becomes a gravel road as you reach Edith Lake. Here, you may catch anglers pulling on their hip waders or standing on the shoreline fishing for rainbow trout.

Four Lakes Trail continues west of Edith Lake, cutting through second-growth forest before reaching the south beach of Alice Lake. This is where you can pump up Debecks Hill (the trail begins at the south end of the road) or follow the flat lakeshore back to the parking area at the north end of the lake. From there, the day is yours to enjoy.

Facing page top: Mountain bikers are regulars on the trails near Squamish.
Facing page bottom: Aside from lakes, the Four Lakes Trail is also vibrant with woodland greenery.
Below: Stump Lake is one of four along the trail.

Anglers cast their lines into all four lakes, fishing for trout. The Freshwater Fisheries Society of BC stocks Stump, Alice, and Edith Lakes with rainbows. Check online for more details: gofishbc.com.

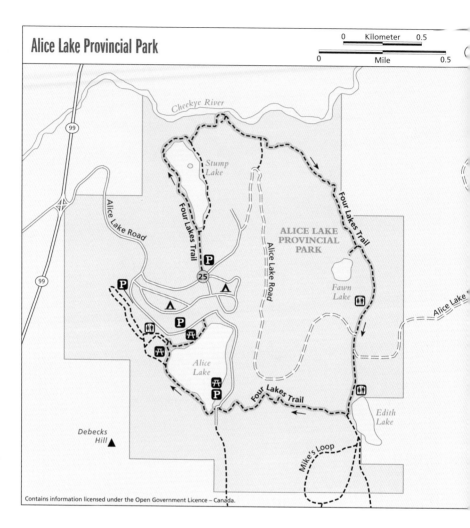

Alice Lake Provincial Park

0   Kilometer   0.5

0   Mile   0.5

Cheekye River

99

Stump Lake

Alice Lake Road

Four Lakes Trail

Four Lakes Trail

ALICE LAKE PROVINCIAL PARK

99

P

A

25

A

P

P

Alice Lake Road

Fawn Lake

Alice Lake

P

Alice Lake

P

Four Lakes Trail

Edith Lake

Debecks Hill ▲

Mike's Loop

Contains information licensed under the Open Government Licence – Canada.

Distances and Directions

0.0 km/0.0 mile Start from the Four Lakes trailhead on Alice Lake Road and head north.

0.3 km/0.2 mile At the trail fork, take the left route to follow the shore of Stump Lake.

1.1 km/0.7 mile On the north side of Stump Lake, keep left (northeast) to continue on Four Lakes Trail. (Continuing straight would take you south back to the road and parking.)

1.5 km/0.9 mile Stop alongside the Cheekye River.

1.6 km/1.0 miles Continue straight (east) at an intersection.

2.8 km/1.7 miles Reach a right spur trail to tiny Fawn Lake to the southwest. After visiting the lakeshore, continue straight (south) toward Edith Lake.

3.5 km/2.2 miles Continue straight at two intersections with the gravel park road.

4.0 km/2.5 miles Stop at Edith Lake and see if any anglers are out for trout.

The banks of the Cheekye River are clogged with tumbled-smooth rocks.

4.3 km/2.7 miles Cut right (west) and head uphill on the Four Lakes Trail. Just a few meters further, make another right toward Alice Lake. (The other routes straight-ahead go to Garibaldi Highlands and Mike's Loop Trail.)

5.2 km/3.2 miles Reach the busy south end of Alice Lake. This, the largest lake, has picnic areas, a beach, a swimming raft, bathrooms, and parking spaces. (***Side-trip:*** For a bit of elevation gain [274 meters (899 feet)], follow the trail up Debecks Hill. The 3-kilometer [1.9-mile] out-and-back hike starts at the south end of the lake parking area.)

5.5 km/3.4 miles Follow the flat shoreline trail clockwise around the lake (northwest).

6.4 km/4.0 miles Amble along the busy northwest shore of the lake. (***Note:*** The Four Lakes Trail is nearly a complete loop, but the final portion follows the park road as there is no trail that links Alice Lake to the Four Lakes trailhead.)

Hike Information

Local Attractions: Motorized boats aren't permitted on the lake, but you can rent canoes, kayaks, and stand-up paddleboards on-site during summer. Sea to Sky Parks; (604) 986-9371; seatoskyparks.com.

Camping: Alice Lake Provincial Park is an exceedingly popular camping destination, especially with families. To snag a site during summer, it's recommended to book as early as possible. Allow for the maximum advance booking—up to 2 months in 2020. (778) 309-1439 or (800) 689-9025; discovercamping.ca.

GREEN TIP
When hiking in a group, walk single file on established trails that are narrow to avoid widening them. If you come upon a sensitive area, spread out so you don't cut one path through the landscape. Don't create new trails where there were none before.

Burnaby to Indian Arm

Ridge walks, lake loops, mountainside routes, and beach treks offer a mixed bag of adventures in the wide and wild region from Burnaby and Port Moody up to the shores of Indian Arm. This is a tucked-away corner of the city, with many communities that are accessible by only a single road.

Parks and hiking trails carry over this set-apart feel. For example, you can only walk or boat in to Buntzen Lake's North Beach, Simon Fraser University sits high up on Burnaby Mountain, and Jug Island Beach requires a hike-in along Belcarra Peninsula.

This prevalence of only-one-way-in destinations is the result of impassable coastal and mountainous geography. The saltwater fjord of Indian Arm divides the North Shore from equally rugged terrain near Burrard Inlet and Port Moody to the south. The glacier-carved inlet boasts one of the Vancouver area's most scenic settings. But there are also no roads along Indian Arm, leaving boat access as the only way in beyond North Vancouver's Deep Cove.

On the southern side near the head of Burrard Inlet, peninsulas, islands, and lakes twist together to create a jigsaw-like landscape. The hikes in this region explore those puzzle pieces, including acres of wilderness in Say Nuth Khaw Yum Provincial Park. Threading through the park, Sendero Diez Vistas Trail offers the most stunning introductory views, with lookouts that also provide a geography lesson as you look down from an undeveloped ridge onto Deep Cove, Belcarra Peninsula, and Indian Arm.

Watch for slugs slowly creeping across the needle-packed trail. Gray-yellow banana slugs are native to BC, but licorice-black slugs arrived from Europe.

While the area is apart from Vancouver, it is certainly not undiscovered. The recreation areas are a natural escape from the close-at-hand cities of Burnaby, Port Moody, Coquitlam, and Port Coquitlam. Buntzen and Sasamat Lakes are a summer pilgrimage, when cool waters and freshwater beaches draw in swimmers. And ocean swimmers aren't left out either, with a sheltered beach at Jug Island at the end of the Belcarra Peninsula.

26 Burnaby Mountain

An intricate trail network surrounds the mountaintop campus of Simon Fraser University. While the woodland paths are a favorite with mountain bikers, they are open to hikers too. Explore the steep slopes of Burnaby Mountain to find quiet routes and simply enjoy the forest. Then post-hike, head up to see the views from Centennial Way and totem poles by an Ainu carver from Japan.

Start: Trailhead off Gaglardi Way
Distance: 5.0-km (3.1-mile) loop
Elevation gain: 184 meters (604 feet)
Hiking time: About 1 hour
Difficulty: Easy due to well-marked forest trails, though a couple of steady steep climbs and descents could pose a moderate challenge
Trail surface: Gravel, forested trail, dirt path, stairs
Best season: Year-round
Other trail users: Mountain bikers, dog-walkers
Canine compatibility: Leashed dogs permitted
Land status: City park, conservation area
Fees and permits: No fees or permits required
Schedule: None, but daylight hours recommended

Maps: The City of Burnaby makes a full trail map available online at burnaby.ca. Government topographic maps include the GeoBC Topographic Map Viewer (gov.bc.ca), as well as map 92G7 in the Atlas of Canada Toporama tool (atlas.gc.ca).
Trail contacts: Burnaby Parks, Recreation and Cultural Services; (604) 294-7450; burnaby.ca
Special considerations: These trails are popular with mountain bikers. With multiuse trails, all groups have to bend a little to consider and accommodate others. As hikers, stay alert while walking and keep to the right-hand side of the trail. Oh, and don't forget to say hello when mountain bikers pass by! There is no water available at the trailhead or along the route.

Finding the trailhead: From the Trans-Canada Highway (Highway 1), take exit 37 for Gaglardi Way. Drive north on Gaglardi, crossing Lougheed Highway and continuing straight (northeast) at the intersection with Broadway. As Gaglardi makes a wide left curve uphill, find a roadside parking spot and walk to the trailhead. Trailhead GPS: N49 16.07' / W122 54.16'

The Hike

Simon Fraser University commands an authoritative vantage on top of Burnaby Mountain—at 370 meters (1,214 feet) above sea level. And while most visitors come for the view on a clear day, rainy weather and low clouds can thwart any plans of admiring the panorama. But on those less-than-ideal days, you can disappear on forest trails and explore under the pleasant forest canopy while getting away from city noise.

Loggers started felling trees on the mountain in the early 1900s. Hikers and hunters moved in (to Snake Hill, as the mountain was then known) during the 1920s. It wasn't until 1965 that students started attending the mountaintop university, its campus from the minds of Vancouver architects Arthur Erickson and Geoffrey Massey.

Left: Burnaby Mountain trails accommodate both mountain bikers and hikers.
Right: A totem pole sculpture frames Vancouver city views from Burnaby Mountain.

This loop hike explores below mountaintop academia, following first a straight, gravel trail that cuts alongside a buried petroleum pipeline—yellow markers warn of the path. The Trans Mountain Pipeline started carrying fuel in 1953 between Edmonton, Alberta, and its Burnaby terminus. Thirteen storage tanks contain crude oil and refined fuel that's headed to a refinery and tanker transport. A more pleasant thought, though, are the pale pink touch-me-nots that bloom here in summer.

Burnaby Mountain trails double as mountain-biking routes, and many have wooden bridges and paving stones that create challenging but smooth rides for two-wheelers. Mountain bikers are also responsible for the quirky (and sometimes intimidating) trail names. While hikers tend toward names that describe vistas or history, mountain bikers crown routes with monikers like Jim's Jungle and Gear Jammer.

Case in point: When the oddly named Dead Moped Trail meets the Trans-Canada, you turn left and follow a short stretch of the national route. The trail network reaches from the Pacific to the Atlantic and to the Arctic, covering 24,000 kilometers (14,913 miles). It was completed in 2017, 25 years after having been started in 1992 to mark Canada's 125th birthday.

This hike turns on Mel's Trail to make the steep climb, but the Trans-Canada Trail continues west to grassy parklands, manicured gardens, and totem poles on Centennial Way. From Burnaby Mountain, the national trail then cuts through the cities of

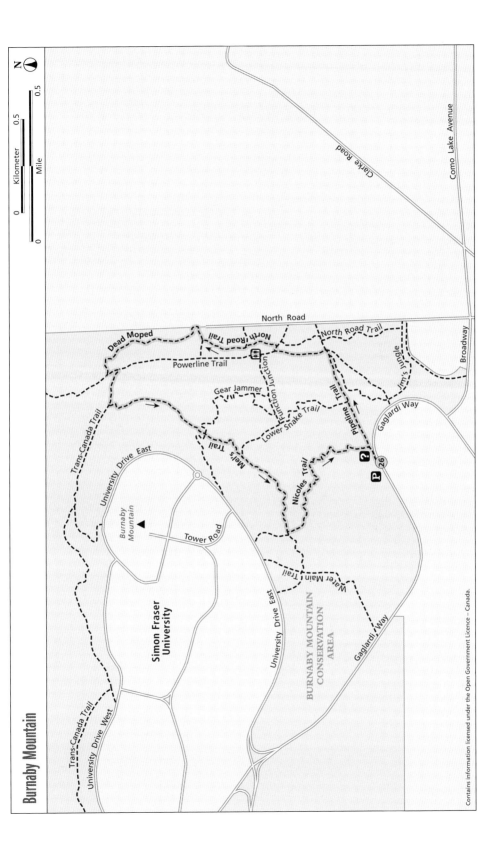

Burnaby Mountain

Contains information licensed under the Open Government Licence – Canada.

Narrow board trails may be designed for mountain bikers, but they are fun for hikers too.

Burnaby and Vancouver, follows the seawall around Stanley Park, and crosses Burrard Inlet to North Vancouver and West Vancouver.

Mel's Trail presents an initial climb but then starts to level off as it intersects winding Gear Jammer and Upper Snake Trails. In 1969, a Kinesiology Department project investigated the effects of exercise on the human condition. The researcher found participants from Skid Row, giving them exercises and monitoring the results. One of those men was named Mel. And since he helped clear some of Burnaby Mountain's trails, this route remembers his efforts.

The second-growth forests are thick and lush on the steep slopes. You really feel the grade as you make a left onto Nicoles Trail—a narrow trail that's considered advanced for mountain bikers. It's not easy for hikers either, especially when muddy, but connects back down to the Gaglardi Way trailhead. (If it's too slick, you can continue straight on Mel's Trail to Water Main, and carefully walk back along Gaglardi Way.)

Distances and Directions

0.0 km/0.0 mile Start from the Gaglardi Way trailhead and walk straight northeast along Pipeline Trail.

0.3 km/0.2 mile Pass the intersection with Lower Snake Trail and continue straight over the bridge.

0.6 km/0.4 mile At Powerline Trail, turn left (north).

0.9 km/0.6 mile Make the next right (east) and then a quick left (north) onto forested North Road Trail. There is also a pit toilet at this junction.

1.1 km/0.7 mile Bear left (north) at the junction with a connector trail, which heads right (east) to North Road.

1.4 km/0.9 mile Make a right (east) and quick left (north) at the fence to follow Dead Moped Trail.

2.2 km/1.4 miles Keep left and then turn left (south) onto the Trans-Canada Trail. Follow the sharp curve east as the trail climbs uphill. Powerline Trail branches off left (south).

2.5 km/1.6 miles Make another left (south) and follow Mel's Trail as you gain more elevation.

3.2 km/2.0 miles Continue straight at the upper and lower sections of Gear Jammer Trail.

4.0 km/2.5 miles Make a left (southeast) onto Nicoles Trail and work your way downhill.

5.0 km/3.1 miles Arrive back at the trailhead.

Options: For a longer hike, continue west on the Trans-Canada Trail to the park area around Centennial Way. Explore a network of short trails before returning along the Trans-Canada (there is no loop that avoids retracing your steps). For some cardio, start down the Velodrome Trail steps.

Hike Information

Local Attractions: Drive or walk to Centennial Way to see a fantastic view of Vancouver and the North Shore Mountains. There are viewpoints, a playground, rose garden, and art pieces all in a compact area. More than a dozen wooden poles form the Kamui Mintara (Playground of the Gods) sculpture. Centennial Way, SFU Campus, Burnaby; burnaby.ca.

Organizations: Burnaby Mountain Biking Association has a hand in keeping the trails in such good shape. bmba.ca.

GREEN TIP
Keep to established trails as much as possible. If there aren't any, stay on surfaces that will be least affected, like rock, gravel, dry grasses, or snow.

27 Buntzen Lake

This moderate loop hike follows the undulating forest shoreline of Buntzen Lake—a BC Hydro–managed recreation area that's a popular spot to cool off in summer. Along the route, you get a sense of the forces harnessed to create clean energy in the province. Dozens of small creeks drain into Buntzen Lake, along with a 3.6-kilometer (2.2-mile) tunnel from Coquitlam Lake. The suspension bridge at the lake's north end is fun to cross.

Start: Buntzen Lake parking lot
Distance: 9.8-km (6.1-mile) loop
Hiking time: About 3 hours
Difficulty: Moderate due to length and undulating trail with a couple steeper climbs
Trail surface: Gravel, forested trail, gravel road, suspension bridge
Best season: Year-round
Other trail users: Dog-walkers, beachgoers
Canine compatibility: Leashed dogs permitted
Land status: Recreation area
Fees and permits: No fees or permits required
Schedule: Varies by season, but generally daylight hours
Maps: BC Hydro has a trail brochure and map available online at bchydro.com. Some trails, including the main Buntzen Lake Trail, are included on the Say Nuth Khaw Yum Provincial

Park map, available online at bcparks.ca. Government topographic maps include the GeoBC Topographic Map Viewer (gov.bc.ca), as well as map 92G7 in the Atlas of Canada Toporama tool (atlas.gc.ca).

Trail contacts: Buntzen Lake Recreation Area Warden, BC Hydro; (604) 469-9679; bchydro .com/community/recreation_areas/buntzen_ lake_trails.html

Special considerations: There is fresh water available near the trailhead, but not during this hike. The water level of Buntzen Lake can change based on BC Hydro's needs. There can be strong current around water intakes and the Coquitlam Lake tunnel outfall. These areas are roped off, but always swim with care and safety in any area of the lake.

Finding the trailhead: From the Trans-Canada Highway (Highway 1), take exit 44 for Lougheed Highway. Follow Lougheed north for 5.5 kilometers (3.4 miles), and then turn left (northwest) onto Barnet Highway. Drive 2.2 kilometers (1.4 miles) and make a right (north) onto Ioco Road. After 700 meters (0.4 mile), continue straight as the street becomes Heritage Mountain Boulevard (Ioco Road heads left). Buntzen Lake signs help you through the following turns. Drive 2.0 kilometers (1.2 miles) and turn right (east) at the roundabout on David Avenue. Make the next left (northeast) onto Forest Park Way, then left again (northwest) onto Aspenwood Drive. The road name changes to E Road as you drive the 2.7 kilometers (1.7 miles) to the junction with Sunnyside Road in Anmore. Turn right (north) and then follow the main road into the park. Trailhead GPS: N49 20.32' / W122 51.40'

The Hike

Ninety-eight percent of British Columbia's electricity comes from hydroelectric infrastructure powered by rivers, falls, and lake reservoirs. It's an astounding and impressive amount, especially when much of the world uses polluting coal and nuclear plants to create power. Most large hydro projects in British Columbia came to fruition in the 1960s and 1970s—but some smaller projects were constructed decades earlier.

Buntzen Lake Powerhouse is one of these, having first used the waters of then-named Lake Beautiful to generate electricity in 1904. Water flowed from the lake to a plant on the shore of Indian Arm, an ocean fjord. Until that point, Vancouver had been relying on steam power.

The first hydroelectricity plant in British Columbia was built near Victoria in 1898.

By 1905, workers had also excavated a tunnel under Eagle Mountain to connect Coquitlam Lake and the renamed Buntzen Lake. Now, more than a century on, hydroelectricity infrastructure, power lines, and artifacts still mark the lakeshore, but are a quiet second to the area's natural beauty.

A suspension bridge crosses Buntzen Lake to reach North Beach.

Some hike, others canoe, the length of Buntzen Lake.

Begin the hike at the huge parking lot, which quickly fills in summer. Walk toward the fenced-in dog beach to pick up the lake trail. As you follow the lakeshore away from South Beach, dozens of wooden bridges span botanically named creeks. These small waterways all help sate Buntzen Lake's thirst.

The narrow trail undulates through pretty forest terrain, with occasional large Douglas firs among cedars and hemlocks. There's little reason to break a steady pace other than a lake viewpoint about a third of the way along.

At the north end of the lake, the forest trail briefly merges with Powerhouse Road. This access road skirts the lake and continues down to a dam and the two Buntzen powerhouses on the coast. These are not accessible to the public, but they are an interesting sight from Indian Arm on the other side of Buntzen Ridge.

Take the narrow path down to the tunnel outlet and see where water surges out, having traveled 3.6 kilometers (2.2 miles) underground from Coquitlam Lake. To construct the tunnel, workers used jackhammers to drill through rock, working from both ends. When the two sides met, 2 years later in 1905, they were almost in exact alignment—less than an inch off. But today's power source came at a great cost. Between 1903 and 1912, more than 100 workers died in accidents during the tunnel's construction and subsequent expansion.

Be aware that the tunnel's outflow is under mechanical control, and currents can be exceedingly strong—even outside the safety area.

There's a second beach at the north end of the lake, where the only access is on foot, by canoe or kayak via the lake, or by bike along Powerhouse Road; crowds are much less here. Picnic tables are well positioned for a barbecue. Immediately west of the beach, a suspension bridge provides a fun way to cross the narrow neck of Buntzen Creek, which connects Buntzen and McCombe Lakes.

Keeping left at the junction with Old Buntzen Lake Trail, follow the lake trail along the west shore. A steep ridge rises between saltwater Indian Arm and you, and the lake lies in a trough between the mountains.

Along the lake's west side, the trail climbs a short but steep hill to power lines before descending and tracing the lake edge through to the Burrard Pumphouse. Here, the trail widens to a gravel road and covers the final 2 kilometers (1.2 miles) to the floating bridge.

Depending on lake levels, the floating bridge could be busy with anglers casting a line for trout or almost out of water and resting close to the lake bottom. With a drawdown you can see lake floor and hewn tree stumps. From the east side of the bridge, trails lead back to the parking lot.

Hikers, bikers, and boaters can all venture to North Beach on Buntzen Lake.

Buntzen Lake

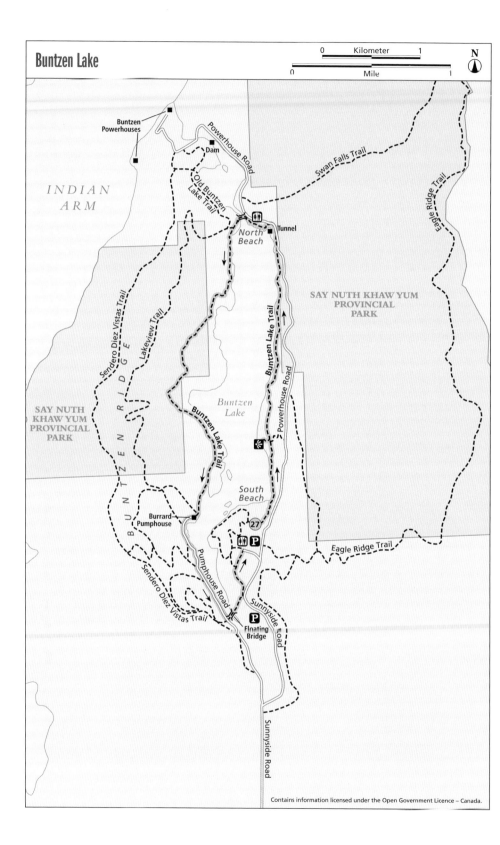

Contains information licensed under the Open Government Licence – Canada.

Distances and Directions

0.0 km/0.0 mile   Start from the Buntzen Lake parking lot and follow gravel paths northeast. The trail at first follows the fence of the dog off-leash area.

0.4 km/0.2 mile   Beyond the dog off-leash area, the gravel trail becomes a forest path and continues along the lake's eastern shore.

1.1 km/0.7 mile   Stop to look out west over the lake from the viewpoint. Then climb up via some easy switchbacks; you'll also pass a connector trail that heads northeast up to Powerhouse Road.

3.5 km/2.2 miles   The trail climbs steeply to briefly meet with gravel Powerhouse Road near the Coquitlam Lake tunnel. Then turn on the left trail (southwest) down to the beach.

3.7 km/2.3 miles   Reach North Beach, a favorite picnicking spot.

3.8 km/2.4 miles   Cross the suspension bridge and continue on Buntzen Lake Trail (southwest).

4.1 km/2.5 miles   Pass a right (north) turn to Old Buntzen Lake and Lakeview Trails. (*Option:* Lakeview Trail adds a moderate challenge to this hike as it follows an undulating route along the hillside.)

7.6 km/4.7 miles   The forest trail becomes a gravel road at Burrard Pumphouse.

7.8 km/4.8 miles   Keep straight on the gravel road as forest trails (including Bear Claw, Saddle Ridge, Horseshoe, and Lakeview Trails) meet this main route over the next kilometer (0.6 mile).

8.9 km/5.5 miles   Turn left (northeast) and cross the floating bridge.

9.5 km/5.9 miles   Follow the short trails back to the parking lot.

9.8 km/6.1 miles   Arrive back at the parking lot.

GREEN TIP

If you're toting a picnic, leave the packaging at home. Repack your provisions in ziplock bags that you can reuse and that can double as garbage bags on the way out of the woods.

28 Sendero Diez Vistas

Nothing tops the fjord viewpoints and lakeshore vistas on this lengthy but worthwhile hike. A challenging climb up Buntzen Ridge elevates you above saltwater Indian Arm. More than 10 viewpoints each provide a different vantage before you return to the Buntzen Lake shoreline. This route direction has been reversed to avoid a detour due to COVID-19 trail restrictions.

Start: Buntzen Lake parking lot
Distance: 12.3-km (7.6-mile) loop
Elevation gain: 418 meters (1,371 feet)
Hiking time: 4–5 hours
Difficulty: Moderate to challenging due to steady climb and technical terrain
Trail surface: Gravel, forested trail, gravel road
Best season: Apr–Nov
Other trail users: Dog-walkers
Canine compatibility: Leashed dogs permitted
Land status: Provincial park, recreation area
Fees and permits: No fees or permits required
Schedule: Varies, but generally during daylight hours
Maps: BC Hydro has a trail brochure and map available online at bchydro.com. Some trails, including the main Diez Vistas Trail, are included on the Say Nuth Khaw Yum Provincial Park map, available online at bcparks.ca. Government topographic maps include the GeoBC Topographic Map Viewer (gov.bc.ca), as well as map 92G7 in the Atlas of Canada Toporama tool (atlas.gc.ca).
Trail contacts: Buntzen Lake Recreation Area Warden, BC Hydro, (604) 469-9679; bchydro .com/community/recreation_areas/buntzen _lake_trails.html; or Say Nuth Khaw Yum Provincial Park, bcparks.ca
Special considerations: There is fresh water available near the trailhead, but not during this hike.

Finding the trailhead: From the Trans-Canada Highway (Highway 1), take exit 44 for Lougheed Highway. Follow Lougheed north for 5.5 kilometers (3.4 miles), and then turn left (northwest) onto Barnet Highway. Drive 2.2 kilometers (1.4 miles) and make a right (north) onto Ioco Road. After 700 meters (0.4 mile), continue straight as the street becomes Heritage Mountain Boulevard (Ioco Road heads left). Buntzen Lake signs help you through the following turns. Drive 2.0 kilometers (1.2 miles) and turn right (east) at the roundabout on David Avenue. Make the next left (northeast) onto Forest Park Way, then left again (northwest) onto Aspenwood Drive. The road name changes to Water Street and then E Road as you drive the 2.7 kilometers (1.7 miles) to the junction with Sunnyside Road in Anmore. Turn right (north) and then follow the main road into the park. Trailhead GPS: N49 20.32' / W122 51.40'

The Hike

A Norwegian by birth, Halvor Lunden is the man who shaped Sendero Diez Vistas Trail—a route that perches you above Indian Arm and delivers view after view of the glacial fjord. Lunden was well known in BC hiking circles for his trails. Though he died in 2008, at the age of 93, Lunden's legacies are the routes he established.

Look down on Belcarra Peninsula from Diez Vistas viewpoints.

The ridge of Diez Vistas travels far above the Indian Arm fjord.

The name Sendero Diez Vistas translates from Spanish as "Path of Ten Views." Not all viewpoints are in prime shape, and there are extras that make that tally a floating number.

This route can be hiked in both directions; however, if one-way restrictions are in place on the floating bridge, it's shortest hiked counterclockwise. In this direction the climb comes in the second half of the hike—a climb that takes you to the heights of Buntzen Ridge, which rises more than 550 meters (1,804 feet) above the saltwater fjord.

But in either direction the views are a treasure, with varying vantages over Indian Arm, Belcarra Peninsula, Jug Island, Deep Cove, and more. Tally up the views as you proceed, stopping at numbered viewpoints.

One of the most popular spots to linger is the viewpoint where you can look down on Indian Arm, Belcarra, and Deep Cove. Burnaby and Vancouver are a faint sight beyond.

As it was a steep climb, so is the descent in either direction.

A benefit to traveling the route clockwise is that North Beach lies at the halfway point and after the intense climb—tempting on a hot summer day with a swim in Buntzen Lake. This option also allows you to pick your pleasure for the return home: Powerhouse Road is a gravel roadway, there are forest trails on both sides of the lake

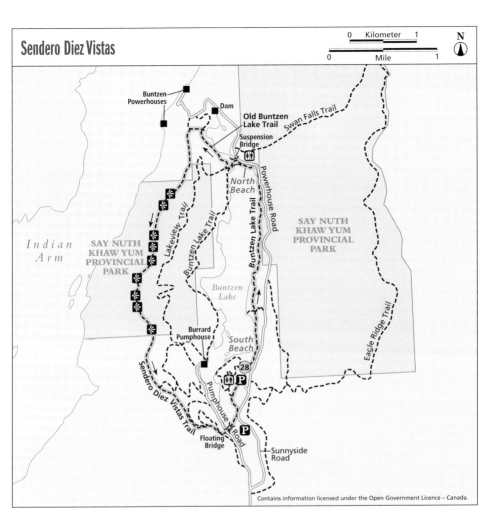

Contains information licensed under the Open Government Licence – Canada.

(the east side was subject to one-way restrictions in 2020), or you can opt for another heart-pumping climb along Lakeview Trail.

Distances and Directions

0.0 km/0.0 mile   Start from the Buntzen Lake parking lot and follow gravel paths northeast. The trail at first follows the fence of the dog off-leash area.

0.4 km/0.2 mile   Beyond the dog off-leash area, the gravel trail becomes a forest path and continues along the lake's eastern shore.

1.1 km/0.7 mile   Stop to look out west over the lake from the viewpoint. Then climb up via some easy switchbacks. A connector trail leads east to Powerhouse Road.

3.4 km/2.1 miles   The trail climbs steeply to briefly meet with gravel Powerhouse Road near the Coquitlam Lake tunnel. Then turn on the left trail (southwest) down to the beach.

3.6 km/2.2 miles   Reach North Beach and then cross the suspension bridge.

4.0 km/2.5 miles Turn right (north) and then keep right at the junction with Lakeview Trail.

4.8 km/3.0 miles Make a left (west) and follow the trail away from the lakeshore.

5.0 km/3.1 miles Turn (southwest) to start Diez Vistas Trail.

6.7 km/4.2 miles After a steep climb, reach the first, if-overgrown vantage, Viewpoint 10.

8.4 km/5.2 miles Stop at a wide viewpoint for particularly excellent views over Indian Arm.

9.3 km/5.8 miles The trail forks. Head right (south), while the left fork heads to a viewpoint over the lake. The trail starts to descend steeply.

9.6 km/6.0 miles Rejoin the Punta del Este Trail.

10.1 km/6.3 miles At powerlines, continue straight (southeast) as spur trails lead to Sasamat Lake (southwest) and Buntzen Lake (northeast).

11.2 km/7.0 mile Keep straight (southeast) at the intersection with Horseshoe Trail.

11.5 km/7.1 mile Near the lakeshore, continue straight ahead (northeast) toward the floating bridge.

11.8 km/7.3 mile Cross the lake over the bridge and then follow trails north toward the parking lot.

12.3 km/7.6 mile Reach the Buntzen Lake Recreation Area parking lot.

Hike Information

Local Events: Should you find Sendero Diez Vistas not challenging enough, it's time to consider the Diez Vista 50-kilometer (31-mile) run. That's a longer distance than a marathon plus about 1,800 meters (6,000 feet) of elevation gain starting from White Pine Beach at Sasamat Lake, following Diez Vistas, and looping around Buntzen Lake. For upcoming event dates, see diezvista.com.

Camping: Anmore Camping has RV sites suited for the family-vacation crowd with an outdoor pool and playground. 3230 Sunnyside Rd., Anmore; (604) 469-2311; anmorecamp-rv.ca.

GREEN TIP
Pack out what you pack in, even food scraps
because they can attract wild animals.

29 Sasamat Lake

Some days, a simple walk around a lake is all you need, perhaps combined with some fishing or a picnic. Sasamat Lake is considered one of the warmest summer swimming lakes near the city, but in winter the floating bridge and loop trail make for a pleasant and quiet forest walk. It also has wilderness appeal, being on the edge of Indian Arm. Nearby, the Village of Belcarra has a long history as an away-from-the-city escape.

Start: White Pine Beach parking lot

Distance: 3.4-km (2.1-mile) loop

Hiking time: Less than 1 hour

Difficulty: Easy due to short length and smooth, flat terrain with occasional stairs

Trail surface: Gravel, forested trail, boardwalk, stairs

Best season: Year-round

Other trail users: Dog-walkers

Canine compatibility: Leashed dogs permitted

Land status: Regional park

Fees and permits: No fees or permits required

Schedule: Daylight hours

Maps: An official park map is available online through Metro Vancouver (metrovancouver.org). Government topographic maps include the GeoBC Topographic Map Viewer (gov.bc.ca), as well as map 92G7 in the Atlas of Canada Toporama tool (atlas.gc.ca).

Trail contacts: Metro Vancouver Regional Parks Central Area Office, 9146 Avalon Ave., Burnaby, V3N 4G8; (604) 520-6442; metrovancouver.org

Finding the trailhead: From the Trans-Canada Highway (Highway 1), take exit 44 for Lougheed Highway. Follow Lougheed for about 5.5 kilometers (3.4 miles), and then turn left (northwest) onto Barnet Highway. After 2.0 kilometers (1.2 miles), turn right (north) onto Ioco Road, following the street as it turns left (northwest) at the junction with Heritage Mountain Boulevard and follows the Port Moody waterfront. Turn right (north) onto 1st Avenue after 4.0 kilometers (2.5 miles). The route becomes Bedwell Bay Road, which twists and turns west all the way to the park. Two kilometers (1.2 miles) from Ioco Road, turn right (north) onto the park road to White Pine Beach. Trailhead GPS: N49 19.39' / W122 53.09'

The Hike

Sasamat Lake is a bit unassuming. A forest trail rings the small lake, where warm swimming waters tempt locals and visitors come summertime. But despite its diminutive size, Belcarra still offers a large dose of wilderness. Belcarra Regional Park, which envelops the lake, is black bear habitat—being on the southern fringe of an uninhabited wilderness, which includes Buntzen Lake Recreation Area, Say Nuth Khaw Yum Provincial Park, and the Coast Mountains beyond.

This simple hike follows the lakeshore in its entirety. In winter, White Pine Beach is empty of beachgoers while in summer it's a true hot spot.

The lake is in view from the sheltered forest trail for most of the route. About a third of the way around the lake is another busy spot in summer: Sasamat Outdoor

BELCARRA COTTAGES AND BOLE HOUSE

The era of the Belcarra cottages began with a murder. During a night of drinking and party-
ing in 1882, John Hall shot and killed his mother-in-law over a financial dispute. His lawyer,
William Bole, mounted a defense but Hall was ultimately found guilty of manslaughter. When
Hall couldn't pay his legal fees, Bole accepted Hall's Belcarra property as payment.

Bole set about creating a summer resort-like property for family and friends, giving it
the Celtic name *Baal* for sun and *Carra* meaning lovely land. He built a two-story home, which
still stands off Belcarra Bay Road, as well as multiple smaller cottages for visitors. These
cottages now lie within the regional park.

Long-term residents have lived in the small, rustic buildings for decades, but Metro
Vancouver's plan to evict residents has led to years of dispute in court. As of 2020 the case
had made it to the BC Supreme Court.

Centre. The center runs kids' camps, and its facilities include a lodge, small cabins, and
yurts, plus an interesting obstacle course.

At the lake's south end, a floating bridge cuts across the narrowest point. It's likely
you'll meet anglers fishing for trout here, as Freshwater Fisheries Society of BC stocks
the lake with rainbow trout in spring and fall. With summer camps, beaches, and

The floating walkway is a popular trout fishing spot.

Bear signs are a reminder of the wilderness that borders Belcarra Regional Park.

fishing, Sasamat can feel like a vacation resort. But again, remember that this area is still wilderness.

In a local history book, *Between Forest and Sea*, the caretaker of a Sasamat Lake camp relates a bear encounter. A Swedish man was walking near the lake, admiring the forest, when he encountered a black bear. Instead of remaining calm, he ran, which enticed the bear to run after him. The man, with bear giving chase, continued running until he reached the lake. On the shore, he edged out on a protruding log. But the bear didn't stop at the water's edge and it started following the man onto the log. With nowhere else to go, the man decided to swim for it. The caretaker recounts cheering the man on as he swam toward the camp dock while the bear watched from the end of the log. Though bears can swim, this one ultimately decided not to take a dip.

Though it's uncommon to see bears on a hike, it is important to always be prepared. "Bear in the area" signs are a common sight at the lake's trailhead.

Avoid an encounter if you can, by making noise (singing, whistling, clapping, or carrying a bear bell) along the trail. If you do see a black bear, stay calm and don't run. Talk softly and start to slowly back away. This is also the time to have your bear spray out and at the ready. Sometimes bears make a false charge. If you are attacked, fight back. Note that these guidelines refer to encountering a black bear. Grizzlies are a whole other matter, but their habitat doesn't stretch into the Vancouver area.

If you see a bear, report the sighting to Conservation Officers at (877) 952-7277.

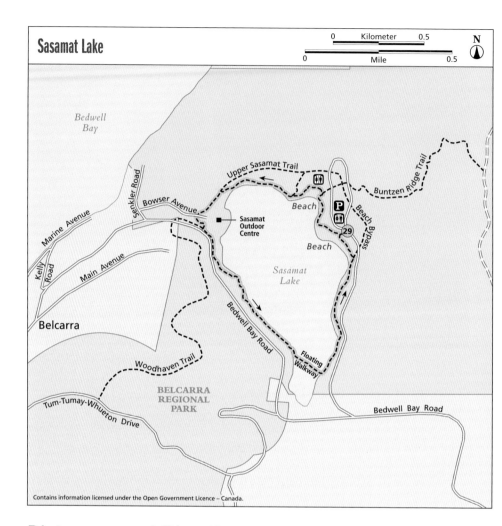

Sasamat Lake

0 Kilometer 0.5
0 Mile 0.5
N

Bedwell
Bay

Upper Sasamat Trail

Buntzen Ridge Trail

Senkler Road

Bowser Avenue

Beach

Beach Bypass

29

Sasamat
Outdoor
Centre

Beach

Marine Avenue

Kelly Road

Main Avenue

Sasamat
Lake

Belcarra

Bedwell Bay Road

Woodhaven Trail

Floating
Walkway

Tum-Tumay-Whueton Drive

BELCARRA
REGIONAL
PARK

Bedwell Bay Road

Contains information licensed under the Open Government Licence – Canada.

Distances and Directions

0.0 km/0.0 mile   Start from the parking lot just east of White Pine Beach and follow any of the short trails that lead down (west) to the lakeshore. Follow the main trail right (northwest) to head counterclockwise around the lake. The water will be to your left.

0.1 km/0.1 mile   Pass White Pine Beach, a favorite with swimmers.

0.4 km/0.2 mile   Pass the second sandy stretch of beach.

0.6 km/0.4 mile   The beach bypass trail joins the lake trail from the right—the bypass keeps dogs away from the beaches in summer.

1.0 km/0.6 mile   Climb the wooden stairs and turn left (southwest) at the Upper Sasamat Trail junction.

1.2 km/0.7 mile   Cross Bowser Avenue, which leads to Sasamat Outdoor Centre on the lakeshore.

1.3 km/0.8 mile   Cross over Windermere Creek and then pass Woodhaven Trail junction, which branches off to the right (west).

1.4 km/0.9 mile   Continue counterclockwise around the lake, passing an obstacle course.

2.2 km/1.4 miles   Turn left (southeast) to cross the southern end of the lake on the floating walkway.

2.4 km/1.5 miles   On the east side of the lake, turn left (northeast) and follow a boardwalk and then a forest trail along the lakeshore.

3.1 km/1.9 miles   On a right branch, the beach bypass trail (for summer dog walkers) climbs up northeast to the road and leaves the lake trail. Continue straight (northwest) along the shoreline.

3.3 km/2.1 miles   Arrive back at White Pine Beach.

3.4 km/2.1 miles   Arrive back at the road-side trailhead.

GREEN TIP

Borrow, rent, or share gear. Many outdoor stores rent less-common items like crampons and climbing equipment.

A floating walkway makes for an interesting route.

30 Jug Island Beach

Tiny Jug Island sits just off the beach at the end of Belcarra Peninsula. Getting there requires hiking a forest trail through the peninsula's center, and though it's an easy hike, it feels like a secreted-away spot. The meditative journey gives time to consider the area's original inhabitants—the Tsleil-Waututh, or the People of the Inlet, who had a large winter village where the park's scenic picnic area now stands.

Start: Belcarra Regional Park picnic area
Distance: 5.2-km (3.2-mile) out-and-back
Hiking time: About 1.5 hours
Difficulty: Easy due to short distance over undulating forest trails
Trail surface: Forested and gravel trails, stairs
Best season: Year-round
Other trail users: Dog-walkers
Canine compatibility: Leashed dogs permitted
Land status: Regional park
Fees and permits: No fees or permits required
Schedule: Daylight hours

Maps: An official park map is available online through Metro Vancouver (metrovancouver.org). Government topographic maps include the GeoBC Topographic Map Viewer (gov.bc.ca), as well as map 92G7 in the Atlas of Canada Toporama tool (atlas.gc.ca).
Trail contacts: Metro Vancouver Regional Parks Central Area Office, 9146 Avalon Ave., Burnaby, V3N 4G8; (604) 520-6442; metrovancouver.org
Special considerations: There is fresh water available near the trailhead, but not during this hike.

Finding the trailhead: From the Trans-Canada Highway (Highway 1), take exit 44 for Lougheed Highway. Follow Lougheed north for 5.5 kilometers (3.4 miles), and then turn left (northwest) onto Barnet Highway. After 2.0 kilometers (1.2 miles), turn right (north) onto loco Road, following the street as it turns left (northwest) at the junction with Heritage Mountain Boulevard and follows the Port Moody waterfront. Turn right (north) onto 1st Avenue after 4.0 kilometers (2.5 miles). The road becomes Bedwell Bay Road, which twists and turns west for 2 kilometers (1.2 miles). Pass the road to Sasamat Lake and continue for 400 meters (0.2 mile) to the stop sign. Make a slight left onto Tum-Tumay-Wheuton, which continues down to the picnic area. Trailhead GPS: N49 18.75' / W122 55.52'

The Hike

For centuries before Europeans arrived, the Tsleil-Waututh used the land now known as Belcarra Regional Park as their winter residence. They called the village here Tum-tumay-whueton, or "Big Place for All the People."

In summer, families spread out along the Indian Arm shoreline to fish, hunt, and gather roots and berries. As winter came, the Tsleil-Waututh would move from those smaller family camps to this large winter residence, bringing with them dehydrated berries, dried sockeye salmon, and meats. It was a safe place and the only flat area in the glacial fjord—protected by the steep mountains of Indian Arm to the north and Buntzen Ridge to the east. The only outlet is through Burrard Inlet to the south.

Jug Island is a dumpling of an island at the end of the trail.

Before beginning the hike to Jug Island, explore the waterfront to see the shell midden here. This and other artifacts show that the Tsleil-Waututh inhabited this site for more than 1,000 years.

The Tsleil-Waututh have a saying: "When the tide goes out the table is set." And Belcarra Bay is still a popular fishing area for crabs and bivalve mollusks. You need a tidal license in order to harvest shellfish here. Check the information board for any posted closures like red tide. Fisheries and Oceans Canada administers tidal licenses (pac.dfo-mpo.gc.ca).

Though the Tsleil-Waututh once numbered up to 10,000 people based here at Belcarra, the effects of colonialism and European diseases like smallpox decimated the nation. The community, now centered on Dollarton Highway reserve lands across Indian Arm, numbers about 500 people.

Starting in the picnic area, you follow a trail to Bedwell Bay Road. The trail continues on the north side of the road. The left branch heads to Jug Island, while the right goes east to sheltered Bedwell Bay. From this point, the forest trail slices through the treed peninsula on a simple path. A familiar mix of second-growth cedars, hemlocks, and firs line the route. Thick mosses and liverworts carpet the rocks and stumps. Though a couple of short hills and stairs offer a slight variation and some climbs, the undulating terrain is unstrenuous.

A woodland trail leads to Jug Island Beach.

Captain George Richards, commanding the HMS *Plumper*, named most of the area features during an 1859 survey. Many, such as Bedwell Bay, are named for ship crew. But Jug Island is different. At one time, a stone handle-like arch protruded from the steep cliff sides of the island, thereby giving it its name.

The pebble beach at the end of the peninsula offers a quiet spot to amble, beach-comb, and relax. A pit toilet provides the bare basics. To head home, simply retrace your steps south to the picnic area.

Distances and Directions

0.0 km/0.0 mile   Start from the Belcarra parking lot and cut northeast across the grassy fields, passing large picnicking shelters, barbecuing areas, and a playground.

0.2 km/0.1 mile   A forested trail leads to Bedwell Bay Road. Cross the road and pick up Jug Island Beach Trail on the northeast side. Midden Road is nearby.

The Belcarra picnic area was a traditional home for the Tsleil-Waututh.

Jug Island Beach

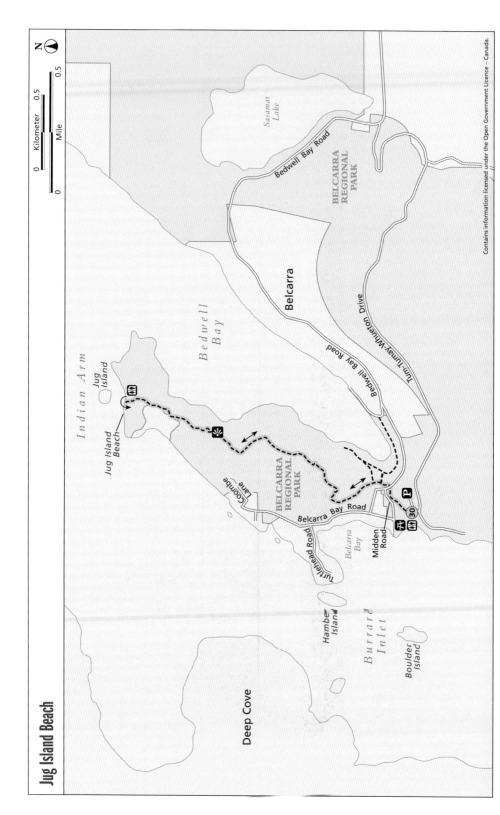

N

| 0 | Kilometer | 0.5 |
| 0 | Mile | 0.5 |

Indian Arm

Jug Island

Jug Island Beach

Bedwell Bay

Belcarra

Sasamat Lake

Bedwell Bay Road

BELCARRA REGIONAL PARK

Tum-tumay-whueton Drive

Bedwell Bay Road

Coombe Lane

Turtlehead Road

BELCARRA REGIONAL PARK

Belcarra Bay Road

Belcarra Bay

Midden Road

P

30

Deep Cove

Hamber Island

Burrard Inlet

Boulder Island

0.3 km/0.2 mile   Bear left to follow Jug Island Beach Trail north. Two spurs of Bedwell Bay Trail head right (east).

1.6 km/1.0 miles   The trail crosses a spur road. Keep right (northeast).

1.9 km/1.2 miles   A viewpoint looks east to Bedwell Bay.

2.6 km/1.6 miles   Descend a final steep stretch to reach Jug Island Beach, at the tip of Belcarra Peninsula.

5.2 km/3.2 miles   Return by the same route to the picnic area and arrive back at the trailhead.

Option: For another, 1.5-hour hike, follow Admiralty Point Trail out to Burns Point—the narrows at the mouth of Port Moody. This 6.0-kilometer (3.7-mile) out-and-back hike offers excellent views of Burrard Inlet throughout the year. It also starts from the Belcarra picnic area.

Hike Information

Local Information: Fisheries and Oceans Canada provides updates on red tide and any closures. (604) 666-2828 or (866) 431-3474; pac.dfo-mpo.gc.ca.

Local Attractions: Takaya Tours offers kayak and stand-up paddleboard rentals from Cates Park, located across Indian Arm, as well as the Belcarra picnic area. (604) 936-0236; takayatours.com.

Other Resources: To read the fantastical tale of George Dyson, an author and kayak builder who lived in a treehouse alongside the historic Judge Bole house for 3 years, pick up *The Starship & the Canoe* by Kenneth Brower. The book weaves Dyson's tale with that of his father, astrophysicist Freeman Dyson, a renowned scientist who drew up plans for spaceships.

GREEN TIP
Rechargeable (reusable) batteries reduce
one source of toxic garbage.

Near the Port Mann and Pitt River Bridges

F ollow the wide, muddy Fraser River east inland from its ocean mouth and the riverbanks become a patchwork of agricultural lands and housing developments. Blueberry bushes, pumpkin patches, and goat dairies thrive in the flat farmers' fields, providing food for the Lower Mainland and other regions. This is where fur traders set up a trading post in 1827, becoming the area's first European settlement.

But the Fraser River and its rolling agricultural lands are only the final leg of the journey for water, nutrients, and animals that transit the river. Branching off to explore the river's tributaries takes you into a more varied terrain of marshlands and sloughs, forests and lakes. It's a landscape rich with migratory birds, salmon, and other animals that depend on the watershed.

The Fraser is the longest river in the province and undammed along its main stem. But some of its many tributaries are essential in British Columbia's hydroelectricity production. Massive dammed lakes, including Hayward Lake and Stave Lake, provide clean, water-generated power for the province.

For these hikes, the Pitt River and Port Mann Bridges are simply the gateway to the area. These bridges are the link between densely populated cities to the west and slightly more rural cities to the east. But I say slightly. It's still common for people to commute to work along Highway 1, or for farmland to become housing developments. Still, when you cross these rivers, the buffer between wilderness and civilization widens a little.

GREEN TIP
Don't take souvenirs home with you. This means
natural materials such as plants, rocks, shells, and
driftwood as well as historic artifacts and fossils.

31 Derby Reach

The mighty Fraser River is a quiet but ever-present force along this hike, which takes you from river's edge to the historic site of a fur trading post and then around a woodland loop. Heritage apple trees, old farm buildings, and salmon anglers transport you from city to country life.

Start: Edgewater Bar parking lot in Derby Reach Regional Park
Distance: 9.3-km (5.8-mile) lollipop
Hiking time: About 2 hours
Difficulty: Easy due to flat gravel trails, though there is some minimal elevation gain along Houston Trail
Trail surface: Gravel, forested trail
Best season: Year-round
Other trail users: Cyclists, dog-walkers, equestrians
Canine compatibility: Leashed dogs permitted
Land status: Regional park

Fees and permits: No fees or permits required
Schedule: Daylight hours
Maps: An official park map is available online through Metro Vancouver (metrovancouver.org), and paper copies are available at the trailhead. Government topographic maps include the GeoBC Topographic Map Viewer (gov.bc.ca), as well as map 92G2 in the Atlas of Canada Toporama tool (atlas.gc.ca).
Trail contacts: Metro Vancouver Regional Parks East Area Office, 1558 200 St., Langley, V2Z 1W5; (604) 530-4983; metrovancouver.org

Finding the trailhead: From the Trans-Canada Highway (Highway 1), take exit 58 for 200 Street. Follow 200 Street north, bearing right (northeast) onto 201 Street. After 450 meters (0.3 mile), make a right (east) turn onto 96 Avenue. Continue on 96 Avenue for 1.2 kilometers (0.7 mile) and then turn left (north) onto 208 Street. After 2.3 kilometers (1.4 miles) the main road bends right (northeast) to become Allard Crescent. Follow Allard Crescent 2.2 kilometers (1.4 miles) along the river to Derby Reach campground at Edgewater Bar. Trailhead GPS: N49 12.48' / W122 37.03'

The Hike

About midway through this hike, a stone cairn with a plaque is the simple marker for an important site: where Hudson's Bay Company established a fur trading post. It was the first European settlement in the Fraser River Valley. Men arrived from Fort Vancouver on the Columbia River in 1827 to clear land and begin trading with First Nations people. The Fraser River was their highway, much as it was for the First Nations people who had been living in the area for thousands of years.

The fur trading post eventually moved 4.0 kilometers (2.5 miles) upriver to Fort Langley in 1839, and that newer location is an active national historic site today with costumed interpreters who may be demonstrating barrel-making, herding goats, growing kitchen gardens, and showing a vast collection of pelts and furs.

Signs of natural and human logging along the Fraser River

In early journals the HBC men tell of eating sturgeon and salmon from the river, and of First Nations people arriving by canoe to trade. This river was survival for this first settlement.

The hike begins at Edgewater Bar, just around the river bend from the original Fort Langley. A large picnicking and camping area is the focus of summertime vacations and fall salmon fishing. An underwater bar forces returning salmon to swim close to the riverbanks—within casting distance of the park. Skirt the action by following

Edge Trail through the woods, admiring the 2.0-meter (6.6-foot)-thick black cottonwoods.

When fur traders were clearing land for the 1827 outpost, the men set fires to burn debris from felled trees. Occasionally the fires got out of control and one in particular "raged with so much violence," writes George Barnston in the fort's daily journal. Three days on, he writes poetically of the blaze's extinction: "Our most dreaded foe has sunk to rest."

James Houston (who farmed this area after an eventful life that included being captured by Maori in New Zealand and being shipwrecked on the Mexican coast) is said to have started the Cariboo Gold Rush in 1857. While near Fort Kamloops, Houston found gold panning Tranquille Creek.

At the east end of the campground, the woodland trail merges with riverside Edge Farm Trail. Gnarled apple trees and Edge Farm barn are remnants of the Edge family farm—first established in 1875. There may be log booms—containing swaths of floating, felled trees—along the river. Watch for any beaver activity too. They are also local lumberjacks.

At the end of the riverfront walk, you reach a stone monument that commemorates the original Fort Langley. James McMillan was in charge of the fort, which was

In summer, Fort Langley National Historic Site has a working-farm feel.

BACK TO THE FUR TRADING POST

Fort Langley National Historic Site sits 4.0 kilometers (2.5 miles) upriver from its original site. Hudson's Bay Company moved their outpost in 1839, signifying a shift in the main purpose: from fur trade to farming and fishing.

Today the 1839 Fort Langley operates as a national historic site. It's one of Parks Canada's flagship attractions, where costumed interpreters wander the grounds in summer giving barrel-making workshops, demonstrating blacksmith techniques, or tending to the farm animals.

One building is still an original—the 1840s storehouse shows off a wide collection of animal furs and pelts. Its musty wooden floors and the oily scent of animal fur certainly create an authentically historical atmosphere.

The national historic site opens year-round, but the guides aren't on-site during winter months.

Fort Langley National Historic Site, 23433 Mavis Ave., Fort Langley; (604) 513-4777; pc.gc.ca/langley

Watch for special messages along many hikes near Vancouver.

Mount Baker is in view of the Fraser River.

established here in 1827. It marked the start of a great change in the lives of local First Nations, who traditionally descended on the Fraser in the fall to fish for salmon.

The gravel Fort-to-Fort Trail continues southeast to Fort Langley, but across Allard Crescent you find another section of park trails. A parking lot and heritage farm buildings surround the trailhead, and one woodland route heads off to make a loop through a lush forest of broadleaf maples, ferns, and blackberry bushes. The trail also passes the eastern edge of Langley Bog on the way.

Either fork takes you around Houston Trail as it loops the immediate area's only hill. There are steep but short-lived sections to the gravel trail. From the end of the loop, the route returns along the river and you walk with the water's flow back to Edgewater Bar.

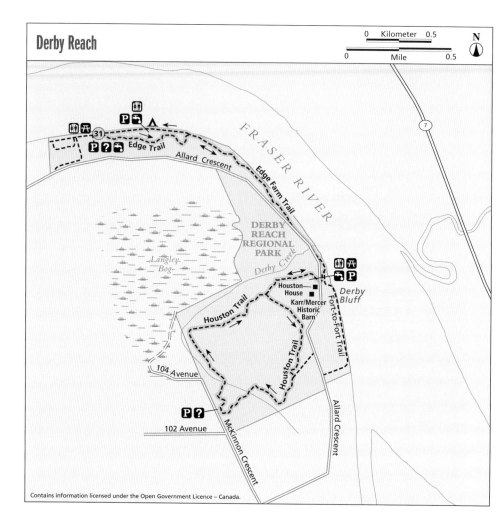

Derby Reach

0 — Kilometer — 0.5
0 — Mile — 0.5
N

FRASER RIVER

Edge Trail
Allard Crescent
Edge Farm Trail

DERBY REACH REGIONAL PARK
Langley Bog
Derby Creek
Houston House
Karr/Mercer Historic Barn
Derby Bluff
Houston Trail
Fort-to-Fort Trail
104 Avenue
Houston Trail
102 Avenue
McKinnon Crescent
Allard Crescent

Contains information licensed under the Open Government Licence – Canada.

Distances and Directions

0.0 km/0.0 mile Start from Derby Reach Regional Park campground registration, near the Edgewater Bar parking lot.

0.1 km/0.1 mile Follow Edge Trail southeast into the woods, as it cuts behind the riverside campground. (This route was one way in 2020 due to COVID-19.)

0.5 km/0.3 mile Pass a campground parking lot.

1.0 km/0.6 mile Reach the end of the campground road and continue right (southeast) along Edge Farm Trail.

1.5 km/0.9 mile Pass through a historic apple orchard and the original site of the Edge family farm. Over the next kilometer (0.6 mile), a number of short spur trails lead down onto the steep riverbanks.

2.5 km/1.6 miles Stop at the Fort Langley historic marker—the main reminder of the BC coast's first European settlement.

2.6 km/1.6 miles Carefully cross Allard Crescent and pass the historic 1909 Houston house and the 1876 Karr/Mercer barn.

2.7 km/1.7 miles When facing the house, head right (north and then west) to follow Houston Trail into the woods.

3.2 km/2.0 miles Take either the left (east) or right (west) fork to start the woodland loop.

6.3 km/3.9 miles Finish the loop and head back northeast toward the heritage farm buildings.

7.0 km/4.3 miles Cross back over Allard Crescent and turn left (northwest) to retrace your steps along the Fraser River. The Fort-to-Fort Trail continues right (southeast) to the Village of Fort Langley.

8.6 km/5.3 miles Continue straight (west) along the campground road and look for salmon anglers. The left trail is your earlier route, the forested Edge Trail.

9.3 km/5.8 miles Arrive back at the trailhead.

Options: If you have a bicycle, consider following the Fort-to-Fort Trail along its 6.0-kilometer (3.7-mile) length—from Derby Reach to Fort Langley. Double the distance to account for the return journey.

Hike Information

Local Information: For information on attractions and dining in the Village of Fort Langley, contact the local tourism board. Tourism Langley, Unit 220, 5385 216 St., Langley; (604) 371-1477; tourism-langley.ca.

Local Attractions: Langley and the Fraser Valley are well known for fertile soils and abundant local produce, which ranges from juicy berries to bright pumpkins. You can find a sampling of the best local goodies at the Fort Langley Village Farmers' Market, held on Saturdays from May to October. 9025 Glover Rd., Fort Langley; fortlangley villagefarmersmarket.org.

Camping: Nearby Brae Island Regional Park has a campground with tent and RV sites. And there's also a lovely 2.1-kilometer (1.3-mile) river walk to Tavistock Point. Fort Camping, 9451 Glover Rd., Fort Langley; (604) 888-3678 or (866) 267-3678; fortcamping.com.

32 UBC Malcolm Knapp Research Forest

University students and researchers study the growth and harvesting of trees in this large research forest north of Maple Ridge. Though trucks and gravel roads can jolt you out of the wilderness, the trails mostly offer a quiet amble along streams, through dense woodlands, and to a viewpoint over the Fraser Valley.

Start: Research forest office
Distance: 7.7-km (4.8-mile) loop
Elevation gain: 180 meters (591 feet)
Hiking time: 2–2.5 hours
Difficulty: Moderate due to limited elevation gain and an at-times rocky trail
Trail surface: Forested trail, gravel road, paved path
Best season: Feb–Nov
Other trail users: Forestry researchers
Canine compatibility: Dogs not permitted
Land status: University-managed research forest
Fees and permits: No fees or permits required
Schedule: Daily 8 a.m. to 4 p.m. (reduced hours due to COVID-19)
Maps: Maps are available online at mkrf .forestry.ubc.ca. Government topographic maps include the GeoBC Topographic Map Viewer (gov.bc.ca), as well as map 92G7 in the Atlas of Canada Toporama tool (atlas.gc.ca).
Trail contacts: UBC Malcolm Knapp Research Forest, 14500 Silver Valley Rd., Maple Ridge; (604) 463-8148; mkrf.forestry.ubc.ca
Special considerations: In some ways, the research forest is a working forestry operation. That means heavy machinery and trucks could be on the move and this route occasionally crosses forestry roads. Keep to the road shoulders at all times and be aware of approaching vehicles. Step off to the side when you do hear one. Your lungs will thank you too for avoiding some of the gravel-road dust. Cougars have also been spotted in the research forest—be sure to travel in groups and keep children close by.

Finding the trailhead: From Lougheed Highway (Highway 7), travel east across Pitt River Bridge to Pitt Meadows. Turn left (northeast) onto Golden Ears Way and the Abernethy Connector. Continue northeast as the road becomes 128 Avenue. About 4 kilometers (2.5 miles) from Lougheed, make a left (north) on 216 Street. Cross the Alouette River and make the next right (east) onto 132 Avenue. Continue for 3 kilometers (1.9 miles) before turning left (north) onto 232 Street. After 1.0 kilometer (0.6 mile) turn right (northeast) onto Silver Valley Road, driving for about 1.5 kilometer (0.9 mile) to the research forest parking lot. Trailhead GPS: N49 15.85' / W122 34.39'

The Hike

Forestry is big business in British Columbia, where about two thirds of the province is cloaked in an evergreen canopy. But harvesting, planting, and managing trees takes delicate expertise—something the University of British Columbia Faculty of Forestry specializes in.

The university manages this 5,157-hectare (12,743-acre) forest, which extends from Pitt Lake in the west to Golden Ears Provincial Park in the east. The landscape's tangle of gravel logging roads is a testament to its history. A fire altered much of the forest's western region in 1868, but loggers still used steam donkeys to haul trees from the deep woods at the turn of the 20th century. Then, a month-long fire in 1931 forced the logging company, Abernethy and Lougheed, to abandon the area. UBC stepped in to manage the area in 1943.

This hike starts from the research forest office, where you can view a map and ask any questions if the office is open to visitors. Trails are well flagged with colored markers. Routings are simply color-coded as blue, yellow, red, or green. This route follows the blue trail, though close to the office it traces the same ground as the red and yellow trails.

Within 0.5 kilometer (0.3 mile) of the research office, the blue trail branches left (northwest) to amble through second-growth forest and over a creek. At G Road you start to get a sense of the forestry operation. The trail cuts through logged and

A small log shelter is a shaded rest point along the Blue Trail.

replanted areas. Since 1987, forestry companies have had to re-plant any and all land that's cut in British Columbia.

As the trail makes twisting turns to gain elevation, so does G Road. You cross the gravel road seven times before heading back in the woods. Once you cross M Road, Blue Trail gets narrower and a touch less well maintained. This section also provides a testing climb to the peak of a small hill that overlooks agricultural lands around Maple Ridge.

Retracing your steps down the hill to Blue Trail, continue east along the hillside route. Some large older-growth trees in this area have escaped fires and axes to shade the trail today.

Three more road crossings (F, A10, and A10 again) bring you to the hike's close. Map in hand, you can choose any route to return to the research office although some trails are more overgrown than others. All lead to the picnic area, where a black-painted steam donkey stands quiet—now replaced by diesel-powered engines.

These steam-powered machines date to the late 1800s, when the machines' winches and wire cables replaced oxen and horse teams in logging operations. They changed the way crews logged BC's forests. And with this history in mind, look around: forestry's future could be in the land surrounding you.

Distances and Directions

0.0 km/0.0 mile Start from the research forest office, following the paved trail west. Within 200 meters (650 feet) you cross a gravel road.

0.4 km/0.2 mile Cross another gravel road and continue straight (west).

0.5 km/0.3 mile Branch left (northwest) leaving the Red and Yellow Trail to follow the Blue Trail.

0.7 km/0.4 mile Head right (north) on the trail as it meets an old road near a clearing and partially obstructed viewpoint.

1.4 km/0.9 mile Cross G Road—the first of seven times. On the seventh crossing, the Blue Trail continues north just to the left of a large information board.

3.3 km/2.1 miles Reach M Road, cross the roadway, and continue on the Blue Trail to the left.

3.6 km/2.2 miles Turn left (north) to start the climb up the steep hill to a viewpoint and log cabin. You'll return to this junction later.

3.8 km/2.4 miles Cross C Road and continue uphill slightly to the right (east).

4.3 km/2.7 miles Reach the viewpoint and look inside the log cabin.

4.9 km/3.0 miles Walk back downhill, cross C Road, and follow the Blue Trail to the familiar junction. This time turn left (southeast).

5.2 km/3.2 miles Cross C Road.

5.4 km/3.4 miles Take the bridge over a stream. The trail follows the stream and then switchbacks up along a rockface.

6.0 km/3.7 miles Cross F Road.

6.2 km/3.9 miles Cross A10 Road.

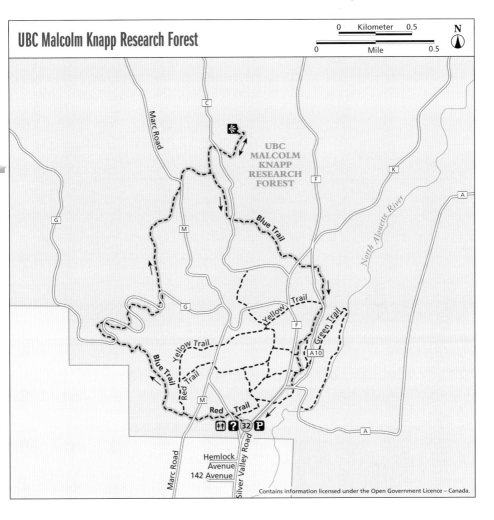

0   Kilometer   0.5

0   Mile   0.5

N

UBC
MALCOLM
KNAPP
RESEARCH
FOREST

Contains information licensed under the Open Government Licence – Canada.

6.4 km/4.0 miles Meet up with a road that's part of Yellow Trail. Head left (south) as another trail heads right. Watch for and follow blue markers.

6.5 km/4.0 miles After a small pond, turn right (southwest) on the trail marked with both Yellow and Blue.

6.8 km/4.2 miles Continue straight on the Yellow Trail as short connectors feed into this main route.

6.9 km/4.3 miles Bear left (south) at the Green Trail, which ends at A10 Road.

7.2 km/4.5 miles Follow F Road back to the research office and pass the historic steam donkey, a technology that's more than a century old.

7.7 km/4.8 miles Arrive back at the trailhead.

Options: The trails at UBC Malcolm Knapp Research Forest are handily color-coded. Red offers the shortest loop, Yellow a little longer, and Green routes along the Alouette River. Mix and match to explore shorter or longer options.

Pit toilets aren't always a delight—but this one's especially cute.

Hike Information

Local Attractions: The Loon Lake Research & Education Centre is not accessible to the general public, but for small groups it offers ropes courses, trails, and a dock on the quiet lake. 14500 Silver Valley Rd., Maple Ridge; (604) 463-8148; loonlake .ubc.ca.

GREEN TIP

On the trail eat grains and veggies instead of meat, which has a higher energy cost.

33 Minnekhada High Knoll Loop

A woodland loop trail climbs above the wetlands of Minnekhada Regional Park to the rocky prominence of High Knoll. It's a tranquil slice of parkland tucked between a quarry and Addington Point on the banks of Pitt River. While Minnekhada is definitely a local favorite for Tri-Cities residents, it's much less known in Vancouver.

Start: Quarry Road parking lot
Distance: 7.1-km (4.4-mile) loop
Elevation gain: 165 meters (541 feet)
Hiking time: 1.5-2 hours
Difficulty: Easy due to rolling forest and fairly flat gravel trails with a moderate climb to the High Knoll viewpoint
Trail surface: Gravel, forested trail
Best season: Year-round
Other trail users: Dog-walkers
Canine compatibility: Leashed dogs permitted
Land status: Regional park
Fees and permits: No fees or permits required
Schedule: Daylight hours

Maps: An official park map is available online through Metro Vancouver (metrovancouver.org), and paper copies are available at the trailhead. Government topographic maps include the GeoBC Topographic Map Viewer (gov.bc.ca), as well as map 92G7 in the Atlas of Canada Toporama tool (atlas.gc.ca).
Trail contacts: Metro Vancouver Regional Parks Central Area Office, 9146 Avalon Ave., Burnaby, V3N 4G8; (604) 520-6442; metro vancouver.org
Special considerations: Note that there is no water available at the Quarry Road trailhead or Minnekhada Lodge.

Finding the trailhead: From the Trans-Canada Highway (Highway 1), take exit 44 and follow signs for Highway 7B, also known as Mary Hill Bypass. Follow the bypass for 5 kilometers (3.1 miles), and then turn left (north) onto Broadway Street. Continue straight and cross the overpass above the large Canadian Pacific Railway yard. At Lougheed Highway (Highway 7), the street becomes Coast Meridian Road. Beyond the railyards, drive straight for nearly 3 kilometers (1.9 miles). Then turn right (east) onto Victoria Drive. Continue for 1.3 kilometers (0.8 mile) and make another left (northeast) to stay on Victoria Drive. Follow the road as it becomes Quarry Road and edges the park. Trailhead GPS: N49 18.00' / W122 42.43'

The Hike

In some places, the past seems to hide under moss and fallen leaves. Minnekhada Regional Park is one of those places as the quiet, present-day park doesn't hint at the lavish country estate and working farm that was once a polo club and a draw for celebrities, politicos, and royals in the 1930s and 1940s.

In 1895 the farm began as a simple 65-hectare (160-acre) tract under George Alderson. A change of ownership later, the land was in the hands of Harry Leroy Jenkins, a lumberman from Minnesota. Buying the farm in 1912,

The name Minnekhada means "rattling water" in the Sioux language. A Minnesota lumberman christened the farm with the moniker in 1912.

207

Knolls, marshes, and woodlands provide diverse scenery in Minnekhada.

Jenkins gave the property the name Minnekhada and increased the land holding tenfold. The farm changed owners many more times through to 1932, when Eric Hamber took ownership. The 1930s saw a succession of improvements at the working farm, the pinnacle of which was the addition of Hamber's lavish country house, completed in 1937.

Hamber was an avid polo player and hosted matches on the farm. Over the decades, some of the many famous guests at Minnekhada have included the Canadian governor general Lord Tweedsmuir, British actress Gracie Fields, and Governor General Earl of Athlone and his wife, Princess Alice. It's even rumored that Princess Elizabeth—later to become Queen Elizabeth II—stayed at the estate.

Today, Minnekhada Lodge stands as the sole testament to that era. But given how tucked away the property feels, it would be near impossible to guess.

This hike begins near the currently-closed-off Minnekhada Farm, and explores cedar forest that feels secluded and deliciously lush. In autumn, richly varied mushrooms line the trail and sprout from decaying logs. In summer, watch for western toadlets on the trail as the minute amphibians move from marsh to forest.

In any season, the lookout at High Knoll is the trip highlight. The view looks down on Pitt River from about 170 meters (558 feet) up. If you are facing south, a

Minnekhada Lodge is a historic gem on the fringes of wilderness.

sunny day pays out double rewards as you picnic on the solar-warmed rocks, and even on gray days, the scene takes in an interesting mix of bird habitats, Pitt River, and low-lying Goose Bar amid the flow.

But the historic lodge built by Hamber comes a close second in reasons to visit.

To see the grand lodge, walk away from the marsh on a paved road. The city-owned heritage building is not generally open to the public, but occasional events do open the historic doors. Open or closed, the elegant façade and pretty gardens are worth the trip.

Finally, return to the edge of Minnekhada Marsh where waterfowl dot the surface and savor the quiet.

Watch for western toadlets on the trail—in summer they move from marsh to forest.

Distances and Directions

0.0 km/0.0 mile Start out from the Quarry Road parking lot and follow the main trail northeast into the forest.

0.1 km/0.1 mile Keep left (northeast) on Meadow Trail, as Lodge Trail branches off right.

0.2 km/0.1 mile Again, keep left (northeast) on the main trail as Meadow Trail branches right (east).

0.4 km/0.2 mile Continue straight (northeast) at the third junction. Here, you follow Quarry Trail as Log Walk heads right (southeast).

1.2 km/0.7 mile Bear right (east) on Quarry Trail as a spur heads left to connect with Quarry Road.

2.2 km/1.4 miles Take the left turn (south) to High Knoll, climbing the steep 500 meter trail to the rocky outlook.

2.7 km/1.7 miles Pause on High Knoll, about 170 meters (558 feet) up. The smooth rock ledges are suited to a picnic, and since the lookout faces south, it catches the full sun on a clear-sky day.

3.2 km/2.0 miles Return down the High Knoll Trail, and then turn left (west) toward the marshes and Low Knoll.

3.7 km/2.3 miles Keep left (south) toward Low Knoll and Addington Lookout. Mid-Marsh Trail to the right cuts between the upper and lower sections of Minnekhada Marsh and offers a shorter route back to Quarry Road.

Lower Marsh, pictured, is home to many species, including coastal painted turtles, sandhill cranes, and western toadlets, among others.

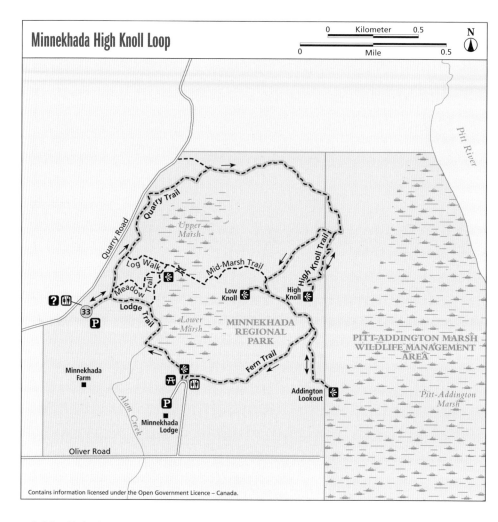

Contains information licensed under the Open Government Licence – Canada.

3.8 km/2.4 miles A spur trail cuts right (west) to Low Knoll. Not as spectacular as High Knoll, this lookout faces west and overlooks Lower Marsh.

4.1 km/2.5 miles Return from Low Knoll and pick up the main trail. Continue right (southeast).

4.4 km/2.7 miles Head left (south) on the 0.5-kilometer (0.3-mile) trail to Addington Lookout.

4.8 km/3.0 miles Peeking out between trees, this lookout point catches snapshots of Addington Point, Pitt River, and raised dike trails—a favorite for bike rides without any elevation gain.

5.3 km/3.3 miles Return from Addington Lookout and head left (southwest) on Fern Trail.

6.1 km/3.8 miles Reach the picnic area. To the left is a paved road that heads south to Minnekhada Lodge and an alternate trailhead. The heritage country-club-style lodge is a 5-minute uphill stroll (southwest) along the single-lane roadway. Back at the main trail, there is a viewing platform alongside Lower Marsh. From this picnic area, Lodge Trail heads right (northwest) to complete the loop back to Quarry Road.

The viewpoint on High Knoll delivers wide views south over Pitt River.

6.5 km/4.0 miles A bridge and a dike trail cut across the wetlands.

6.7 km/4.2 miles Keep left (west) at two trail junctions (200 meters [0.1 mile] apart) to return to the parking lot.

7.1 km/4.4 miles Arrive back at the trailhead.

Options: To shorten the hike, return to Quarry Road via Mid-Marsh Trail. This route cuts between the upper and lower sections of Minnekhada Marsh. If you're taking this option (and picking between the upper and lower half-loops), the upper loop includes High Knoll with its steeper climb and a bigger payoff, while the lower Addington Lookout loop has less impressive views, less elevation gain, and passes Minnekhada Lodge.

Hike Information

Organizations: Minnekhada Park Association advocates for Minnekhada Regional Park. For details about current events, see minnekhada.ca.

34 Katzie Marsh Loop

Wetlands and dike trails create an active environment alongside tidal Pitt Lake. In spring, find Canada geese goslings, bright purple lupines, and slowly ripening thimbleberries along the quiet trails that encircle Katzie Marsh. Bird-watchers especially love the area for the more than 200 species of birds including herons, eagles, and tundra swans. Viewing towers allow even children to get a good view over the landscape.

Start: Grant Narrows parking lot
Distance: 6.5-km (4.0-mile) loop
Hiking time: 1.5–2 hours
Difficulty: Easy due to completely flat trails and short distance
Trail surface: Gravel, dirt path
Best season: Year-round
Other trail users: Cyclists, dog-walkers, bird-watchers
Canine compatibility: Leashed dogs permitted
Land status: Wildlife management area
Fees and permits: No fees or permits required

Schedule: Daylight hours
Maps: Information signs display a trail map near the parking lot. Government topographic maps include the GeoBC Topographic Map Viewer (gov.bc.ca), as well as map 92G7 in the Atlas of Canada Toporama tool (atlas.gc.ca).
Trail contacts: Ministry of Environment, Regional Headquarters; (604) 582-5200; gov .bc.ca/gov/content/environment
Special considerations: There is no water available at Pitt Lake.

Finding the trailhead: From the Trans-Canada Highway (Highway 1), take exit 44. Follow signs for Highway 7B, also known as Mary Hill Bypass. Follow the bypass for 7.0 kilometers (4.3 miles), and then keep right (southeast) onto Lougheed Highway (Highway 7 East). Cross the river on Pitt River Bridge and turn left (northeast) at the lights onto Old Dewdney Trunk Road. About 2.0 kilometers (1.2 miles) on, turn left (north) onto Harris Road and drive for 3.0 kilometers (1.9 miles). Make a right (east) onto McNeil Road, following it through farmlands for about 4.0 kilometers (2.5 miles). At Rannie Road, turn left (north) and follow the long, straight farm road past Pitt Polder Ecological Reserve. Rannie Road ends at Grant Narrows and Pitt Lake. Trailhead GPS: N49 20.95' / W122 36.89'

The Hike

Each day, tidal salt waters work their way up from the Strait of Georgia, along the Fraser River, up Pitt River, and into Pitt Lake. It's a funny thought: a river essentially flowing backward. But the action makes 24-kilometer-long (15-mile-long) Pitt Lake the world's largest tidal freshwater lake. It also creates an unfortunate challenge for unaware boaters, some of whom get stranded in shallow areas as the water level drops with the tides.

This hike over the flat dike trails escapes from the weekend-frenzy of Grant Narrows parking lot, where trucks and trailers line up to launch powerboats. Start along the lakeshore, head east with the lake to your left and stop at the first viewing tower to climb the stairs and look out over the landscape. To the north lies Pitt Lake, its blue surface dotted with ducks, boats, and the occasional kayak. To the west of the lake lies Pinecone Burke Provincial Park. Malcolm Knapp Research Forest and Golden Ears Provincial Park are to the east.

To the north this terrain is an impenetrable barrier with no roads or communities. A look south reveals a different landscape still. Over Katzie and Pitt Marshes a network of canals and shrub-covered dikes create an almost country-estate feel. The Pitt Polder area was first diked and drained in the 1870s, when Dutch immigrants expanded the natural system to prevent flooding and gain farmland.

Back on the Pitt Lake shore, continue along the lakefront road. Near the end of the road, a private sign dissuades you from exploring farther, so head southwest along the only dike trail. Watch in the tall grasses and reeds for Canada geese, blue-winged teal ducks, and mallard ducks. Among the greenery, bright patches of lupines and tall columbines are a fresh sight in spring. One warm summer evening, I saw swarms of dragonflies dancing to catch insects here.

Sandhill cranes nest in these marshlands; it's one of only a handful of nesting sites in the Lower Mainland. The lanky cranes resemble herons but are gray with a red patch on their foreheads. The birds are large, standing over a meter [3.3 feet] tall, and build massive nests (up to 1.5 meters [5.0 feet] across). When it's nesting season, from spring to midsummer, wildlife managers close certain areas of the marshlands to give the birds space.

Winter is the best season to spot waterfowl. Trumpeter swans, northern pintails, and American wigeons appear in the colder months.

Viewing towers provide a higher vantage over the dike trails.

A warm summer evening may bring swarms of dragonflies.

Keeping right at all trail intersections provides a reasonably short triangular–shaped loop with lots of time and space for bird-watching. Nature Dike Trail, which returns to the parking lot from the second viewing tower, is a narrow thread through lush vegetation. Look for thimbleberries, a large white flower in spring that turns into a fragile, seedy berry in summer—but leave the spoils for the birds.

GREEN TIP
Go out of your way to avoid birds and animals that
are mating or taking care of their young.

Katzie Marsh Loop

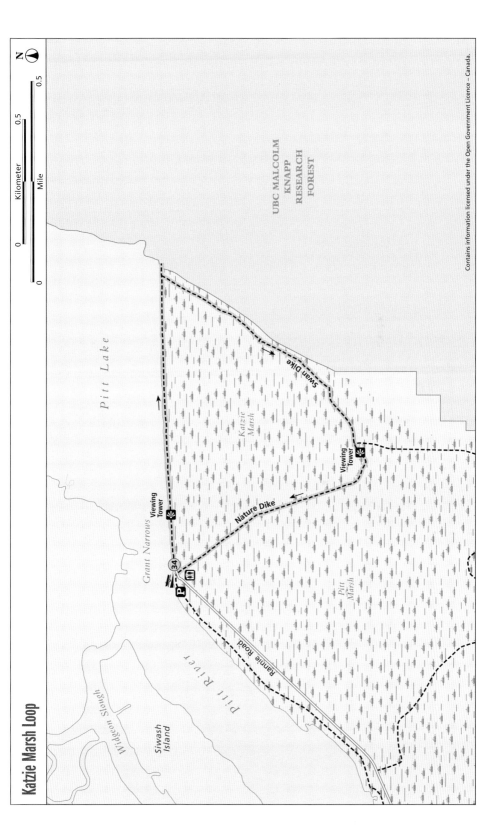

Pitt Lake

UBC MALCOLM
KNAPP
RESEARCH
FOREST

Katzie
Marsh

Swan Dike

Viewing
Tower

Grant Narrows

Viewing
Tower

Nature Dike

34

P

Pitt
Marsh

Rannie Road

Pitt River

Widgeon Slough

Siwash
Island

Kilometer

Mile

N

LEGEND OF THE LOST CREEK MINE

In the late 1880s, when fortunes were made and lost in British Columbia's gold fields, a man named Slumach would arrive in New Westminster laden with gold nuggets. He'd drink and spend the spoils, but never tell the secret location of his gold source. People tried to follow his trail as he headed back into the mountains, but to no avail.

In 1890 Slumach shot a man near Pitt River. The gold miner escaped without being caught, though the wilderness slowly took its toll and Slumach returned to civilization in rough shape. He was hanged for the murder in New Westminster, taking the unknown location of his gold mine to his grave.

People still remember the legend of Slumach's gold, and newspapers even sent reporters searching for it in the 1950s. But the gold has never been found. Still, that doesn't stop people from searching for it to this day.

Distances and Directions

0.0 km/0.0 mile Start from the Grant Narrows parking lot. Follow the lakefront road straight (east) along the shore, keeping the lake to your left.

0.4 km/0.2 mile Reach the first covered viewing tower.

2.3 km/1.4 miles Turn right (southwest) onto Swan Dike Trail and venture through Katzie Marsh.

4.0 km/2.5 miles Keep right (west) as the route meets with a spur trail that heads left (east) to a dead-end.

4.5 km/2.8 miles Again, keep right (southwest) at a dike trail.

4.6 km/2.9 miles Climb the second viewing tower.

4.7 km/2.9 miles Head northwest from the viewing tower and return to the parking lot along Nature Dike Trail.

6.0 km/3.7 miles Sadly one of the COVID-19 impacts—closing the pit toilets near the parking lot—had turned this final section of the trail into a bathroom in 2020. I hope, for your sake, the situation has improved!

6.5 km/4.0 miles Arrive back at the trailhead.

Option: Easy sightlines, few intersecting trails, and flat terrain make it ideal to explore farther on these dike trails. To double the length of your walk, take a left (south) just before the second viewing tower. Continue for about 1.5 kilometers (0.9 mile) before turning right (west) onto a dike trail. Make the next right (northwest) onto Crane Dike, which connects with Rannie Road. For a pleasant route back to the parking lot, cross the road and follow the river trail northeast.

Hike Information

Local Information: Check tides with Fisheries and Oceans before boating. tides.gc .ca/eng/find/zone/10.

35 Widgeon Falls

A canoe paddle through a low-lying slough followed by a short hike makes the perfect summer weekend day trip. Lace your way through Widgeon Slough, leave the canoe on a sandy beach, and make the easy walk through the woods to powerful Widgeon Falls. As the creek tumbles over a rocky drop, it creates a refreshing rainbow of spray and a stunning view.

Start: Grant Narrows parking lot

Distance: 6.1-km (3.8-mile) lollipop, plus a 9.4-km (5.8-mile) out-and-bank canoe paddle

Trip time: About 4–5 hours

Difficulty: Easy due to flat but sometimes undulating forest trails with a moderate canoe paddle through Widgeon Slough

Trail surface: Gravel road, forested trail, stairs

Best season: Year-round

Other trail users: Powerboats, kayakers, dog-walkers

Canine compatibility: Leashed dogs permitted

Land status: Provincial park, national wildlife area

Fees and permits: Canoe rental, but no other fees or permits required

Schedule: Daylight hours

Maps: Information signs display a trail map near the parking lot. Check with the City of Pitt Meadows for more information, available online at pittmeadows.ca. Government topographic maps include the GeoBC Topographic Map Viewer (gov.bc.ca), as well as map 92G7 in the Atlas of Canada Toporama tool (atlas.gc.ca).

Trail contacts: Pinecone Burke Provincial Park, bcparks.ca; or Canadian Wildlife Service, Environment and Climate Change Canada, 5421 Robertson Rd., Delta, (800) 668-6767, ec.gc.ca

Special considerations: You need a canoe or kayak to cross Grant Narrows and reach the trailhead. Though it was closed in 2020, contact Pitt Lake Canoe Rentals at (604) 836-7117 for rental availability and reservations. The logistics are trickier, but Deer Lake Boat Rentals has good rates for offsite rentals as well as transportation kits—contact them at (604) 521-3183 or deerlakeboatrentals.com. Note that there is no water available at the Grant Narrows parking lot or at the campground trailhead.

Finding the trailhead: From the Trans-Canada Highway (Highway 1), take exit 44. Follow signs for Highway 7B, also known as Mary Hill Bypass. Follow the bypass for 7.0 kilometers (4.3 miles), and then keep right (southeast) onto Lougheed Highway (Highway 7 East). Cross the river on Pitt River Bridge and turn left (northeast) at the lights onto Old Dewdney Trunk Road. About 2.0 kilometers (1.2 miles) on, turn left (north) onto Harris Road and drive for 3.0 kilometers (1.9 miles). Make a right (east) onto McNeil Road, following it through farmlands for about 4.0 kilometers (2.5 miles). At Rannie Road, turn left (north) and follow the long, straight farm road past Pitt Polder Ecological Reserve. Rannie Road ends at Grant Narrows and Pitt Lake. Trailhead GPS: N49 20.95' / W122 36.98'

Powerful Widgeon Falls eventually flows into the calm waters of Widgeon Slough.

The Hike

Paddling canoes, hiking to waterfalls—you can't get more picturesquely Canadian than this. And yet Widgeon Falls and the approach through the snaking slough are fairly unvisited, especially when comparing numbers with the lineup of trucks and motorboats that launch into Pitt Lake on summer weekends.

Via canoe, kayak, or stand-up paddleboard, depart from the dock at the south end of Pitt Lake. This tidal freshwater lake is the largest of its kind in the world. As the tide comes in, the lake level rises, and as the tide falls so does the lake level. See if you notice a difference between the paddle in and the paddle out.

Cross Pitt Lake at Grant Narrows, the bottleneck between the lake and Pitt River. On the far shore, the canoe route passes between Siwash Island to the left and the mainland to the right. Keep right and head north into Widgeon Slough. This area is protected as Widgeon Valley National Wildlife Area and no powerboats are permitted in these waters, only those under oar or paddle power. The scenery is spectacular both under and above the water. Shelves of plant matter lie below the surface; grasses and mountain rise above. The wetlands are important habitat for migratory birds and waterfowl. Look for mallards, wood ducks, and Canada geese year-round. In spring, there are cinnamon teals and northern pintails in the area. Pied-billed grebes frequent the area in spring and summer. You may also spot sandhill cranes fishing in the slough waters; the lanky cranes resemble herons but are gray with a red patch on their foreheads and stand over a meter [3.3 feet] tall.

As the creek bends in the final approach to the beach, the water flow may intensify. In spring, you'll need all hands on the paddles to reach the sandy beach while in late summer it's an easy arrival. This midpoint has a small campground, pit toilets, and the hiking trailhead. Rest and relax, or step right onto the hiking trail. An old gravel road leads north, making a gentle ascent. At a fork, opt for the forest trail that winds through the woods to touch the banks of Widgeon Creek. In some stretches the bridges on this trail may be in rough shape so take careful, slow steps.

The trail pops out at the large, rushing waterfall where the fast waters have worn many smooth paths through the rock. The spray is refreshing after the paddle and hike. Bask on the smooth rocks and picnic, and then return to the campground via the gravel road. It's a more leisurely paddle back to Pitt Lake—this time with the river's flow.

Paddlers explore the many channels of Widgeon Slough.

The spring freshet is an impressive sight at Widgeon Falls.

Widgeon Falls

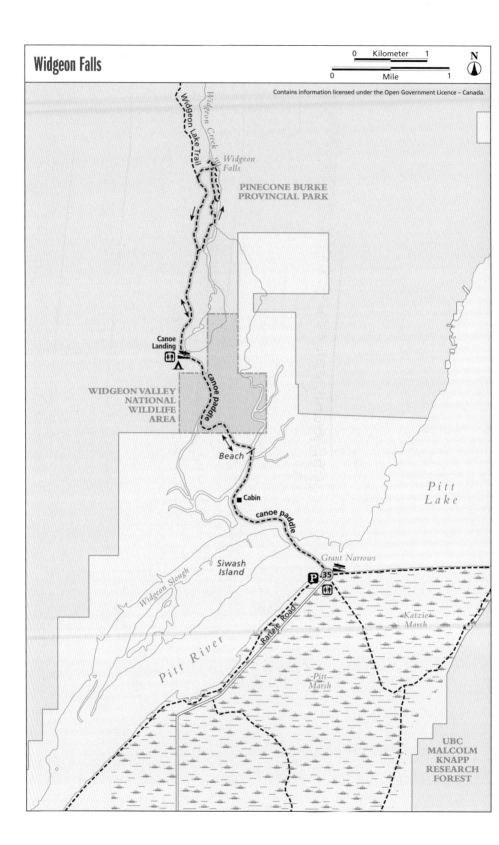

Contains information licensed under the Open Government Licence – Canada.

Widgeon Lake Trail

Widgeon Creek

Widgeon Falls

PINECONE BURKE
PROVINCIAL PARK

Canoe
Landing

canoe paddle

WIDGEON VALLEY
NATIONAL
WILDLIFE
AREA

Beach

Cabin

Pitt
Lake

canoe paddle

Siwash
Island

Grant Narrows

Widgeon Slough

P 35

Rannie Road

Katzie
Marsh

Pitt River

Pitt
Marsh

UBC
MALCOLM
KNAPP
RESEARCH
FOREST

Canoeing Distances and Directions

0.0 km/0.0 mile   Start from the Pitt Lake dock, and paddle northwest across Grant Narrows.

0.7 km/0.4 mile   Near the far shore, head straight (northwest) to slip between low-lying Siwash Island and the forested mainland.

1.9 km/1.2 miles   A small cabin in disrepair sits on the east bank.

2.6 km/1.6 miles   Bear left (northwest) at a beach.

3.5 km/2.2 miles   Round a sharp bend and paddle up Widgeon Creek.

4.7 km/2.9 miles   Dock on the beach at Widgeon Creek Campground.

Note: As you're paddling against the flow of Widgeon Creek, take solace that the return journey is an easier paddle.

Distances and Directions

0.0 km/0/0 mile   Start from the campground beach.

0.1 km/0.1 mile   Stop for a bathroom break at the pit toilets. Then, when facing the toilets, turn right (northeast) onto the gravel road.

1.5 km/0.9 mile   At a junction, make a right (northeast) and follow the forest trail.

2.0 km/1.2 miles   Reach a clearing alongside Widgeon Creek.

2.3 km/1.4 miles   Keep left (north), following the trail markers, when the faint old trail heads right.

2.9 km/1.8 miles   At a trail junction, head right (northeast) to Widgeon Falls.

3.1 km/1.9 miles   Reach the main falls. Explore, rest, and then start to retrace your route.

3.3 km/2.1 miles   On the return journey, keep straight (southwest) at the first trail junction, taking a different route back to the campground.

3.6 km/2.2 miles   Turn left (south) to follow the gravel road back toward the campground. The right (north) trail leads to Widgeon Lake. (*Side-trip:* Plan to return with camping gear and make the hike into Widgeon Lake. The lake is about 16 kilometers [10 miles] round-trip from the campground.)

4.6 km/2.9 miles   Continue straight (south) as the forest trail rejoins the gravel road.

6.1 km/3.8 miles   Arrive back at the campground trailhead.

Hike Information

Local Information: For canoe rentals and paddling directions, contact Pitt Lake Canoe Rentals at (604) 836-7117 to check availability. Alternately, offsite rentals and transportation kits are available from Deer Lake Boat Rentals (5435 Sperling Ave., Burnaby; 604-521-3183; deerlakeboatrentals.com).

GREEN TIP
Donate used gear to a nonprofit kids' organization like Take a Hike Youth at Risk Foundation (takeahikefoundation.org).

36 Gold Creek Falls

Golden Ears Provincial Park has a wilderness feel you find in the national parks in the Rocky Mountains, with its evergreen forests, a wide lake, and a single parkway providing access. After nearly a century of being protected from logging, the park's forest is thick and lush. This very easy hike's end point—thunderous Gold Creek Falls—is a roaring torrent of power and cold water in spring.

Start: Gold Creek parking lot, Golden Ears Provincial Park
Distance: 5.5-km (3.4-mile) out-and-back
Hiking time: 1–1.5 hours
Difficulty: Easy due to gently inclining (but often muddy) forest trails
Trail surface: Forested trail
Best season: Year-round
Other trail users: Dog-walkers
Canine compatibility: Leashed dogs permitted with some off-leash areas
Land status: Provincial park
Fees and permits: In 2020, this route required reserving a day-use pass (discovercamping.ca) due to COVID-19 restrictions.
Schedule: Daylight hours

Maps: An official Golden Ears Provincial Park map is available online at bcparks.ca. Government topographic maps include the GeoBC Topographic Map Viewer (gov.bc.ca), as well as map 92G8 in the Atlas of Canada Toporama tool (atlas.gc.ca).
Trail contacts: Golden Ears Provincial Park; (604) 466-8325; bcparks.ca and alouette parks.ca
Special considerations: Drinking water is only available during camping season. Also, take caution near the falls. Though the pool above the falls is a frequented swimming hole, swimmers have been carried away over the falls and died at higher water levels. It's safest to save the swimming for the calm waters and sandy beaches along Alouette Lake.

Finding the trailhead: From the Trans-Canada Highway (Highway 1), take exit 44. Follow signs for Highway 7B, also known as Mary Hill Bypass. Follow the bypass for 7.0 kilometers (4.3 miles), and then keep right (southeast) on Lougheed Highway (Highway 7 East). Cross over the Pitt River Bridge, continuing on Lougheed Highway for about 9.0 kilometers (5.6 miles). Make a left (north) onto 216 Street. After 3 kilometers (1.9 miles), turn right (east) on 132 Avenue and follow the route past two roundabouts. The road becomes Fern Crescent and then Golden Ears Parkway to lead into the provincial park. Follow signs for Gold Creek Campground. The parking lot is about 13.0 kilometers (8.1 miles) from the park entrance. Trailhead GPS: N49 20.01' / W122 27.46'

The Hike

When the government set aside Garibaldi Provincial Park in 1927, they included the area around Mount Blanshard (also known as Golden Ears) within the vast protected area. But the two peaks (Garibaldi and Blanshard) are more than 60 kilometers (37 miles) apart. The access areas are so vastly different, it would take about 2 hours to drive from one to the other.

So, a few decades on, in 1967, the Golden Ears section became its own provincial park—taking its name from the twin snow-covered peaks of Mount Blanshard. The mountain is a landmark in the Fraser Valley, with special significance to local First Nations who once predicted weather and salmon runs by the mountain's hue.

There is an intense Golden Ears summit route in the park, but this short hike experiences the gentler pace—ambling along the riverbanks of Gold Creek. On a quiet off-season day, when the campgrounds are empty, it feels like meditation in practice.

Leaving the Gold Creek parking lot, head north along Lower Falls Trail. This flat, forest route gives a few hints at its logging past. Much of the valley was logged in the 1920s, and a fire blazed through in 1931. But from the ashes and nearly a century of peace the park seems to have risen again as wilderness. Some of the remaining red cedar stumps are the size of a small car.

About halfway along the route, a beach area sits at a river bend. It's a favorite picnic spot due to the flat sandy area and shallow waters. Take in the mountain views before heading back into the cool, damp, moss-cloaked forest.

Gold Creek is as tranquil as the trail.

Top: A giant stump amid second-growth cedars
Bottom: Gold Creek Falls is a wide, thundering waterfall.

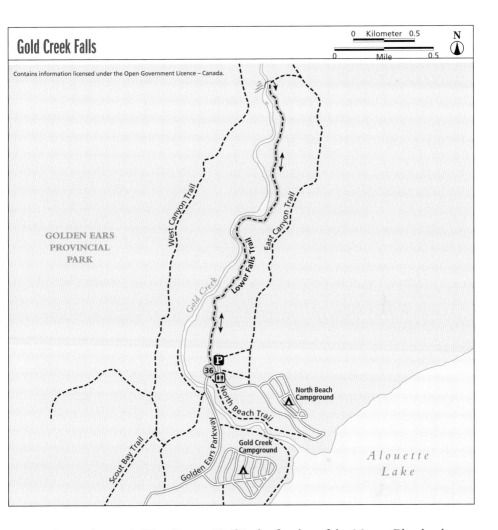

Gold Creek Falls

Contains information licensed under the Open Government Licence – Canada.

0   Kilometer   0.5

0   Mile   0.5

N

West Canyon Trail

East Canyon Trail

GOLDEN EARS
PROVINCIAL
PARK

Gold Creek

Lower Falls Trail

P

36

North Beach Trail

North Beach
Campground

Gold Creek
Campground

Scout Bay Trail

Golden Ears Parkway

Alouette
Lake

Across the creek, West Canyon Trail is the first leg of the Mount Blanshard summit hike. East Canyon Trail runs parallel to this Gold Creek Falls Trail, though the steep connector between the two is tricky to find from the lower trail (it's much clearer when starting out on East Canyon Trail). It's easiest to head out-and-back along the same trail. A bridge connects East and West Canyon Trails about 1 kilometer (0.6 mile) upstream.

How the name Gold Creek came about I don't know. Most tales of Gold Rush fever come from more northern regions, such as the Yukon and Cariboo. Vancouver was one of the staging grounds, where prospectors bought a literal ton of supplies and started the journey north. While there are a few tales of gold finds along Pitt River, stories of Gold Creek's treasures seem to be lost to time.

Though you may be keen to find a nugget yourself, prospecting is illegal in provincial parks. There are a dozen or so recreational panning reserves in the province, including in Cayoosh Creek in Lillooet along the Sea to Sky Highway, in Lytton and Yale along the Fraser River, in Hope just off the Trans-Canada, and in Princeton just east of Manning Provincial Park.

To follow recreational panning guidelines, you must keep the equipment simple (a pan, shovel, and gloves will get you started). More information is available from the Ministry of Energy and Mines (gov.bc.ca).

Distances and Directions

0.0 km/0.0 mile   Start from Gold Creek parking lot.

0.1 km/0.1 mile   Follow Lower Falls Trail north.

1.4 km/0.9 mile   A pebbly, sandy creekside beach marks the halfway point.

2.7 km/1.7 miles Reach the Lower Falls viewing area.

2.8 km/1.7 miles Climb the hill to reach a higher viewing point.

5.5 km/3.4 miles Retrace your route along the same trail and arrive back at the trailhead. (*Side-trip:* Once you reach the parking lot, cross Golden Ears Parkway and follow North Beach Trail southeast down to the shores of Alouette Lake—about 1.2 kilometers [0.7 mile] one way. The trail follows Gold Creek, which has slowed to a saunter at this point. Flat rocks beckon a break, as does the sandy beach on the lakeshore.)

Option: On the west side of Gold Creek, West Canyon Trail leads to a backcountry camping area at Alder Flats. This is a favorite, and fairly easy, trek for a backpacking trip. From Alder Flats, you can make an epic hike to Golden Ears—though you need crampons and mountaineering skills to reach the summit safely. The journey covers 24 kilometers (14.9 miles) round-trip and gains 1,500 meters (4,921 feet) elevation. Though extremely fit hikers complete the route in one very long day, most cover the distance over two.

Hike Information

Local Information: Maple Ridge is quite hidden from Vancouver, tucked between the Fraser River and the peaks of Golden Ears Provincial Park. For information on local attractions, contact Tourism Maple Ridge. 11995 Haney Place, Maple Ridge; (604) 467-7320; mapleridge.ca.

Camping: Golden Ears Provincial Park is a favorite for tent and RV campers, in no small part due to the serene setting along Alouette Lake. There are three front-country campgrounds: Alouette, Gold Creek, and North Beach. All have reservable spaces through the Discover Camping system. (778) 309-1439 or (800) 689-9025; discovercamping.ca.

GREEN TIP
Pack out your dog's waste and dispose of it in a trash can.

37 Hayward Lake

Hayward Lake Reservoir sits on the downstream side of Stave Falls and Blind Slough Dams, two of many BC hydroelectricity projects. Because water levels can vary, the landscape can range from an apocalyptic lake bottom to tranquil recreation area. This woodland hike, moderate due to its length, leads to spectacular Steelhead Falls and then follows the lakeshore through a lesser-traveled tract of forest.

Start: Reservoir Trail parking lot at the northeast end of Hayward Lake
Distance: 14.2-km (8.8-mile) out-and-back
Hiking time: 3–3.5 hours
Difficulty: Moderate due to length and undulating terrain, though the elevation gain is on the return journey
Trail surface: Forested trail
Best season: Year-round
Other trail users: Dog-walkers
Canine compatibility: Leashed dogs permitted
Land status: Recreation area
Fees and permits: No fees or permits required
Schedule: Daylight hours
Maps: A BC Hydro online map of Hayward and Stave Lakes is available at bchydro.com.

Government topographic maps include the GeoBC Topographic Map Viewer (gov.bc.ca), as well as map 92G1 in the Atlas of Canada Toporama tool (atlas.gc.ca).
Trail contacts: BC Hydro, (604) 462-7533; bchydro.com/community/recreation_areas/hayward_lake.html
Special considerations: There is no fresh water available at the trailhead or during this hike. BC Hydro locks the parking lot gates from dusk to dawn (exact hours change with the season). Hours are posted at the parking lot gates. Be sure to allow plenty of time to avoid getting locked in.

Finding the trailhead: From the Trans-Canada Highway (Highway 1), take exit 44. Follow signs for Highway 7B, also known as Mary Hill Bypass. Follow the bypass northeast for 7.0 kilometers (4.3 miles), and then keep right (southeast) on Lougheed Highway (Highway 7 East). Cross Pitt River Bridge, continuing on Lougheed Highway for 6.0 kilometers (3.7 miles). Turn left (east) onto Dewdney Trunk Road, driving 25 kilometers (15.5 miles). Dewdney Trunk Road takes you through Maple Ridge, through Websters Corner, and then past the powerhouse visitor center and across Stave Falls Dam. Hayward Lake parking lot is a right turn on the east side of the dam. Trailhead GPS: N49 13.79' / W122 20.85'

The Hike

More than a century ago, the Powerhouse at Stave Falls began generating hydroelectric power for BC residents. Today, three dams produce power on Hayward Lake. At the north end of the reservoir water flows in through the Stave Falls Main Dam and Blind Slough Dam. During construction, a consulting engineer complimented the dam's "imperishable character."

Watch for unique sightings along Reservoir Trail.

At the south end, water leaves Hayward Lake through Ruskin Dam, which was added in 1929. But there's also something unseen at work. A 1.0-kilometer (0.6-mile) tunnel pipes in extra water flow from Alouette Lake to the northwest in Golden Ears Provincial Park. It's a rather complex and large system, one that helps BC draw 98 percent of its electricity from waterpower.

This lovely forest hike follows Reservoir Trail along the lake's eastern shore, reaching a waterfall, pretty picnic area, and finally a floating bridge. The trail cuts an undulating profile, with plenty of short ups and downs to keep things interesting. But on the way southwest, there's an overall decline.

Steelhead Falls has a beautiful, tapered cascade.

Ferns and second-growth forest line the Reservoir Trail.

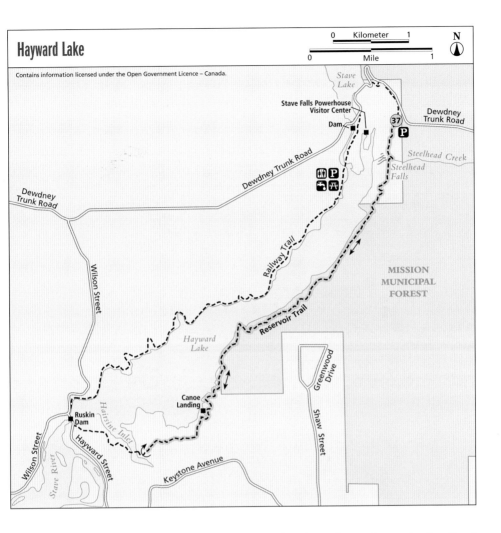

Hayward Lake

Contains information licensed under the Open Government Licence – Canada.

Stave Lake

Stave Falls Powerhouse Visitor Center

Dam

Dewdney Trunk Road

37

Steelhead Creek

Steelhead Falls

Dewdney Trunk Road

Dewdney Trunk Road

Railway Trail

MISSION MUNICIPAL FOREST

Reservoir Trail

Hayward Lake

Greenwood Drive

Wilson Street

Canoe Landing

Ruskin Dam

Hatzic Inlet

Shaw Street

Wilson Street

Stave River

Hayward Street

Keystone Avenue

When you cross the wide, fast-moving Steelhead Creek, you know the Steelhead Falls junction lies just ahead. Cut right and hike down the short trail to the falls. A wooden platform provides a viewing area and benches. It's rare to have such a spectacular, face-on view of a waterfall. Often viewing points seem to land at odd angles. After admiring the roughly 20-meter (66-foot) falls, retrace your steps up the hill to the main trail.

Mossy stumps show where the area was logged in the early 1900s, but the most interesting stumps are those that appear from the lake bottom at low-water levels. Regular water levels cover what was once the Stave River Valley and forest. During drawdown, you can see the lake's underbelly exposed. Thin stumps, perhaps a meter or two high, seem cut off at the knees. They stand as a ghost forest on the bottom of the reservoir.

HOW TO FIND A HIKING BUDDY

True, it's safest to hike in a group. But it can also be fun to share knowledge about the landscape, swap war stories, and perhaps make a new friend.

Sometimes getting your friends out on the trail might be a challenge, or perhaps you want to head out at the last minute because the weather looks good. Or maybe your work schedule varies from the usual Monday-to-Friday set. Whatever the reason, it's handy to have a few sources of company for a hike.

Lace up and get out on the trail with a hiking buddy—new or old.

Hiking appeals to a wide variety of people. As such, you'd be surprised at who might be keen to hit the trail. A simple Facebook status post looking for company could introduce you to some hikers you already know.

There are also many local organizations, groups, and websites that are focused on getting people together to go hiking. The BC Mountaineering Club (bcmc.ca) started as a Vancouver-area hiking and mountaineering club in 1907. From the beginning, its goals have been exploring and preserving the area mountains. That started with a series of hiking trips, like treks up to Grouse Mountain before the days of bridges, and has expanded to include mountain climbing and rock climbing. Its newsletter is available by email, which is the norm for most hiking groups that use websites, email lists, and social media to easily connect with members.

A similar club that's been around a little longer is the Alpine Club of Canada (accvancouver .ca). The club runs family hikes, day trips, backcountry excursions, and social activities for more than 1,000 members. Another well-established group is the North Shore Hikers (northshore hikers.org), which focuses on hikes close to Vancouver.

Nature Vancouver (naturevancouver.ca) started out as the Vancouver Natural History Society. While its focus is more on the environment, members explore the outdoors through hikes, walks, and other activities. The pace tends to be slower, with lots of stopping and looking, but the knowledgeable folks make for great conversation.

Other nature-minded organizations run regular guided hikes and walks. There may be a small fee for these, you may need to buy a membership, or they may be free. In Vancouver you can join city-led tours of the area watersheds through Metro Vancouver (metrovancouver.org), join a nature walk with the Stanley Park Ecology Society (stanleyparkecology.ca), or go mushroom hunting with the Vancouver Mycology Society (vanmyco.com).

ONLINE HIKING GROUPS

A variety of hiking-themed websites share knowledge about Vancouver-area trails and have active forums where people comment on trail conditions and find hiking partners. A few worth investigating for hiking buddies include:

Clubtread.com: The website maintains a hiking database for a range of areas including British Columbia. This is a great resource for hikes farther from the city.

Wanderung.ca: A community of hikers with an active Facebook group.

Meetup.com: This website focuses on bringing people who have similar interests together. Just in the Vancouver area alone, there are Meetup groups dedicated to age groups, women's hiking, slower-paced hikers, and more.

Canoe Landing, 5.9 kilometers (3.7 miles) along the trail, is an easy spot to get near the water for a picnic. From here, you can hike along to the turnaround point at the floating bridge. The bridge across Hairsine Inlet to Ruskin Dam has been closed about a decade (as of 2020). But if the trails are open, it would then be possible to make a loop over Ruskin Dam and back along the Railway Trail on the west side of the lake.

In addition to its lakeshore hiking trails, Hayward is a popular spot for outdoor recreation. There is a busy beach area along Railroad Trail. Canoes, kayaks, and non-motorized boats are permitted in the waters.

Distances and Directions

0.0 km/0.0 mile   Start from Hayward Lake parking lot off Dewdney Trunk Road.

0.1 km/0.1 mile   Turn left (southwest) at two junctions, as trails feed in from the right (north). Follow the main trail.

0.8 km/0.5 mile   Turn right (northwest) down to Steelhead Falls.

0.9 km/0.6 mile   View Steelhead Falls. (***Bail-out:*** As with all out-and-back trails, you can turn around at any point. Turning around at Steelhead Falls provides a nice and scenic short hike of about 1.8 kilometers [1.1 miles] round-trip from the parking lot.)

1.0 km/0.6 mile   Return to the main trail and turn right (south).

3.7 km/2.3 miles   Continue straight past a trail that spurs off to your left (south).

5.9 km/3.7 miles   Turn right (northwest) down to a viewpoint and picnic area known as Canoe Landing. Walk out on the small dock to admire the lake landscape. (***Bail-out:*** The picnic area, about three-quarters of the way along the trail, also makes a well-timed turnaround for an 11.6-kilometer [7.2-mile] hike.)

7.2 km/4.5 miles   Follow the trail to the floating bridge—which remained closed as of 2020.

14.2 km/8.8 miles   Retrace your steps northeast along the trail and arrive back at the trailhead.

Options: Railway Trail is a more developed route on the west side of the reservoir, traveling 16 kilometers (9.9 miles) from the main beach recreation area to Ruskin Dam and back. This trail has a level grade and wide, flat surface. It's a similar distance to the Reservoir Trail, though there is road access at both ends if you'd prefer a point-to-point walk.

Hike Information

Local Attractions: See the inner workings of a hydroelectricity dam and the powerhouse's original century-old turbines and generators at Powerhouse at Stave Falls Visitor Centre. There is a small admission fee charged. Check for hours. 31338 Dewdney Trunk Rd., Mission; (604) 462-1222; bchydro.com/community/recreation_areas/stave_falls_visitor_centre.html.

South, Over the Fraser River

Richmond and Delta mostly sit at sea level, on drained peat moss bog and sediment that has, over millennia, been washed down the Fraser River and collected where the river meets the saltwater. When Captain Vancouver sailed these waters in 1792, he didn't notice the Fraser River. But to be fair, at its murky mouth it doesn't really exude the grandeur you'd expect of BC's longest river at 1,375 kilometers (854 miles). Waterways in more than a quarter of the province drain into the Fraser.

Agricultural fields, housing developments, and tidal flats sum up a quick lay of the land. As such, it's not the place to go for a strenuous, heart-pumping hike or technical terrain. But for bird-watchers, cyclists, and nature lovers, the area is a huge draw.

Trails make use of the long, flat expanses available. Many of the region's trails top the dikes that keep the waters of the Strait of Georgia and the Fraser River at bay.

In this section, a walk around Brunswick Point west of Ladner does just that and rates as spectacular when upwards of 80,000 snow geese flock to the area from November through March. Also with no elevation gain (but strong on-shore winds), Iona Jetty offers another flat walk, using the long runway of a wastewater treatment facility pipe to cross the shallow flats. It's a fishing spot, though not for humans: eagles, herons, and occasionally even a seal make use of the jetty's vantage.

Sweeping beaches in Boundary Bay, just north of the 49th Parallel, are also a haven for birds. About 1.5 million birds visit the bay each year. A dune hike takes you through protected birding areas and by a busy sandy beach.

And to get a sense of what was here before development paved it over, head to the Delta Nature Reserve section of Burns Bog. A small, protected corner lets you take a peek at an approximately 3,000-hectare (7,413-acre) peat bog.

Trails in this area don't demand hiking boots. Opt for lighter footwear and a slower pace, and be sure to bring binoculars, cameras, and bird guides.

38 Iona Jetty

The walk along this 4.0-kilometer (2.5-mile) jetty jutting into the Strait of Georgia can be deceiving. When the gusts pick up and blast in from the west, it feels like you're walking into a wind tunnel. But it's worth battling this invisible force to spot harbor seals, catch a close-up glimpse of an eagle, and stand at this westerly point and take in a panorama of mainland, islands, and mountains.

Start: Parking lot of Iona Beach Regional Park
Distance: 8.0-km (5.0-mile) out-and-back
Hiking time: About 2 hours
Difficulty: Easy due to moderate length and flat, gravel path
Trail surface: Gravel path, gravel road
Best season: Year-round
Other trail users: Bikes, runners, and dog-walkers
Canine compatibility: Due to COVID-19 restrictions in 2020, dogs were not permitted off-leash on the jetty's lower road.
Land status: Regional park
Fees and permits: No fees or permits required

Schedule: Daylight hours
Maps: Maps are available online at metro-vancouver.org. Government topographic maps include the GeoBC Topographic Map Viewer (gov.bc.ca), as well as map 92G3 in the Atlas of Canada Toporama tool (atlas.gc.ca).
Trail contacts: Metro Vancouver Regional Parks West Area Office, Suite 130, 1200 W. 73rd Ave., Vancouver, V6P 6G5; (604) 224-5739; metrovancouver.org
Special considerations: There is fresh water available near the trailhead, but not during this hike.

Finding the trailhead: From Granville Street, drive south and follow signs to the airport, crossing the Arthur Laing Bridge and continuing straight onto Grant McConachie Way. Turn right (north) onto Templeton Street, which becomes Ferguson Road at Grauer Road. Continue west along Ferguson Road for about 6.0 kilometers (3.7 miles) to Iona Beach Regional Park. Trailhead GPS: N49 13.02' / W123 12.74'

The Hike

The end is almost immediately in sight as you walk out the very straight 4.0 kilometers (2.5 miles) to the end of Iona Jetty. Your footsteps follow the wide concrete pipeline discharging treated wastewater from Iona Island Wastewater Treatment Plant, which provides a very essential service for 600,000 people in the city. The plant breaks down organic materials, producing methane gas and biosolids. Treated wastewater is then released into the tide-scoured Strait of Georgia.

Frankly, it's not always a pleasant-smelling location. But that's when you can truly appreciate the strong westerly winds that blow in from across the water. On especially

Facing page top: The flat terrain provides easy walking, running, and cycling.
Facing page bottom: There are 360-degree views throughout the walk along Iona Jetty.

Walkers commonly spot bald eagles near the jetty.

windy days, bring something (whether it's a toque or hooded jacket) to cover your ears.

In any season, the views from Iona Jetty are terrific. Mount Baker hovers to the southeast beyond Vancouver International Airport, mountains on the Gulf Islands and Vancouver Island rise in the west, the peaks around Howe Sound stand to the north-west, and Vancouver's North Shore Mountains are also clearly in view.

In the ponds near the trailhead, you can see Canada geese and ducks swimming in the wetlands—a habitat that once covered much more of Sea Island. Most local marsh areas have been developed, primarily as the Vancouver International Airport. In late spring, yellow-headed blackbirds nest in the area. They are rare locally, but well known for their looks and sounds. They have an unmistakable sunny-golden head and a white patch on their wings, and the males make a screeching, buzz-saw-like noise.

Tidal flats on both sides of the jetty attract more than 300 bird species to the area, and it's a stopover for many migratory species.

The mouth of the North Arm of the Fraser River provides rich feeding grounds. Blue herons and boisterous seagulls are regular visitors. A seal may be lingering off shore. If your timing is right, you might get fairly close to a bald eagle sitting on the jetty's deck. Their hulking black bodies are impressive; their 1.8-meter (5.9-foot) or larger wingspans even more so. Bucking the trend of the animal kingdom, female eagles are actually about 30 percent heavier than males.

The scene changes as you near the end of the jetty. A final viewing tower looks out to the Gulf Islands and Vancouver Island mountains behind. Then, turning back to the land, you see the forests of Pacific Spirit Park and planes circling to land at the airport.

Distances and Directions

0.0 km/0.0 mile   Start from the information sign and walk out southwest along the jetty on the upper path. If COVID-19 restrictions are in place, you'll walk out on the upper road and return on the lower road, which is also wheelchair accessible and open to cyclists. If restrictions are not in place, the lower road is open to off-leash dogs as well.

1.4 km/0.9 mile   Reach the first of two wind shelters.

2.7 km/1.7 miles   Continue southwest along the jetty at the second wind shelter.

4.0 km/2.5 miles   Climb up to the final viewing tower and look out over the Strait of Georgia. Turn around and return northeast along the lower road of the jetty.

8.0 km/5.0 miles   Arrive back at the trailhead. (***Note:*** This out-and-back route can be shortened to any length—an especially attractive option in the face of strong winds.)

There is a Coast Guard station in Richmond—south of Iona Jetty.

Iona Jetty

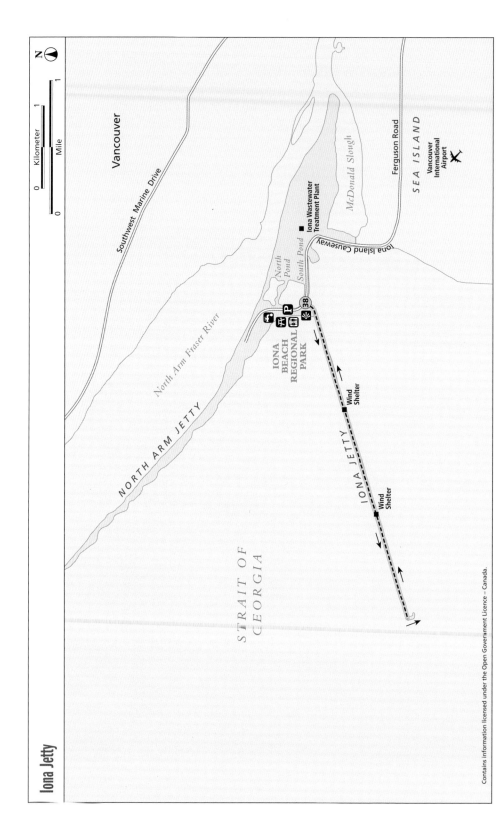

Options: The North Arm Jetty is also open to hikers. There are no trails, but you can walk along the beach, staying below the high-tide line. Check the tides before setting out for the 6.0-km (3.7-mile) out-and-back hike.

On the way home from Iona Beach, try your hand at a little plane spotting. Avid and casual plane spotters hang out at the intersection of Ferguson and Grauer Roads, which sits directly under the approach for YVR's north runway. Plane spotters love the airport's variety of international airlines.

Hike Information

Local Information: For information about attractions and events in Richmond, contact the Tourism Richmond Visitor Centre. 3811 Moncton St., Richmond, BC, V7E 3A7; (604) 271-8280 or toll free (877) 247-0777; tourismrichmond.com.

Local Attractions: The Vancouver International Airport isn't just for catching a flight. Besides the on-site hotel and various restaurants, there are many First Nations artworks on display. Most prominent is Bill Reid's *Jade Canoe*, located in the departures area of the International Terminal. 3211 Grant McConachie Way, Richmond; (604) 207-7077; yvr.ca.

Restaurants: The Flying Beaver, on the south shore of Sea Island, is a favorite for its pub fare and micro-brewed beers. A sunny patio has a vantage of seaplanes landing on the middle arm of the Fraser River. 4760 Inglis Dr., Richmond; (604) 273-0278; mjg.ca/flying-beaver.

GREEN TIP
When hiking at the beach, stay off dunes
and away from nesting areas.

39 Brunswick Point

Though this 7.4-km (4.6-mile) hike atop flat, gravel dike trails isn't a challenge, it's big on rewards: especially the 360-degree view of snowcapped mountains. During winter, snow geese flock to the surrounding fields and other migratory birds feed on the mudflats of Roberts Bank. For serious bird-watchers, there's an island bird sanctuary nearby.

Start: Cul-de-sac at the far western end of River Road
Distance: 7.4-km (4.6-mile) out-and-back
Hiking time: 1.5–2 hours
Difficulty: Easy due to completely flat, gravel trails
Trail surface: Gravel dike trail
Best season: Year-round
Other trail users: Bikes, dog-walkers
Canine compatibility: Dogs permitted—it's best to keep your dog on a leash so he/she doesn't disturb the birdlife.
Land status: City trail
Fees and permits: No fees or permits required

Schedule: Daylight hours
Maps: A Delta routes (trails and cycling) map is available online at delta.ca. Government topographic maps include the GeoBC Topographic Map Viewer (gov.bc.ca), as well as map 92G3 in the Atlas of Canada Toporama tool (atlas.gc.ca).
Trail contacts: N/A
Special considerations: The area at the trail's east end is subject to hunting. Tsawwassen First Nation hunting season runs from Sept to Mar. There are no sources of water or restrooms along the trail.

Finding the trailhead: From Highway 99, take exit 28. Keep right and follow signs for Highway 17A toward the Tsawwassen ferry terminal. Drive south for about 2.0 kilometers (1.2 miles) and turn right (west) onto Ladner Trunk Road. The route passes through Ladner's business district, and at Arthur Drive the road becomes 47A Avenue and then River Road West. About 6.0 kilometers (3.7 miles) from Ladner town center, you arrive at a metal gate that marks the road end. Trailhead GPS: N49 04.09' / W123 09.12'

The Hike

This gently sloped dike is a line in the sand between the swells of ocean tides and the farmland of Brunswick Point peninsula. The trail affords an easy journey over a flat gravel surface with plenty of opportunities for bird-watching. Indeed, birders have spotted nearly 300 species in the area.

As the south arm of the Fraser River empties into the ocean, it deposits nutrients in the wide mudflats. Migratory birds like sandpipers and snow geese flock to the area to feed, fueling up for long migration routes. The western sandpiper, for example, may fly up to 20,000 kilometers (12,427 miles) in 1 year.

From about November to March, upwards of 80,000 snow geese flock to this area (though many spend late December to February south of the border on the

Top: A researcher crosses Roberts Bank mudflats.
Bottom: Snow geese flock to Brunswick Point and other nearby fields during winter.

Skagit estuary). These impressive birds have flown south for the winter, escaping harsh Arctic temperatures. During the summer, when they are flightless, they spend the season northwest of Alaska on Wrangel Island, Russia.

As these birds have flocked here to feed up and gain strength, it's essential to their survival that you keep your distance and avoid disturbing them. Dogs also can cause harm simply by scaring the feeding birds.

Just to the north of the dike, across Canoe Passage, the George C. Reifel Migratory Bird Sanctuary is a favorite bird-watching destination. Westham Island, a one-time resort and farming operation for the Reifel family, was first leased as a bird sanctuary in the 1960s. It has grown and garnered more protection

Wild beach peas are a bright beacon along the dike trails.

since then. Both the migratory bird sanctuary and Alaksen National Wildlife Area are protected areas on the island.

Year-round, hawks and eagles circle on drafts of air, waiting perhaps for a mouse scurrying in the farm fields. And with summer's warmth, garter snakes sun on the darker stretches of gravel before disappearing into rock crevasses.

BC'S MIGHTY RIVER

The muddy waters of the Fraser River can seem unimpressive at first glance. But when you consider that river deposits are growing land at the river mouth by up to 3.0 meters (9.8 feet) each year, there might be something greater at work.

The Fraser is undammed along its main stem—the longest such river in North America, south of the Arctic. It transports incredible amounts of fresh water from inland British Columbia to the Strait of Georgia (not to mention logs, fish, and pleasure boats).

For millennia First Nations groups from around the area shared in the river's salmon resources. They gathered in fall to catch salmon and dry the fish as winter food stocks.

First Nations people also fished for the prehistoric-looking white sturgeon. These massive fish can reach 6.0 meters (19.7 feet) in length and weigh up to 600 kilograms (1,323 pounds). Beyond their immense size, razor-sharp scutes (or bony plates) make them tough to handle. The sturgeon is now protected in BC.

Brunswick Point sits in an out-of-the-way corner of the Lower Mainland.

Dikes protect farmland in Ladner and other areas of the Lower Mainland.

Overall, the route is a simple one, rounding Brunswick Point and then cutting a straight course southeast along the Roberts Bank shoreline. The turnaround point is just before a busy truck and rail route to container terminal Deltaport. But in both directions on this walk, hazy, snowcapped mountains form a perfect panorama. To the north you see Grouse and Seymour ski hills on the North Shore Mountains and Vancouver Island peaks to the west.

Brunswick Point

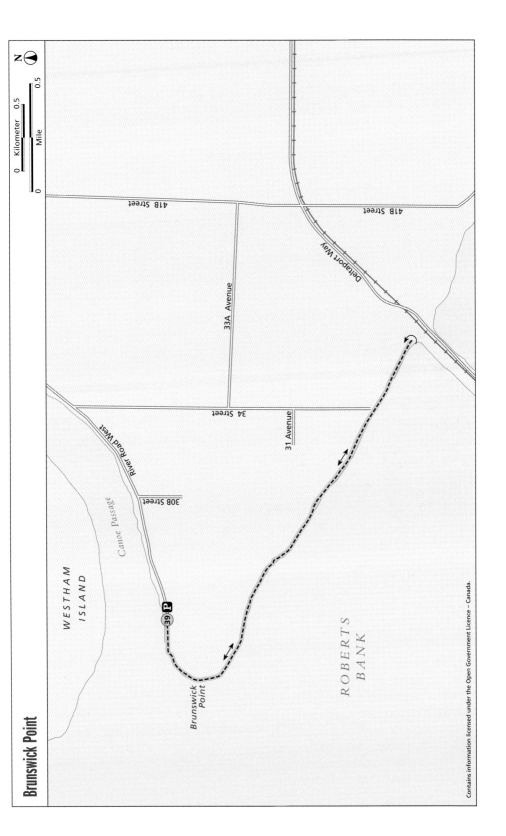

N

0 Kilometer 0.5

0 Mile 0.5

41B Street

33A Avenue

34 Street

31 Avenue

Deltaport Way

41B Street

River Road West

30B Street

Canoe Passage

WESTHAM ISLAND

Brunswick Point

ROBERTS BANK

39 P

Distances and Directions

0.0 km/0.0 mile   Start from the western end of River Road and pick up the dike trail heading west.

0.3 km/0.2 mile   A gravel section of River Road joins the trail from the left.

0.7 km/0.4 mile   Pass benches at the end of Brunswick Point as the trail bends southeast. (*Bail-out:* This out-and-back route means you can turn around at any time. The bench sitting area at Brunswick Point is just a 10-minute walk from the parking area.)

2.2 km/1.4 miles   There are more benches along the trail.

3.1 km/1.9 miles   Reach start of the Tsawwassen First Nation hunting area.

3.7 km/2.3 miles   Turn around before reaching the road and rail lines to the busy container terminal.

7.4 km/4.6 miles   Retrace your steps along the dike trail and arrive back at the trailhead.

Options: If you've caught the Audubon bug, make an extra trip to the George C. Reifel Migratory Bird Sanctuary. It's located at 5191 Robertson Rd., Delta. The turnoff is 2.5 kilometers (1.6 miles) east of the hike trailhead, off River Road. (604) 946-6980, reifelbirdsanctuary.com.

Hike Information

Local Events: Optimistically, Ladner May Days kicks off the summer season in the town, although it was canceled due to COVID-19 in 2020. Memorial Park, ladner maydays.com.

Restaurants: A pub near Ladner's Government Wharf serves up fine seafood and has a patio. Sharkey's Seafood Bar and Grille, 4953 Chisholm St., Ladner; (604) 946-7793; sharkeys.ca.

GREEN TIP
Observe wildlife from a distance. Don't interfere in their lives—both of you will be better for it.

40 Burns Bog

A boardwalk amble guides you through the more-than-meets-the-eye terrain of Burns Bog. From spring skunk cabbage to fall bog cranberries, the nature reserve is rich with plant life. The habitat is important to migratory birds like endangered greater sandhill cranes, which nest here, but it's just as important to us humans—the peat bog absorbs carbon dioxide and Fraser River floodwaters. In fact, it's the largest urban wilderness in North America.

Start: Planet Ice parking lot, 10388 Nordel Court, Delta
Distance: 3.5-km (2.2-mile) lollipop
Hiking time: 45 minutes-1 hour
Difficulty: Easy due to flat, gravel trails and well-maintained boardwalks
Trail surface: Gravel, boardwalk, paved path
Best season: Year-round
Other trail users: Cyclists, dog-walkers
Canine compatibility: Leashed dogs permitted
Land status: City nature reserve
Fees and permits: No fees or permits required

Schedule: None, but daylight hours recommended
Maps: Info signs at the nature reserve include a trail map. Government topographic maps include the GeoBC Topographic Map Viewer (gov.bc.ca), as well as map 92G2 in the Atlas of Canada Toporama tool (atlas.gc.ca).
Trail contacts: Metro Vancouver Central Area Office, 9146 Avalon Ave., Burnaby, V3N 4G8; (604) 520-6442; metrovancouver.org
Special considerations: There are no washrooms or freshwater sources at the trailhead.

Finding the trailhead: From Knight Street, drive south over the Fraser River. Follow signs for Highway 91 East, and merge onto the East-West Connector. Continue on Highway 91 East, over Annacis Island and the Alex Fraser Bridge. On the south side of the bridge, take the first exit. Keep right (west) for River Road and follow the exit ramp onto Nordel Way. After just 600 meters (0.4 mile) make a right (east) onto Nordel Court. Drive straight into the large Planet Ice parking lot. Trailhead GPS: N49 08.94' / W122 56.12'

The Hike

Ask someone to name North America's largest, undeveloped urban wilderness, and I'd bet money they won't say Burns Bog. This peat bog on the Fraser River Delta covers about 3,000 hectares (7,413 acres). And its only access is this short gravel path and boardwalk trail in the northeastern corner, an area called the Delta Nature Reserve. The rest of the bog is off-limits, left to rare species like the Mariposa copper butterfly and Arctic plants like cloudberries. Since peat fires can smolder underground for years (yes, years!), it's important to minimize human impact on this disappearing habitat.

Environmentally, the bog acts like a sponge, soaking up floodwaters and absorbing carbon dioxide by turning it into plant matter. Culturally, the bog is equally important. First Nations people gathered blueberries, salal berries, cranberries, and blackberries on the bog's fertile landscape. Traditional medicines grow in the bog too,

Top left: Skunk cabbage flowers burst through the mud in spring.
Top right: Boardwalk trails venture through the thick growth of Burns Bog.
Bottom: First Nations people traditionally gathered berries (including salmonberries) from Burns B

Boardwalk trails venture throughout the forest of Burns Bog.

like Labrador tea, rich in vitamin C, and sphagnum moss that people dried and used as wound dressings and baby diapers. The bog's quicksand-like peat and a possible underground waterway to the ocean make it the feature of First Nations legends too.

So with this idea of urban wilderness, it feels almost fitting that the hike begins in a parking lot, behind an ice-skating rink. A paved trail is also a greenway—expect to encounter bicycles—and cuts under a thundering highway before reaching a creek. From here, the traffic noises start to fade, though never completely. In early spring, bright yellow skunk cabbage flowers poke up from the marshy ground. Another name for the plant is swamp lantern, and seeing the beacon of color gives weight to the name. The plant's soft, skunky scent lingers in the damp air. You might think skunk cabbage looks a lot like a calla lily, and you're right. Both are members of the arum family. Skunk cabbage even creates its own heat.

As you continue the walk along the trails and boardwalk, benches provide a spot to sit and wait for bird sightings. The terrain changes from wetland to hardhack meadows and cedar forest. The hike's final loop follows a short trail to where a bulldozer sits almost completely swallowed up by peat bog. The tale goes that someone stole the machinery from a construction site and drove it into the bog. After just 1 day the bulldozer sank 3.0 meters (9.8 feet) down, and no amount of hauling could pull it out.

As you can see, it's still there.

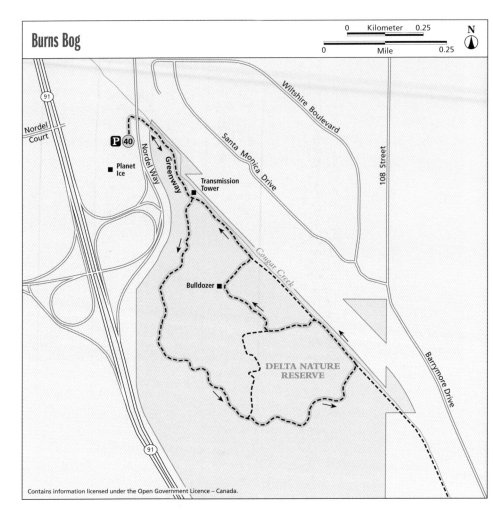

Contains information licensed under the Open Government Licence – Canada.

Distances and Directions

0.0 km/0.0 mile   Start from the southeast end of the Planet Ice parking lot and turn left (north) along the paved trail.

0.1 km/0.1 mile   Follow the curved path to pass under Nordel Way and turn right (southeast). Leaving the paved path, you follow a gravel trail branching left along Cougar Creek.

0.4 km/0.2 mile   Just past the transmission tower, turn right (south) onto a boardwalk trail

1.7 km/1.1 miles   Continue straight at a boardwalk trail. It's a shortcut to the nature reserve's inner trail.

2.0 km/1.2 miles   Rejoin the creek trail and turn left (northwest). A bridge heads right (northeast) over the creek.

2.2 km/1.4 miles   Turn left (west) and follow the small arc of a shorter boardwalk trail.

2.3 km/1.4 miles   Continue straight (west) when the woodland boardwalk splits off to the left.

2.6 km/1.6 miles   See the sunken bulldozer.

There's a unique affection for the unique habitat of Burns Bog.

2.7 km/1.7 miles Reach Cougar Creek again and turn left (northwest) to return to the trailhead.

3.4 km/2.1 miles Turn left (south), passing under Nordel Way and rejoining the paved path.

3.5 km/2.2 miles Arrive back at the trailhead.

Hike Information

Local Information: Burns Bog Conservation Society runs events and guided walks to support bog conservation efforts. 4-7953 120 St., Delta, BC, V4C 6P6; (604) 572-0373; burnsbog.org.

GREEN TIP
Be green and stylish too—wear clothing made of organic cotton and other recycled products.

41 Boundary Bay

Boundary Bay has gone to the birds—snowy owls, hawks, plovers, and trumpeter swans to name a few. This is one of the Vancouver area's most important habitats for migratory birds, and 1.5 million birds make a journey to the wide, sandy bay just north of the 49th Parallel each year. A flat, gravel trail takes you on an easy shoreline hike and past protected areas before looping back to Centennial Beach.

Start: Centennial Beach concession
Distance: 3.8-km (2.4-mile) loop
Hiking time: 1–1.5 hours
Difficulty: Easy due to flat trails over dunes and wetlands
Trail surface: Gravel, dirt path, boardwalk, sand
Best season: Year-round
Other trail users: Cyclists, beachgoers, dog-walkers, bird-watchers
Canine compatibility: Leashed dogs permitted
Land status: Regional park
Fees and permits: No fees or permits required

Schedule: Daylight hours
Maps: An official park map is available online at metrovancouver.org. Government topographic maps include the GeoBC Topographic Map Viewer (gov.bc.ca), as well as map 92G3 in the Atlas of Canada Toporama tool (atlas.gc .ca).
Trail contacts: Metro Vancouver Central Area Office, 9146 Avalon Ave., Burnaby, V3N 4G8; (604) 520-6442; metrovancouver.org
Special considerations: There is fresh water available near the trailhead, but not during this hike.

Finding the trailhead: From Highway 99 South, take exit 28 for Highway 17A. This highway connects to the Tsawwassen ferry terminal, and though you turn off the highway sooner, the ferry signs are easy to follow. Drive south on Highway 17A and then as it becomes Highway 17 for a total of about 7.0 kilometers (4.3 miles), and then turn left (south) onto 56 Street. Drive 2.0 kilometers (1.2 miles) and turn left (east) onto 12 Avenue. The main route hangs a sharp right bend and becomes Boundary Bay Road. After 1.6 kilometer (1.0 mile), watch for the park entrance on the left (east). Trailhead GPS: N49 00.89' / W123 02.41'

The Hike

Boundary Bay is a 16-kilometer-wide (10-mile-wide) sweeping curve, just north of the 49th Parallel north. While you'd expect huge Centennial Beach to be packed in summer and near desolate in winter, that's not quite so. When it's not beach season at Boundary Bay, it's birding season.

About 1.5 million birds, coming from a collection of twenty countries, feed in the bay's tidal flats, wetlands, and grasslands each year. The park is fairly small with a varied mix of habitats, including shoreline, grasslands, and wetlands. But it sits next to an 11,470-hectare (28,343-acre) tract of mudflats: the Boundary Bay Wildlife Management Area.

With a beach and wide paths, the park is a lovely spot to linger until the sun sets.

This attracts an interesting mix of feathered friends. Peregrine falcons and hawks circle above the grasslands waiting to spot some small, tasty prey. Ponds provide habitat for wood ducks, tundra swans, and mergansers. And thickets are a safe home for small perching, or passerine, birds like finches, warblers, and thrushes. You can spot different birds in each season. Though year-round you're likely to see ducks, great blue herons, goldfinches, and bald eagles.

Generally, shorebirds, waterfowl, and raptors stay in the area from September through April or May. Flocks of shorebirds are easy to spot, though often far away, at low tide. Semipalmated plovers, sandpipers, and killdeer are best-spotted in spring and fall—some of the many birds that travel the Pacific Flyway migratory route.

On rare years, snowy owls leave their Arctic home and come to Boundary Bay. It's known as an interruption year and thought to occur when food is short in the Arctic. These impressive birds migrate south to feed on ducks and other tasty prey.

Volunteers maintain a rare bird alert service in the province. It's available through birding.bc.ca.

The majestic, mostly white birds came to the Fraser Delta hunting grounds in both 2012 and 2013. If the owls are around when you are, you won't need to strain your eyes to see them. Most likely a group of birders, long camera lenses and binoculars protruding, will alert you to the birds. And if not, the owls' pretty white plumage

More than a million birds feed in Boundary Bay each year.

stands out against the grasslands. Watch for them perched on fence posts and barn roofs.

Bird-watching etiquette dictates that you don't get too close. Flushing a bird, or causing it to fly away, uses up calories that are essential for that bird's survival.

Distances and Directions

0.0 km/0.0 mile   Start from the concession and turn left (northwest) to follow 12 Avenue Dyke Trail, running parallel to the beach.

0.2 km/0.1 mile   At an information sign, turn right (northeast) onto Dune Trail Loop. Follow the path through the sandy grasses.

0.5 km/0.3 mile   Rejoin 12 Avenue Dyke Trail and continue northwest.

0.6 km/0.4 mile   Keep right (northeast) on Dyke Trail as the route forks. Raptor Trail spurs off to the left.

0.9 km/0.6 mile   Pass Raptor Trail on your left.

1.0 km/0.6 mile   Climb the viewing tower for a better vantage across Boundary Bay. Then, continue northwest along the shore. A fenced-off wildlife reserve lies to the west and there are mudflats, at low tide, to the east.

1.8 km/1.1 miles   Reach a second observation area.

1.9 km/1.2 miles   Follow Raptor Trail as it turns left (south), inland. Beach Grove Lagoon is off to the north.

2.0 km/1.2 miles The trail forks. Take the left (south) trail.

2.1 km/1.3 miles Keep left (southeast) on Raptor Trail as the route splits again.

2.3 km/1.4 miles As trail branches rejoin this trail, continue straight (east) and over a bridge.

2.5 km/1.6 miles With protected wildlife areas on both sides, walk slowly and watch carefully for birds.

2.6 km/1.6 miles The trail forks. Take either trail as they rejoin a short distance on.

3.0 km/1.9 miles At the four-way intersection keep right (south) briefly on Raptor Trail (a turn left [north] would take you along a boardwalk). After just 20 meters (66 feet) leave Raptor Trail and turn right (southwest) onto Savannah Trail. Raptor Trail continues to the southeast.

3.1 km/1.9 miles Continue south on Savannah Trail toward the parking lot.

3.5 km/2.2 miles Reach the parking lot. Head left (east) back toward the beach and 12 Avenue Dyke Trail.

3.8 km/2.4 miles Arrive back at the concession.

The flat, gravel trails in Boundary Bay Regional Park weave through rich grassland, wetland, and mudflat habitats.

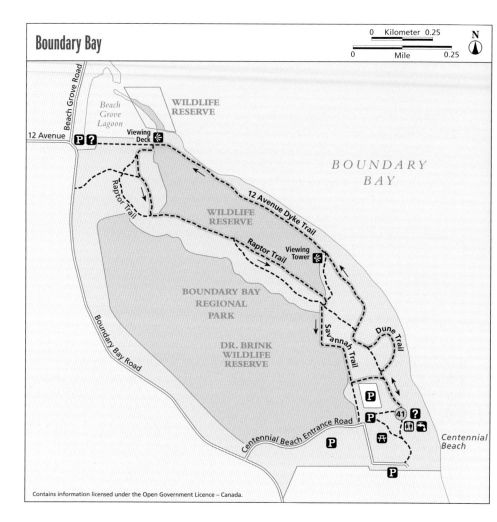

0   Kilometer 0.25

0   Mile   0.25

N

BOUNDARY
BAY

Beach Grove Road

12 Avenue

Beach
Grove
Lagoon

Viewing
Deck

WILDLIFE
RESERVE

Raptor Trail

WILDLIFE
RESERVE

12 Avenue Dyke Trail

Raptor Trail

Viewing
Tower

BOUNDARY BAY
REGIONAL
PARK

Boundary Bay Road

DR. BRINK
WILDLIFE
RESERVE

Savannah Trail

Dune Trail

P

P

41

P

Centennial Beach Entrance Road

P

P

Centennial
Beach

P

Contains information licensed under the Open Government Licence – Canada.

Hike Information

Local Events: Birding clubs have held regular bird-watching events at Boundary Bay over the years. Start with Nature Vancouver to find out about any current opportunities. naturevancouver.ca.

Local Events: The Christmas Bird Count is a North American tradition, started in 1900. The first Vancouver-area count happened in 1954. The National Audubon Society assesses tallies from across the Western Hemisphere. audubon.org.

Organizations: The Ministry of Environment provides information about viewing sites and birding checklists. env.gov.bc.ca/fw/wildlife/viewing.

Art of Hiking

When standing nose to nose with a black bear, you're probably not too concerned with the issue of ethical behavior in the wild. No doubt you're just terrified. But let's be honest. How often are you nose to nose with a bear? For most of us, a hike into the "wild" means loading up the SUV with expensive gear and driving to a toileted trailhead. Sure, you can mourn how civilized we've become—how GPS units have replaced natural instinct and Gore-Tex stands in for true grit—but the silly gadgets of civilization aside, we have plenty of reason to take pride in how we've matured. With survival now on the back burner, we've begun to understand that we have a responsibility to protect, no longer just conquer, our wild places: that they, not we, are at risk. So please, do what you can. The following section will help you understand better what it means to "do what you can" while still making the most of your hiking experience. Anyone can take a hike, but hiking safely and well is an art requiring preparation and proper equipment.

Trail Etiquette

Leave no trace. Always leave an area just like you found it—if not better than you found it. Avoid camping in fragile, alpine meadows and along the banks of streams and lakes. Use a camp stove versus building a wood fire. Pack up all of your garbage and extra food. Bury human waste at least 61 meters (200 feet) from water sources under 15 to 20 centimeters (6 to 8 inches) of topsoil. Don't bathe with soap in a lake or stream—use prepackaged moistened towels to wipe off sweat and dirt, or bathe in the water without soap.

Stay on the trail. It's true, a path anywhere leads nowhere new, but purists will just have to get over it. Paths serve an important purpose; they limit impact on natural areas. Straying from a designated trail may seem innocent, but it can cause damage to sensitive areas—damage that may take years to recover, if it can recover at all. Even simple shortcuts—like cutting between switchbacks—can be destructive, causing erosion and more damage that requires repairs or rehabilitation. So, please, stay on the trail.

Leave no weeds. Invasive species tend to overtake other plants, which in turn affects animals and birds that depend on them for food. To minimize the spread of nonnative invaders, hikers should regularly clean their boots, tents, packs, and hiking poles of mud and seeds. Also brush your dog to remove any weed seeds before heading off into a new area.

Keep your dog under control. You can buy a retractable leash that allows your dog to go exploring along the trail, while allowing you the ability to reel him in should another hiker approach or should he decide to chase a squirrel. Always obey leash laws and be sure to bury your dog's waste or pack it out in resealable plastic bags.

Respect other trail users. Often you're not the only one on the trail. With the rise in popularity of multiuse trails, you'll have to learn a new kind of respect, beyond the nod and "hello" approach you may be used to. First investigate whether you're on a multiuse trail, and assume the appropriate precautions. When you encounter motorized vehicles (logging trucks, ATVs, motorcycles, and 4WDs), be alert. Though they should always yield to the hiker, often they're going too fast or are too lost in the buzz of their engine to react to your presence. If you hear activity ahead, step off the trail just to be safe. Note that you're not likely to hear a mountain biker coming, so be prepared and know ahead of time whether you share the trail with them. Cyclists should always yield to hikers, but that's little comfort to those on foot. Be aware. When you approach horses or pack animals on the trail, always step quietly off the trail, preferably on the downhill side, and let them pass. If you're wearing a large backpack, it's often a good idea to sit down. To some animals, a hiker wearing a large backpack might appear threatening.

Getting into Shape

Unless you want to be sore—and possibly have to shorten your trip or vacation—be sure to get in shape before a big hike. If you're terribly out of shape, start a walking program early, preferably 8 weeks in advance. Start with a 15-minute walk during your lunch hour or after work and gradually increase your walking time to an hour. You should also increase your elevation gain. Walking briskly up hills really strengthens your leg muscles and gets your heart rate up. If you work in a storied office building, take the stairs instead of the elevator. If you prefer going to a gym, walk the treadmill or use a stair machine. You can further increase your strength and endurance by walking with a loaded backpack. Stationary exercises you might consider are squats, leg lifts, sit-ups, and push-ups. Other good ways to get in shape include biking, running, yoga, body-weight exercises, and, of course, short hikes. Stretching before and after a hike keeps muscles flexible and helps avoid injuries, as does seeking medical advice before making big changes to your fitness regime.

Preparedness

It's been said that failing to plan means planning to fail. So do take the necessary time to plan your trip. Whether going on a short day hike or an extended backpacking trip, always prepare for the worst. You need to do your best to prevent problems from arising in the first place. In order to survive—and to stay reasonably comfortable—you need to concern yourself with the basics: water, food, and shelter. Don't go on a hike without having these bases covered. And don't go on a hike expecting to find these items in the woods.

Water. Even in frigid conditions, you need at least 2 liters/2 quarts of water a day to function efficiently. Add heat and taxing terrain and you can bump that figure up another 1 liter/1 quart or more. That's simply a base to work from—your metabolism and your level of conditioning can raise or lower that amount. Unless you know your level, assume that you need 4 liters/1 gallon of water a day. Now, where do you plan on getting the water?

Preferably not from natural water sources. These sources can be loaded with intestinal disturbers, such as bacteria, viruses, and fertilizers. *Giardia lamblia,* the most common of these disturbers, is a protozoan parasite that lives part of its life-cycle as a cyst in water sources. The parasite spreads when mammals defecate in water sources. Once ingested, *Giardia* can induce cramping, diarrhea, vomiting, and fatigue within 2 days to 2 weeks after ingestion. Giardiasis is treatable with prescription drugs. If you believe you've contracted giardiasis, see a doctor immediately.

Treating water. The most reliable solution to avoid polluted water is to carry your water with you. Yet, depending on the nature of your hike and the duration, this may not be an option—4 liters/1 gallon of water weighs 4 kg/8.8 pounds. In that case, you'll need to look into treating water. Regardless of which method you choose, you should always carry some water with you in case of an emergency. Save this reserve until you absolutely need it.

There are three methods of treating water: boiling, chemical treatment, and filtering. If you boil water, it's recommended that you do so for at least 1 minute, and for 3 minutes if you're above 2,000 meters (6,562 feet). This is often impractical because you're forced to exhaust a great deal of your fuel supply. You can opt for chemical treatment, which will kill *Giardia* but will not take care of other chemical pollutants. Another drawback to chemical treatments is the unpleasant taste of the water after it's treated. You can remedy this by adding powdered drink mix to the water. Filters are the preferred method for treating water. Many filters remove *Giardia,* organic and inorganic contaminants, and don't leave an aftertaste. Water filters are far from perfect as they can easily become clogged or leak if a gasket wears out. It's always a good idea to carry a backup supply of chemical treatment tablets in case your filter decides to quit on you.

Food. If we're talking about survival, you can go days without food, as long as you have water. But we're also talking about comfort. Try to avoid foods that are high in sugar and fat like candy bars and potato chips. These food types are harder to digest and are low in nutritional value. Instead, bring along foods that are easy to pack, nutritious, and high in energy (e.g., bagels, nutrition bars, dehydrated fruit, gorp, and jerky). If you are on an overnight trip, easy-to-fix dinners include rice mixes, dehydrated potatoes, corn, pasta with cheese sauce, and soup mixes. For a tasty breakfast, you can fix hot oatmeal with brown sugar and reconstituted milk powder topped off with banana chips. If you like a hot drink in the morning, bring along herbal tea bags or hot chocolate. If you are a coffee junkie, you can purchase coffee that is instant as well as packaged like tea bags. You can prepackage all of your meals in heavy-duty resealable plastic bags to keep food from spilling in your pack. These bags can be reused to pack out trash.

Shelter. The type of shelter you choose depends less on the conditions than on your tolerance for discomfort. Shelter comes in many forms—tent, tarp, lean-to, bivy sack, cabin, cave, and so on. If you're camping in the desert, a bivy sack may suffice, but if you're above the tree line and a storm is approaching, a better choice is a three- or four-season tent. Tents are the logical and most popular choice for most backpackers as they're lightweight and packable—and you always have shelter from the elements. Before you leave on your trip, anticipate what the weather and terrain will be like and plan for the type of shelter that will work best for your comfort level (see Equipment later in this section).

Finding a campsite. If there are established campsites, stick to those. If not, start looking for a campsite early—around 3:30 or 4:00 p.m., depending on sunset. Stop at the first decent site you see. Depending on the area, it could be a long time before you find another suitable location. Pitch your camp in an area that's level. Make sure the area is at least 61 meters (200 feet) from fragile areas like lakeshores, meadows, and stream banks. And try to avoid areas thick in underbrush, as they can harbor insects and provide cover for approaching animals.

If you are camping in stormy, rainy weather, look for a rock outcrop or a shelter in the trees to keep the wind from blowing your tent all night. Be sure that you don't camp under trees with dead limbs that might break off on top of you. Also, try to find an area that has an absorbent surface, such as sandy soil or forest duff. This, in addition to camping on a surface with a slight angle, will provide better drainage. By all means, don't dig trenches to provide drainage around your tent—remember you're practicing zero-impact camping.

If you're in bear country, steer clear of creekbeds or animal paths. If you see any signs of a bear's presence (i.e., scat, footprints), relocate. You'll need to find a campsite near a tall tree where you can hang your food and other items that may attract bears such as deodorant, toothpaste, or soap. Carry a lightweight nylon rope with which to hang your food. As a rule, you should hang your food at least 4 meters (13.1 feet) from the ground and 1.5 meters (5.0 feet) away from the tree trunk. You can put food and other items in a waterproof stuff sack and tie one end of the rope to the stuff sack. To get the other end of the rope over the tree branch, tie a good-size rock to it, and gently toss the rock over the tree branch. Pull the stuff sack up until it reaches the top of the branch and tie it off securely. Don't hang your food near your tent! If possible, hang your food at least 50 meters (164 feet) away from your campsite. The same distance goes for your cooking and eating areas. Alternatives to hanging your food are bear-proof plastic tubes and metal bear boxes, and you can check ahead as some campsites (such as those in provincial parks) may have these available.

Lastly, think of comfort. Lie down on the ground where you intend to sleep and see if it's a good fit. For morning warmth (and a nice view to wake up to), have your tent face east.

First Aid

I know you're tough, but get 16 kilometers (10 miles) into the woods and develop a blister and you'll wish you had carried that first-aid kit. Face it, it's just plain good sense. Many companies produce lightweight, compact first-aid kits. Just make sure yours contains at least the following:

- adhesive bandages
- moleskin or duct tape
- various sterile gauze and dressings
- white surgical tape
- elastic bandage
- antihistamine
- aspirin
- antiseptic
- first-aid book
- antacid tablets
- tweezers
- scissors
- antibacterial wipes
- antibiotic ointment
- plastic gloves
- sterile cotton tip applicators
- thermometer
- wire splint

Here are a few tips for dealing with and hopefully preventing certain ailments.

Sunburn. Take along sunscreen or sun block, protective clothing, and a wide-brimmed hat. If you do get a sunburn, treat the area with aloe vera gel, and protect the area from further sun exposure. At higher elevations, the sun's radiation can be particularly damaging to skin. Remember that your lips and eyes are vulnerable to this radiation as well. Sunglasses can be a good way to prevent headaches and permanent eye damage from the sun, especially in places where light-colored rock or patches of snow reflect light up in your face.

Blisters. Be prepared to take care of these hike-spoilers by carrying moleskin (a lightly padded adhesive), gauze and tape, or adhesive bandages. An effective way to apply moleskin is to cut out a circle of moleskin and remove the center—like a doughnut—and place it over the blistered area. Cutting the center out will reduce the pressure applied to the sensitive skin. Other products can help you combat blisters. Some are applied to suspicious hot spots before a blister forms to help decrease friction to that area, while others are applied to the blister after it has popped to help prevent further irritation.

Insect bites and stings. You can treat most insect bites and stings by applying hydrocortisone 1% anti-itch cream topically and taking a pain medication such as ibuprofen or acetaminophen to reduce swelling. If you forgot to pack these items, a cold compress or a paste of mud and ashes can sometimes assuage the itching and discomfort. Remove any stingers by using tweezers or scraping the area with your fingernail or a knife blade. Don't pinch the area as you'll only spread the venom.

Some hikers are highly sensitive to bites and stings and may have a serious allergic reaction that can be life threatening. Symptoms of a serious allergic reaction can include wheezing, an asthmatic attack, and shock. The treatment for this severe type of reaction is epinephrine. If you know that you are sensitive to bites and stings, carry a prepackaged epinephrine autoinjector, which can be obtained only by prescription from your doctor.

Ticks. Ticks can carry diseases such as Lyme disease and Rocky Mountain spotted fever. The best defense is, of course, prevention. If you know you're going to be hiking through an area littered with ticks, wear long pants and a long-sleeved shirt. You can apply a permethrin repellent to your clothing (or buy tick and mosquito repellent clothing) and use a DEET repellent on exposed skin. At the end of your hike, do a spot check for ticks (and insects in general). If you do find a tick, grab the head of the tick firmly—with a pair of tweezers if you have them—and gently pull it away from the skin with a twisting motion. Sometimes the mouth parts linger, embedded in your skin. If this happens, try to remove them with a disinfected needle. Clean the affected area with an antibacterial cleanser and then apply triple-antibiotic ointment. Monitor the area for a few days. If irritation persists or a white spot develops, see a doctor for possible infection.

Poison ivy, oak, and sumac. These skin irritants can be found most anywhere in North America and come in the form of a bush or a vine, having leaflets in groups of three, five, seven, or nine. Learn how to spot the plants. The oil they secrete can cause an allergic reaction in the form of blisters, usually about 12 hours after exposure. The itchy rash can last from 10 days to several weeks. The best defense against these irritants is to wear clothing that covers the arms, legs, and torso. For summer, zip-off cargo pants come in handy. There are also nonprescription lotions you can apply to exposed skin that guard against the effects of poison ivy/oak/sumac and can be washed off with soap and water. If you think you were in contact with the plants, after hiking (or even on the trail during longer hikes), wash with soap and water. Taking a hot shower with soap after you return home from your hike will also help to remove any lingering oil from your skin. Should you contract a rash from any of these plants, use an antihistamine to reduce the itching. If the rash is localized, create a light bleach/water wash to dry up the area. If the rash has spread, either tough it out or see your doctor about getting a dose of cortisone (available both orally and by injection).

Snakebites. Snakebites are rare in North America. Unless startled or provoked, the majority of snakes will not bite. If you are wise to their habitats and keep a careful eye on the trail, you should be just fine. When stepping over logs, first step on the log, making sure you can see what's on the other side before stepping down. Though your chances of being struck are slim, it's wise to know what to do in the event you are.

If a *nonpoisonous* snake bites you, allow the wound to bleed a small amount and then cleanse the wounded area with an antiseptic solution. Rinse the wound with clean water (preferably) or fresh urine (it might sound ugly, but it's sterile). Once the area is clean, cover it with triple-antibiotic ointment and a clean bandage. Remember, most residual damage from snakebites, poisonous or otherwise, comes from infection, not the snake's venom. Keep the area as clean as possible and get medical attention immediately.

If somebody in your party is bitten by a *poisonous* snake, follow these steps:

1. Calm the patient.
2. Remove jewelry, watches, and restrictive clothing, and immobilize the affected limb. Do not elevate the injury. Medical opinions vary on whether the area should be lower or level with the heart, but the consensus is that it should not be above it.
3. Make a note of the circumference of the limb at the bite site and at various points above the site as well. This will help you monitor swelling.
4. Evacuate your victim. Ideally he or she should be carried out to minimize movement. If the victim appears to be doing okay, he or she can walk. Stop and rest frequently, and if the swelling appears to be spreading or the patient's symptoms increase, change your plan and find a way to get your patient transported.
5. If you are waiting for rescue, make sure to keep your patient comfortable and hydrated (unless he begins vomiting).

Snakebite treatment is rife with old-fashioned remedies: You used to be told to cut and suck the venom out of the bite site or to use a suction cup extractor for the same purpose; applying an electric shock to the area was even in vogue for a while. Do not do any of these things. Do not apply ice, do not give your patient painkillers, and do not apply a tourniquet. All you really want to do is keep your patient calm and get help. If you're alone and have to hike out, don't run—you'll only increase the flow of blood throughout your system. Instead, walk calmly.

Dehydration. Have you ever hiked in hot weather and had a roaring headache and felt fatigued after only a few miles? More than likely you were dehydrated. Symptoms of dehydration include fatigue, headache, and decreased coordination and judgment. When you are hiking, your body's rate of fluid loss depends on the outside temperature, humidity, altitude, and your activity level. On average, a hiker walking in warm weather will lose 4 liters (4 quarts) of fluid a day. That fluid loss is easily replaced by normal consumption of liquids and food. However, if a hiker is walking briskly in hot, dry weather and hauling a heavy pack, he or she can lose 1 to 3 liters

(1 to 3 quarts) of water an hour. It's important to always carry plenty of water and to stop often and drink fluids regularly, even if you aren't thirsty.

Heat exhaustion is the result of a loss of large amounts of electrolytes and often occurs if a hiker is dehydrated and has been under heavy exertion. Common symptoms of heat exhaustion include cramping, exhaustion, fatigue, lightheadedness, and nausea. You can treat heat exhaustion by getting out of the sun and drinking an electrolyte solution made up of 1 teaspoon salt and 1 tablespoon sugar dissolved in a liter of water. Drink this solution slowly over a period of 1 hour. Drinking plenty of fluids (preferably an electrolyte solution/sports drink) can prevent heat exhaustion. Avoid hiking during the hottest parts of the day, and wear breathable clothing, a wide-brimmed hat, and sunglasses.

Hypothermia is one of the biggest dangers in the backcountry, especially for day hikers in the summertime. That may sound strange, but imagine starting out on a hike in midsummer when it's sunny and 25°C/80°F out. You're clad in nylon shorts and a cotton T-shirt. About halfway through your hike, the sky begins to cloud up, and in the next hour a light drizzle begins to fall and the wind starts to pick up. Before you know it, you are soaking wet and shivering—the perfect recipe for hypothermia. More advanced signs include decreased coordination, slurred speech, and blurred vision. When a victim's temperature falls below 32°C/90°F, moderate hypothermia symptoms include low blood pressure and slowed heart rate. Severe hypothermia, a body temperature below 28°C/82°F, can lead to unconsciousness.

To avoid hypothermia, always bring a windproof/rainproof shell, a fleece jacket, long underwear made of a breathable, synthetic fiber, gloves, and hat when you are hiking in the mountains. Learn to adjust your clothing layers based on the temperature. If you are climbing uphill at a moderate pace, you will stay warm, but when you stop for a break, you'll become cold quickly, unless you add more layers of clothing.

If a hiker is showing advanced signs of hypothermia, dress him or her in dry clothes and make sure he or she is wearing a hat and gloves. Place the person in a sleeping bag in a tent or shelter that will protect him or her from the wind and other elements. Give the person warm fluids to drink and keep him or her awake.

Frostbite. When the mercury dips below 0°C/32°F, your extremities begin to chill. If a persistent chill attacks a localized area, say, your hands or your toes, the circulatory system reacts by cutting off blood flow to the affected area—the idea being to protect and preserve the body's overall temperature. And so it's death by attrition for the affected area. Ice crystals start to form from the water in the cells of the neglected tissue. Deprived of heat, nourishment, and now water, the tissue literally starves. This is frostbite.

Prevention is your best defense against this situation. Most prone to frostbite are your face, hands, and feet, so protect these areas well. Wool is the traditional material of choice because it provides ample air space for insulation and draws moisture away from the skin. Synthetic fabrics, however, have made great strides in the cold weather clothing market. Do your research. A pair of light silk liners under your regular gloves is a good trick for keeping warm. They afford some additional warmth, but more importantly they'll allow you to remove your mitts for tedious work without exposing the skin.

If your feet or hands start to feel cold or numb due to the elements, warm them as quickly as possible. Place cold hands under your armpits or bury them in your crotch. If your feet are cold, change your socks. If there's plenty of room in your boots, add another pair of socks. Do remember, though, that constricting your feet in tight boots can restrict blood flow and actually make your feet colder more quickly. Your socks need to have breathing room if they're going to be effective. Dead air provides insulation. If your face is cold, place your warm hands over your face, or simply wear a head stocking.

Should your skin go numb and start to appear white and waxy, chances are you've got or are developing frostbite. Don't try to thaw the area unless you can maintain the warmth. In other words, don't stop to warm up your frostbitten feet only to head back on the trail. You'll do more damage than good. Tests have shown that hikers who walked on thawed feet did more harm, and endured more pain, than hikers who left the affected areas alone. Do your best to get out of the cold entirely and seek medical attention—which usually consists of performing a rapid rewarming in water for 20 to 30 minutes.

The overall objective in preventing both hypothermia and frostbite is to keep the body's core warm. Protect key areas where heat escapes, like the top of the head, and maintain the proper nutrition level. Foods that are high in calories aid the body in producing heat. Never smoke or drink when you're in situations where the cold is threatening. By affecting blood flow, these activities ultimately cool the body's core temperature.

Altitude sickness (AMS). High lofty peaks, clear alpine lakes, and vast mountain views beckon hikers to the high country. But those who like to venture high may become victims of altitude sickness (also known as Acute Mountain Sickness—AMS). Altitude sickness is your body's reaction to insufficient oxygen in the blood due to decreased barometric pressure. While some hikers may feel lightheaded, nauseous, and experience shortness of breath at 2,133 meters (7,000 feet), others may not experience these symptoms until they reach 3,000 meters (10,000 feet) or higher.

Slowing your ascent to high places and giving your body a chance to acclimatize to the higher elevations can prevent altitude sickness. For example, if you live at sea level and are planning a weeklong backpacking trip to elevations between 2,133 meters (7,000 feet) and 3,650 meters (12,000 feet), start by staying below 2,133 meters (7,000 feet) for one night, then move to between 2,133 meters (7,000 feet) and 3,000 meters (10,000 feet) for another night or two. Avoid strenuous exertion and alcohol to give your body a chance to adjust to the new altitude. It's also important to eat light food and drink plenty of nonalcoholic fluids, preferably water. Loss of appetite at altitude is common, but you must eat!

Most hikers who experience mild to moderate AMS develop a headache and/or nausea, grow lethargic, and have problems sleeping. The treatment for AMS is simple: stop heading uphill. Keep eating and drinking water and take meds for the headache. You actually need to take more breaths at altitude than at sea level, so breathe a little faster without hyperventilating. If symptoms don't improve over 24 to 48 hours, descend. Once a victim descends about 600 to 900 meters (2,000 to 3,000 feet), the signs will usually begin to diminish.

Severe AMS comes in two forms: High Altitude Pulmonary Edema (HAPE) and High Altitude Cerebral Edema (HACE). HAPE, an accumulation of fluid in the lungs, can occur above 2,400 meters (8,000 feet). Symptoms include rapid heart rate, shortness of breath at rest, AMS symptoms, dry cough developing into a wet cough, gurgling sounds, flulike or bronchitis symptoms, and lack of muscle coordination. HAPE is life threatening so descend immediately, at least 600 to 1,200 meters (2,000 to 4,000 feet). HACE usually occurs above 3,650 meters (12,000 feet) but sometimes occurs above 3,000 meters (10,000 feet). Symptoms are similar to HAPE but also include seizures, hallucinations, paralysis, and vision disturbances. Descend immediately—HACE is also life threatening.

Hantavirus Pulmonary Syndrome (HPS). Deer mice spread the virus that causes HPS, and humans contract it from breathing it in, usually when they've disturbed an area with dust and mice feces from nests or surfaces with mice droppings or urine. Exposure to large numbers of rodents and their feces or urine presents the greatest risk. As hikers, we sometimes enter old buildings like cabins, and often deer mice live in these places. We may not be around long enough to be exposed, but do be aware of this disease. About half the people who develop HPS die. Symptoms are flulike and appear about 2 to 3 weeks after exposure. After initial symptoms, a dry cough and shortness of breath follow. Breathing is difficult. If you even think you might have HPS, see a doctor immediately!

Natural Hazards

Besides tripping over a rock or tree root on the trail, there are some real hazards to be aware of while hiking. Even if where you're hiking doesn't have a plethora of poisonous snakes and plants, there are a few weather conditions and predators you may need to take into account.

Lightning. Lightning is generated by thunderheads and can strike without warning, even several miles away from the nearest overhead cloud. The best rule of thumb is to start leaving exposed peaks, ridges, and canyon rims by about noon. This time can vary a little depending on storm buildup. Keep an eye on cloud formation and don't underestimate how fast a storm can build. The bigger they get, the more likely a thunderstorm will happen. Lightning takes the path of least resistance, so if you're the high point, it might choose you. Ducking under a rock overhang is dangerous as you form the shortest path between the rock and ground. If you dash below tree line, avoid standing under the only or the tallest tree. If you are caught above tree line, stay away from anything metal you might be carrying, Move down off the ridge slightly to a low, treeless point and squat until the storm passes. If you have an insulating pad, squat on it. Avoid having both your hands and feet touching the ground at once and never lie flat. If you hear a buzzing sound or feel your hair standing on end, move quickly as an electrical charge is building up.

Bears. The Vancouver area does not have a grizzly bear population save for some very remote areas of the Coast Mountains. Black bears are plentiful, however. Here are some tips in case you and a bear scare each other. Most of all, avoid surprising a bear. Talk or sing where visibility or hearing are limited, such as along a rushing creek or in thick brush. In grizzly country especially, carry bear spray in a holster on your pack belt where you can quickly grab it. While hiking, watch for bear tracks (five toes), droppings (sizable with leaves, partly digested berries, seeds, and/or animal fur), or rocks and roots along the trail that show signs of being dug up (this could be a bear looking for bugs to eat). Keep a clean camp, hang food or use bearproof storage containers, and don't sleep in the clothes you wore while cooking. Be especially careful to avoid getting between a mother and her cubs. In late summer and fall, bears are busy eating to fatten up for winter, so be extra careful around berry bushes. If you do encounter a bear, move away slowly while facing the bear, talk softly, and avoid direct eye contact. Give the bear room to escape. Since bears are very curious, it might stand upright to get a better whiff of you, and it may even charge you to try to intimidate you. Try to stay calm. If a black bear attacks you, fight back with anything you have handy. If a grizzly bear attacks you, your best option is to "play dead" by lying face down on the ground and covering the back of your neck and head with your hands. Unleashed dogs have been known to come running back to their owners with a bear close behind. Keep your dog on a leash or leave it at home.

Cougars. Cougars appear to be getting more comfortable around humans as long as deer (their favorite prey) are in an area with adequate cover. Usually elusive and quiet, cougars rarely attack people. If you meet a cougar, give it a chance to escape. Stay calm and talk firmly to it. Back away slowly while facing the animal. If you run, you'll only encourage the cat to chase you. Make yourself look large by opening a jacket, if you have one, or waving your hiking poles. If the cougar behaves aggressively, throw stones, sticks, or whatever you can while remaining tall. If a cougar does attack, fight for your life with anything you can grab.

Moose. Because moose have very few natural predators, they don't fear humans like other animals. You might find moose in sagebrush and wetter areas of willow, aspen, and pine, or in beaver habitats. Mothers with calves, as well as bulls during mating season, can be particularly aggressive. If a moose threatens you, back away slowly and talk calmly to it. If a moose charges you, run in a zigzag and duck behind trees—moose have poor eyesight. Keep your pets away from moose.

Other considerations. Hunting is a popular pastime, especially during fall. Hiking is still enjoyable in those months in many areas, so just take a few precautions. First, learn when the different hunting seasons start and end in the area in which you'll be hiking. During this time frame, be sure to wear at least a blaze orange hat, and possibly put an orange vest over your pack. Don't be surprised to see hunters in camo outfits carrying bows or rifles around during their season. If you would feel more comfortable without hunters around, hike in national parks, provincial parks, and city parks where hunting is not allowed.

Navigation

Whether you are going on a short hike in a familiar area or planning a weeklong backpack trip, you should always be equipped with the proper navigational equipment—at the very least a detailed map and a sturdy compass.

Maps. There are many different types of maps available to help you find your way on the trail. Easiest to find are National Topographical System maps. These maps tend to cover large areas, so be sure they are detailed enough for your particular trip. Online topographical options include the GeoBC Topographic Map Viewer (gov.bc .ca), as well as the Atlas of Canada Toporama tool (atlas.gc.ca). You can also obtain park maps as well as high-quality maps from private companies and trail groups. These maps can be obtained either from outdoor stores or ranger stations.

If you want to check out the high-tech world of maps, you can purchase topographic maps digitally. These software-mapping programs let you select a route on your computer, print it out, then take it with you on the trail. Many mapping programs also let you insert symbols and labels, download waypoints from a GPS unit, and export the maps.

Smartphone apps are also making leaps in functions that allow you to see local area trails, download maps for use offline, and track your adventures. Two I can recommend are Gaia GPS (gaiagps.com) and Topo Maps+ (glacierpeak.app).

Orientation. The art of map reading is a skill that you can develop by first practicing in an area you are familiar with. To begin, orient the map so the map is lined up in the correct direction (i.e., north on the map is lined up with true north). Next, familiarize yourself with the map symbols and try to match them up with terrain features around you such as a high ridge, mountain peak, river, or lake. If you are practicing with a topographical map, notice the contour lines. On gentler terrain these contour lines are spaced farther apart, and on steeper terrain they are closer together. Pick a short loop trail, and stop frequently to check your position on the map. As you practice map reading, you'll learn how to anticipate a steep section on the trail or a good place to take a rest break, and so on.

Compasses. First off, the sun is not a substitute for a compass. So, what kind of compass should you have? Here are some characteristics you should look for: a rectangular base with detailed scales, a liquid-filled housing, protective housing, a sighting line on the mirror, luminous alignment and back-bearing arrows, a luminous north-seeking arrow, and a well-defined bezel ring.

You can learn compass basics by reading the detailed instructions included with your compass. If you want to fine-tune your compass skills, sign up for an orienteering class or purchase a book on compass reading. Once you've learned the basic skills of using a compass, remember to practice these skills before you head into the backcountry.

GPS. If you are a klutz at using a compass, you may be interested in checking out the technical wizardry of a GPS (Global Positioning System) device. GPS was developed by the Pentagon and works off 24 NAVSTAR satellites, which were designed to guide missiles to their targets. A GPS device is a handheld unit that calculates your latitude and longitude with the easy press of a button. The Department of Defense used to scramble the satellite signals a bit to prevent civilians (and spies!) from getting extremely accurate readings, but that practice was discontinued in May 2000, and GPS units now provide nearly pinpoint accuracy (within 9 to 18 meters [30 to 60 feet]).

There are many different types of GPS units available and they range in price from $100 to $400. In general, all GPS units have a display screen and keypad where you input information. In addition to acting as a compass, the unit allows you to plot your route, easily retrace your path, track your traveling speed, find the mileage between waypoints, and calculate the total mileage of your route.

Before you purchase a GPS unit, keep in mind that these devices don't pick up signals indoors, in heavily wooded areas, on mountain peaks, or in deep valleys. Also, batteries can wear out or other technical problems can develop. A GPS unit should be used in conjunction with a map and compass, not in place of those items.

Activity trackers. Fitness trackers and pedometers are small, clip-on or wearable units with a digital display that calculate your hiking distance in miles or kilometers based on your walking stride. Some also calculate the calories you burn and your total hiking time. Basic options are available at most large outdoor stores and online for around $20 to $40.

Trip Planning

Planning your hiking adventure begins with letting a friend or relative know your trip itinerary so they can call for help if you don't return at your scheduled time. Your next task is to make sure you are outfitted to experience the risks and rewards of the trail. This section highlights gear and clothing you may want to take with you to get the most out of your hike.

Day Hikes

- bear repellent spray (if hiking in black bear country)
- bear bell
- camera
- cell phone with charged battery
- compass, plus an optional GPS unit
- daypack
- emergency shelter, such as a tarp or large orange plastic bag

- first-aid kit
- fitness tracker/pedometer
- food
- guidebook
- headlamp/flashlight with extra batteries and bulbs
- hat
- insect repellent
- knife/multipurpose tool
- map
- matches in waterproof container and fire starter
- fleece jacket
- rain gear
- space blanket
- sunglasses
- sunscreen
- swimsuit and/or fishing gear (if hiking to a lake)
- watch
- water and water bottles/water hydration system
- whistle

Overnight Trip

In addition to the day hike essentials above:
- backpack and waterproof rain cover
- backpacker's trowel
- bandana
- biodegradable soap
- collapsible water container (8–12 liter [2–3 gallon] capacity)
- clothing—extra wool socks, shirt, and shorts
- cook set/utensils
- ditty bags to store gear
- extra plastic resealable bags
- gaiters
- garbage bag
- ground cloth
- journal/pen
- long underwear
- nylon rope to hang food

- permit (if required)
- pot scrubber
- rain jacket and pants
- sandals to wear around camp and to ford streams
- sleeping bag
- sleeping pad
- small bath towel
- stove and fuel
- tent
- toiletry items
- water filter
- waterproof stuff sack

Equipment

With the outdoor market currently flooded with products, many of which are pure gimmickry, it seems impossible to both differentiate and choose. Do I really need a tropical-fish-lined collapsible shower? (No, you don't.) The only defense against the maddening quantity of items thrust in your face is to think practically—and to do so before you go shopping. The worst buys are impulsive buys. Since most name brands will differ only slightly in quality, it's best to know what you're looking for in terms of function. Buy only what you need. You will, don't forget, be carrying what you've bought on your back. Here are some things to keep in mind before you go shopping.

Clothes. Clothing is your armor against Mother Nature's little surprises. Hikers should be prepared for any possibility, especially when hiking in mountainous areas. Adequate rain protection and extra layers of clothing are a good idea. In summer, a wide-brimmed hat can help keep the sun at bay. In the winter months the first layer you'll want to wear is a "wicking" layer of long underwear that keeps perspiration away from your skin. Wear long underwear made from synthetic fibers that wick moisture away from the skin and draw it toward the next layer of clothing, where it then evaporates. Avoid wearing long underwear made of cotton as it is slow to dry and keeps moisture next to your skin.

The second layer you'll wear is the "insulating" layer. Aside from keeping you warm, this layer needs to "breathe" so you stay dry while hiking. A fabric that provides insulation and dries quickly is fleece. It's interesting to note that this one-of-a-kind fabric is made out of recycled plastic. Purchasing a zip-up jacket made of this material is highly recommended.

The last line of layering defense is the "shell" layer. You'll need some type of waterproof, windproof, breathable jacket that will fit over all of your other layers. It should have a large hood that fits over a hat. You'll also need a good pair of rain pants made from a similar waterproof, breathable fabric. Some Gore-Tex jackets cost as much as $500, but you should know that there are more affordable fabrics out there that work just as well.

Now that you've learned the basics of layering, you can't forget to protect your hands and face. In cold, windy, or rainy weather, you'll need a hat made of wool or fleece and insulated, waterproof gloves that will keep your hands warm and toasty. As mentioned earlier, buying an additional pair of light silk liners to wear under your regular gloves is a good idea.

Footwear. If you have any extra money to spend on your trip, put that money into boots or trail shoes. Poor shoes will bring a hike to a halt faster than anything else. To avoid this annoyance, buy shoes that provide support and are lightweight and flexible. A lightweight hiking boot is better than a heavy, leather mountaineering boot for most day hikes and backpacking. Trail running shoes provide a little extra cushion and are made in a sneaker style that many people wear for hiking. These running shoes are lighter, more flexible, and more breathable than hiking boots. If you know you'll be hiking in wet weather often, purchase boots or shoes with a Gore-Tex liner, which will help keep your feet dry.

When buying your boots, be sure to wear the same type of socks you'll be wearing on the trail. If the boots you're buying are for cold weather hiking, try the boots on while wearing two pairs of socks. Speaking of socks, a good cold weather sock combination is to wear a thinner sock made of wool or polypropylene covered by a heavier outer sock made of wool or a synthetic/wool mix. The inner sock protects the foot from the rubbing effects of the outer sock and prevents blisters. Many outdoor stores have some type of ramp to simulate hiking uphill and downhill. Be sure to take advantage of this test, as toe-jamming boot fronts can be very painful and debilitating on the downhill trek.

Once you've purchased your footwear, be sure to break them in before you hit the trail. New footwear is often stiff and needs to be stretched and molded to your foot.

Hiking poles. Hiking poles help with balance, and more importantly take pressure off your knees. The ones with shock absorbers are easier on your elbows and knees. Some poles even come with a camera attachment to be used as a monopod. And heaven forbid you meet a cougar, bear, or unfriendly dog, the poles can make you look a lot bigger.

Backpacks. No matter what type of hiking you do, you'll need a pack of some sort to carry the basic trail essentials. There are a variety of backpacks on the market, but let's first discuss what you intend to use it for. Day hikes or overnight trips?

If you plan on doing a day hike, a daypack should have some of the following characteristics: a padded hip belt that's at least 5 centimeters (2 inches) in diameter (avoid packs with only a small nylon piece of webbing for a hip belt); a chest strap (the chest strap helps stabilize the pack against your body); external pockets to carry water and other items that you want easy access to; an internal pocket to hold keys, a knife, a wallet, and other miscellaneous items; an external lashing system to hold a jacket; and, if you so desire, a hydration pocket for carrying a hydration system (which consists of a water bladder with an attachable drinking hose).

For short hikes, some hikers like to use a fanny pack to store just a camera, food, a compass, a map, and other trail essentials. Most fanny packs have pockets for two water bottles and a padded hip belt.

If you intend to do an extended, overnight trip, there are multiple considerations. First off, you need to decide what kind of framed pack you want. There are two backpack types for backpacking: the internal frame and the external frame. An internal frame pack rests closer to your body, making it more stable and easier to balance when hiking over rough terrain. An external frame pack is just that, an aluminum frame attached to the exterior of the pack. Some hikers consider an external frame pack to be better for long backpack trips because it distributes the pack weight better and allows you to carry heavier loads. It's often easier to pack, and your gear is more accessible. It also offers better back ventilation in hot weather.

The most critical measurement for fitting a pack is torso length. The pack needs to rest evenly on your hips without sagging. A good pack will come in two or three sizes and have straps and hip belts that are adjustable according to your body size and characteristics.

When you purchase a backpack, go to an outdoor store with salespeople who are knowledgeable in how to properly fit a pack. Once the pack is fitted for you, load the pack with the amount of weight you plan on taking on the trail. The weight of the pack should be distributed evenly and you should be able to swing your arms and walk briskly without feeling out of balance. Another good technique for evaluating a pack is to walk up and down stairs and make quick turns to the right and to the left to be sure the pack doesn't feel out of balance. Other features that are nice to have on a backpack include a removable daypack or fanny pack, external pockets for extra water, and extra lash points to attach a jacket or other items.

Sleeping bags and pads. Sleeping bags are rated by temperature. You can purchase a bag made with synthetic insulation, or you can buy a goose down bag. Goose down bags are more expensive, but they have a higher insulating capacity by weight and will keep their loft longer. You'll want to purchase a bag with a temperature rating that fits the time of year and conditions you are most likely to camp in. One caveat: The techno-standard for temperature ratings is far from perfect. Ratings vary from manufacturer to manufacturer, so to protect yourself you should purchase a bag rated 5 to 10°C/10 to 15°F below the temperature you expect to be camping in. Synthetic bags are more resistant to water, while down bags are also more compressible and take up less room in your pack, which is an important consideration if you are planning a multiday backpack trip. Features to look for in a sleeping bag include a mummy-style bag, a hood you can cinch down around your head in cold weather, and draft tubes along the zippers that help keep heat in and drafts out.

You'll also want a sleeping pad to provide insulation and padding from the cold ground. There are different types of sleeping pads available, from the more expensive self-inflating air mattresses to the less expensive closed-cell foam pads. Self-inflating air mattresses are usually heavier than closed-cell foam mattresses and are prone to punctures.

Tents. The tent is your home away from home while on the trail. It provides protection from wind, rain, snow, and insects. A three-season tent is a good choice for backpacking and can range in price from $150 to $500 or more. These lightweight and versatile tents provide protection in all types of weather, except heavy snowstorms or high winds, and can weigh less than 1 kilogram (2.2 pounds). Look for a tent that's easy to set up and will easily fit two people with gear. Dome-type tents usually offer more headroom and places to store gear. Other handy tent features include a vestibule where you can store wet boots and backpacks. Some nice-to-have items in a tent include interior pockets to store small items and lashing points to hang a clothesline. Most three-season tents also come with stakes so you can secure the tent in high winds. Before you purchase a tent, set it up and take it down a few times to be sure it is easy to handle. Also, sit inside the tent and make sure it has enough room for you and your gear.

Cell phones. Many hikers carry their cell phones into the backcountry these days in case of emergency. That's fine and good, but please know that cell phone coverage is often poor to nonexistent in valleys, canyons, and thick forest. More importantly people have started to call for help because they're tired or lost. Let's go back to being prepared. You are responsible for yourself in the backcountry. Use your brain to avoid problems, and if you do encounter one, first use your brain to try to correct the situation. Only use your cell phone, if it works, in true emergencies. If it doesn't work down low in a valley, try hiking to a high point where you might get reception.

Before heading out on the trail, be sure your battery is fully charged. Keeping your phone in "airplane" mode is the best way to preserve battery life. Search and rescue services also recommend knowing how to use your phone to find your GPS coordinates or via a website such as https://yourlo.ca/tion.

Hiking with Children

Hiking with children isn't a matter of how many miles you can cover or how much elevation gain you make in a day; it's about seeing and experiencing nature through their eyes.

Kids like to explore and have fun. They like to stop and point out bugs and plants, look under rocks, jump in puddles, and throw sticks. If you're taking a toddler or young child on a hike, start with a trail that you're familiar with. Trails that have interesting things for kids, like piles of leaves to play in or a small stream to wade through during the summer, will make the hike much more enjoyable for them and will keep them from getting bored.

You can keep your child's attention if you have a strategy before starting on the trail. Using games is not only an effective way to keep a child's attention, it's also a great way to teach him or her about nature. Quiz children on the names of plants and animals. Pick up a family-friendly outdoor hobby like geocaching (geocaching.com), which combines the outdoors, clue-solving, and treasure hunting. If your children are old enough, let them carry their own daypack filled with snacks and water. So that you are sure to go at their pace and not yours, let them lead the way. Playing follow the leader works particularly well when you have a group of children. Have each child take a turn at being the leader.

With children, a lot of clothing is key. The only thing predictable about weather is that it will change. Especially in mountainous areas, weather can change dramatically in a very short time. Always bring extra clothing for children, regardless of the season. In the winter, have your children wear wool socks and warm layers such as long underwear, a fleece jacket and hat, wool mittens, and good rain gear. It's not a bad idea to have these along in late fall and early spring as well. Good footwear is also important. A sturdy pair of running shoes or lightweight hiking boots are the best bet for little ones. If you're hiking in the summer near a lake or stream, bring along a pair of old sneakers that your child can put on when he or she wants to go exploring in the water. Remember when you're near any type of water, always watch your child at all times. Also, keep a close eye on teething toddlers who may decide a rock or leaf of poison oak is an interesting item to put in their mouth.

From spring through fall, you'll want your kids to wear a wide-brimmed hat to keep their face, head, and ears protected from the hot sun. Also, make sure your children wear sunscreen at all times. If you are hiking with a child younger than 6 months, don't use sunscreen or insect repellent. Instead, be sure that their head, face, neck, and ears are protected from the sun with a wide-brimmed hat, and that all other skin exposed to the sun is protected with the appropriate clothing.

Remember that food is fun. Kids like snacks so it's important to bring a lot of munchies for the trail. Stopping often for snack breaks is a fun way to keep the trail interesting. Raisins, apples, granola bars, crackers and cheese, cereal, and trail mix all make great snacks. Also, a few of their favorite candy treats can go a long way toward heading off a fit of fussing. If your child is old enough to carry his or her own backpack, let him or her fill it with some lightweight "comfort" items such as a doll, a small stuffed animal, or a little toy (you'll have to draw the line at bringing the 10-pound Tonka truck). If your kids don't like drinking water, you can bring some powdered drink mix or a juice box.

Avoid poorly designed child-carrying packs—you don't want to break your back carrying your child. Most child-carrying backpacks are designed to carry an 18-kilogram (40-pound) child plus the weight of diapers and other items. Some have an optional rain/sun hood.

Hiking with Your Dog

Bringing your furry friend with you is always more fun than leaving him behind. Our canine pals make great trail buddies because they never complain and always make good company. Hiking with your dog can be a rewarding experience, especially if you plan ahead.

Getting your dog in shape. Before you plan outdoor adventures with your dog, make sure he's in shape for the trail. Getting your dog into shape takes the same discipline as getting yourself into shape, but, luckily, your dog can get in shape with you. Take your dog with you on your daily runs or walks. If there is a park near your house, hit a tennis ball or play Frisbee with your dog.

Swimming is also an excellent way to get your dog into shape. If there is a lake or river near where you live and your dog likes the water, have him retrieve a tennis ball or stick. Gradually build your dog's stamina up over a 2- to 3-month period. A good rule of thumb is to assume that your dog will travel twice as far as you will on the trail. If you plan on doing an 8-kilometer (5-mile) hike, be sure your dog is in shape for a 16-kilometer (10-mile) hike.

Training your dog for the trail. Before you go on your first hiking adventure with your dog, be sure he has a firm grasp on the basics of canine etiquette and behavior. Make sure he can sit, lie down, stay, and come. One of the most important commands you can teach your canine pal is to "come" under any situation. It's easy for your friend's nose to lead him astray or possibly get lost. Another helpful command is the "get behind" command. When you're on a hiking trail that's narrow, you can have your dog follow behind you when other trail users approach. Nothing is more bothersome than an enthusiastic dog that runs back and forth on the trail and disrupts the peace of the trail for others—or, worse, jumps up on other hikers and gets them muddy. When you see other trail users approaching you on the trail, give them the right-of-way by quietly stepping off the trail and making your dog lie down and stay until they pass.

Equipment. The most critical pieces of equipment you can invest in for your dog are proper identification and a sturdy leash. Flexi-leads work well for hiking because they give your dog more freedom to explore but still leave you in control. Make sure your dog has identification that includes your name and address and a number for your veterinarian. Other forms of identification for your dog include a tattoo or a microchip. You should consult your veterinarian for more information on these last two options.

The next piece of equipment you'll want to consider is a pack for your dog. By no means should you hold all of your dog's essentials in your pack—let him carry his own gear! Dogs that are in good shape can carry 30 to 40 percent of their own weight.

Most packs are fitted by a dog's weight and girth measurement. Companies that make dog packs generally include guidelines to help you pick out the size that's right for your dog. Some characteristics to look for when purchasing a pack for your dog include a harness that contains two padded girth straps, a padded chest strap, leash attachments, removable saddlebags, internal water bladders, and external gear cords.

You can introduce your dog to the pack by first placing the empty pack on his back and letting him wear it around the yard. Keep an eye on him during this first introduction. He may decide to chew through the straps if you aren't watching him closely. Once he learns to treat the pack as an object of fun and not a foreign enemy, fill the pack evenly on both sides with a few ounces of dog food in resealable plastic bags. Have your dog wear his pack on your daily walks for a period of 2 to 3 weeks. Each week add a little more weight to the pack until your dog will accept carrying the maximum amount of weight he can carry.

You can also purchase collapsible water and dog food bowls for your dog. These bowls are lightweight and can easily be stashed into your pack or your dog's. If you are hiking on rocky terrain or in the snow, you can purchase footwear for your dog that will protect his feet from cuts and bruises.

Always carry plastic bags to remove feces from the trail. It is a courtesy to other trail users and helps protect local wildlife.

The following is a list of items to bring when you take your dog hiking: collapsible water/food bowls, a comb, a collar and a leash, dog food, plastic bags for feces, a dog pack, flea/tick powder, paw protection, water, and a first-aid kit that contains eye ointment, tweezers, scissors, stretchy foot wrap, gauze, antibacterial wash, sterile cotton tip applicators, antibiotic ointment, and cotton wrap.

First aid for your dog. Your dog is just as prone—if not more prone—to getting in trouble on the trail as you are, so be prepared. Here's a rundown of the more likely misfortunes that might befall your little friend.

Bees and wasps. If a bee or wasp stings your dog, remove the stinger with a pair of tweezers and place a mudpack or a cloth dipped in cold water over the affected area.

Porcupines. One good reason to keep your dog on a leash is to prevent it from getting a nose full of porcupine quills. You may be able to remove the quills with pliers, but a veterinarian is the best person to do this nasty job because most dogs need to be sedated.

Heat stroke. Avoid hiking with your dog in really hot weather. Dogs with heat stroke will pant excessively, lie down and refuse to get up, and become lethargic and disoriented. If your dog shows any of these signs on the trail, have him lie down in the shade. If you are near a stream, pour cool water over your dog's entire body to help bring his body temperature back to normal.

Heartworm. Dogs get heartworms from mosquitoes, which carry the disease in the prime mosquito months of July and August. Giving your dog a monthly pill prescribed by your veterinarian easily prevents this condition.

Plant pitfalls. One of the biggest plant hazards for dogs on the trail are foxtails. Foxtails are pointed grass seed heads that bury themselves in your friend's fur, between his toes, and even get in his ear canal. If left unattended, these nasty seeds can work their way under the skin and cause abscesses and other problems. If you have a long-haired dog, consider trimming the hair between his toes and giving him a summer haircut to help prevent foxtails from attaching to his fur. After every hike, always look over your dog for these seeds—especially between his toes and his ears.

Other plant hazards include burrs, thorns, thistles, and poison oak. If you find any burrs or thistles on your dog, remove them as soon as possible before they become an unmanageable mat. Thorns can pierce a dog's foot and cause a great deal of pain. If you see that your dog is lame, stop and check his feet for thorns. Dogs are immune to poison oak but they can pick up the sticky, oily substance from the plant and transfer it to you.

Protect those paws. Be sure to keep your dog's nails trimmed so he avoids getting soft tissue or joint injuries. If your dog slows and refuses to go on, check to see that his paws aren't torn or worn. You can protect your dog's paws from trail hazards such as sharp gravel, foxtails, lava scree, and thorns by purchasing dog boots.

Sunburn. If your dog has light skin, he is an easy target for sunburn on his nose and other exposed skin areas. You can apply a nontoxic sunscreen to exposed skin areas that will help protect him from overexposure to the sun.

Ticks and fleas. Ticks can easily give your dog Lyme disease, as well as other diseases. Before you hit the trail, treat your dog with a flea and tick spray or powder. You can also ask your veterinarian about a once-a-month pour-on treatment that repels fleas and ticks.

Mosquitoes and deer flies. These little flying machines can do a job on your dog's snout and ears. Best bet is to spray your dog with pet-friendly fly repellent to discourage both pests.

Giardia. Dogs can get *Giardia*, which results in diarrhea. It is usually not debilitating, but it's definitely messy.

Mushrooms. Make sure your dog doesn't sample mushrooms along the trail. They could be poisonous to him, but he doesn't know that.

When you are finally ready to hit the trail with your dog, keep in mind that some parks and wilderness areas do not allow dogs on trails. Your best bet is to hike in provincial parks and on Crown land—and to bring a leash. Always check ahead to see what the restrictions are.

Clubs and Trail Groups

Hiking Clubs

Alpine Club of Canada, alpineclubofcanada.ca

Alpine Club of Canada (Vancouver), accvancouver.ca

British Columbia Mountaineering Club, PO Box 20042, Vancouver, BC, V5Z 0C1; bcmc.ca

Federation of Mountain Clubs of BC, (604) 873-6096; mountainclubs.org

Nature Vancouver, naturevancouver.ca

North Shore Hikers, northshorehikers.org

Search and Rescue

Dial 911 for all emergencies and ask for the police.

Coquitlam Search and Rescue, 1300 Pinetree Way, Coquitlam, BC, V3B 7S4; (604) 927-3484; coquitlam-sar.bc.ca

Lions Bay Search and Rescue, PO Box 629, Lions Bay, BC, V0N 2E0; lbsar.com

North Shore Rescue, 63 Bewicke Ave., North Vancouver, BC, V7M 3B6; (778) 338-6300; northshorerescue.com

Ridge Meadows Search and Rescue, 23598 Jim Robson Way, Maple Ridge, BC, V2W 1B8; (604) 463-4891; rmsar.bc.ca

Squamish Search and Rescue Society, PO Box 1666, Garibaldi Highlands, BC, V0N 1T0; (604) 815-5071, squamishsar.org

South Fraser Search and Rescue, sfsar.ca

Advocacy Groups

BC Wildlife Federation, 101-9706 188th St., Surrey, BC, V4N 3M2; (604) 882-9988, toll free (888) 881-2293; bcwf.bc.ca

Burns Bog Conservation Society, 4-7953 120 St., Delta, BC, V4C 6P6; (604) 572-0373; burnsbog.org

Friends of Cypress Provincial Park, cypresspark.ca

Outdoor Recreation Council of BC, (604) 873-5546; orcbc.ca

Parks and Recreation Areas

BC Parks, bcparks.ca

Discover Camping, (778) 309-1439, toll free (800) 689-9025; discovercamping.ca

Outdoor Gear Stores

Arc'teryx Factory Store, 2155 Dollarton Hwy., #100, North Vancouver, BC, V7H 3B2; (604) 960-3119; arcteryx.com

Mountain Equipment Co-op, 111 East 2nd Ave., Vancouver, BC, V5T 1B4; (604) 872-7858; mec.ca

Rent Outdoors, (604) 357-4770; rentoutdoors.com

Taiga Works, 3454 Bridgeway St., Vancouver, BC, V5K 1B6; (604) 875-6644; taiga works.ca

Valhalla Pure, 88 W. Broadway, Vancouver, BC, V5Y 1P2; (604) 872-8872; vpo.ca

Hike Index

Acadia and Tower Beaches, 37
Alice Lake Provincial Park, 160
Beaver Lake, 14
Boundary Bay, 258
Brunswick Point, 246
Buntzen Lake, 172
Burnaby Mountain, 167
Burns Bog, 253
Capilano Pacific Trail, 84
Cypress Falls, 99
Deep Cove to Lynn Canyon, 69
Derby Reach, 195
Eagle Bluff, 118
Goat Mountain, 47
Gold Creek Falls, 226
Grouse Grind, 42
Hayward Lake, 231
Hollyburn Ridge, 106
Iona Jetty, 240
Jug Island Beach, 188
Katzie Marsh Loop, 214

Killarney Lake, 125
Lighthouse Park, 93
Lions Binkert, The, 136
Lynn Peak, 59
Lynn Valley to Grouse Mountain, 54
Minnekhada High Knoll Loop, 207
Mount Gardner, 131
Mount Seymour, 76
Norvan Falls, 64
Pacific Spirit Loop, 32
Petgill Lake, 142
Saint Mark's Summit, 112
Sasamat Lake, 183
Sea to Summit, 148
Sendero Diez Vistas, 178
Spanish Banks, 26
Stanley Park Seawall, 20
Stawamus Chief, 154
UBC Malcolm Knapp Research
    Forest, 202
Widgeon Falls, 219

About the Author

As a travel writer since 2006, **Chloë Ernst** has skied on the slopes overlooking her Vancouver home, retraced the Gold Rush in the Cariboo region, and caught waves on the Pacific coast. She loves to do the things she writes about, especially when it means canoeing in Widgeon Slough or reaching the summit of Goat Mountain. Chloë has written guidebooks for Globe Pequot, Fodor's, and Frommer's, as well as hundreds of articles for the *Toronto Star*, ZAGAT, and travelandleisure.com.